FOUR MODERN PLAYS

FOUR MODERN PLAYS

FIRST SERIES

REVISED EDITION

HENRIK IBSEN

Hedda Gabler

BERNARD SHAW

Pygmalion

EUGENE O'NEILL

The Emperor Jones

ANTON CHEKHOV

The Cherry Orchard

HOLT, RINEHART AND WINSTON, INC. NEW YORK, TORONTO

23924–0213

Typography by Stefan Salter

Printed in the United States of America, 1962

Library of Congress Catalog Card Number: 62-21767

CONTENTS

FOUR MODERN PLAYS

HENRIK IBSEN

Hedda Gabler

TRANSLATED FROM THE NORWEGIAN BY EDMUND GOSSE AND WILLIAM ARCHER

CAST

GEORGE TESMAN

HEDDA TESMAN, *his wife*

MISS JULIANA TESMAN, *his aunt*

MRS. ELVSTED

JUDGE BRACK

EILERT LÖVBORG

BERTA, *servant at the Tesmans'*

SCENE: *The action is Tesman's villa, in the west end of Christiania*

ACT I

SCENE: *A spacious, handsome, and tastefully furnished drawing room, decorated in dark colors. In the back, a wide doorway with curtains drawn back, leading into a smaller room decorated in the same style as the drawing room. In the right-hand wall of the front room, a folding door leading out to the hall. In the opposite wall, on the left, a glass door, also with curtains drawn back. Through the panes can be seen part of a veranda outside, and trees covered with autumn foliage. An oval table, with a cover on it, and surrounded by chairs, stands well forward. In front, by the wall on the right, a wide stove of dark porcelain, a high-backed armchair, a cushioned footrest, and two footstools. A settee, with a small round table in front of it, fills the upper right-hand corner. In front, on the left, a little way from the wall, a sofa. Farther back than the glass door, a piano. On either side of the doorway at the back a whatnot with terra-cotta and majolica ornaments. Against the back wall of the inner room a sofa, with a table, and one or two chairs. Over the sofa hangs the portrait of a handsome elderly man in a General's uniform. Over the table a hanging lamp, with an opal glass shade. A number of bouquets are arranged about the drawing room, in vases and glasses. Others lie upon the tables. The floors in both rooms are covered with thick carpets. Morning light. The sun shines in through the glass door.*

MISS JULIANA TESMAN, *with her bonnet on and carrying a parasol, comes in from the hall, followed by* BERTA, *who carries a bouquet wrapped in paper.* MISS TESMAN *is a comely and pleasant-looking lady of about sixty-five. She is nicely but simply dressed in a gray walking costume.* BERTA *is a middle-aged woman of plain and rather countrified appearance.*

MISS TESMAN [*Stops close to the door, listens, and says softly.*] Upon my word, I don't believe they are stirring yet!

BERTA [*Also softly.*] I told you so, Miss. Remember how late the steamboat got in last night. And then, when they got home!—good Lord, what a lot the young mistress had to unpack before she could get to bed.

MISS TESMAN Well, well—let them have their sleep out. But let us see that they get a good breath of the fresh morning air when they do appear. [*She goes to the glass door and throws it open.*]

BERTA [*Beside the table, at a loss what to do with the bouquet in her hand.*] I declare, there isn't a bit of room left. I think I'll put it down here, Miss. [*She places it on the piano.*]

MISS TESMAN So you've got a new mistress now, my dear Berta. Heaven knows it was a wrench to me to part with you.

BERTA [*On the point of weeping.*] And do you think it wasn't hard for me, too, Miss? After all the blessed years I've been with you and Miss Rina.

MISS TESMAN We must make the best of it, Berta. There was nothing else to be done. George can't do without you, you see—he absolutely can't. He has had you to look after him ever since he was a little boy.

BERTA Ah, but, Miss Julia, I can't help thinking of Miss Rina lying helpless at home there, poor thing. And with only that new girl, too! She'll never learn to take proper care of an invalid.

MISS TESMAN Oh, I shall manage to train her. And, of course, you know I shall take most of it upon myself. You needn't be uneasy about my poor sister, my dear Berta.

BERTA Well, but there's another thing, Miss. I'm so mortally afraid I shan't be able to suit the young mistress.

MISS TESMAN Oh, well—just at first there may be one or two things . . .

BERTA Most like she'll be terrible grand in her ways.

MISS TESMAN Well, you can't wonder at that—General Gabler's daughter! Think of the sort of life she was accustomed to in her father's time. Don't you remember how we used to see her riding down the road along with the General? In that long black habit—and with feathers in her hat?

BERTA Yes, indeed—I remember well enough!—But, good Lord, I should never have dreamt in those days that she and Master George would make a match of it.

MISS TESMAN Nor I. But by the by, Berta—while I think of it: in future you mustn't say Master George. You must say Dr. Tesman.

BERTA Yes, the young mistress spoke of that, too—last night—the moment they set foot in the house. Is it true then, Miss?

MISS TESMAN Yes, indeed it is. Only think, Berta—some foreign university has made him a doctor—while he has been abroad, you understand. I hadn't heard a word about it, until he told me himself upon the pier.

BERTA Well, well, he's clever enough for anything, he is. But I didn't think he'd have gone in for doctoring people, too.

MISS TESMAN No, no, it's not that sort of doctor he is. [*Nods significantly.*] But let me tell you, we may have to call him something still grander before long.

BERTA You don't say so! What can that be, Miss?

MISS TESMAN [*Smiling.*] H'm—wouldn't you like to know! [*With emotion.*] Ah, dear, dear—if my poor brother could only look up from his grave now, and see what his little boy has grown into! [*Looks around.*] But bless me, Berta—why have you done this? Taken the chintz covers off all the furniture?

BERTA The mistress told me to. She can't abide covers on the chairs, she says.

MISS TESMAN Are they going to make this their everyday sitting room then?

BERTA Yes, that's what I understood—from the mistress. Master George—the doctor—he said nothing.

[GEORGE TESMAN *comes from the right into the inner room, humming to himself, and carrying an unstrapped empty portmanteau. He is a middle-sized, young-looking man of thirty-three, rather stout, with a round, open, cheerful face, fair hair and beard. He wears spectacles, and is somewhat carelessly dressed in comfortable indoor clothes.*]

MISS TESMAN Good morning, good morning, George.

TESMAN [*In the doorway between the rooms.*] Aunt Julia! Dear Aunt Julia! [*Goes up to her and shakes hands warmly.*] Come all this way—so early! Eh?

MISS TESMAN Why, of course I had to come and see how you were getting on.

TESMAN In spite of your having had no proper night's rest?

MISS TESMAN Oh, that makes no difference to me.

TESMAN Well, I suppose you got home all right from the pier? Eh?

MISS TESMAN Yes, quite safely, thank goodness. Judge Brack was good enough to see me right to my door.

TESMAN We were so sorry we couldn't give you a seat in the carriage. But you saw what a pile of boxes Hedda had to bring with her.

MISS TESMAN Yes, she had certainly plenty of boxes.

BERTA [*To* TESMAN.] Shall I go in and see if there's anything I can do for the mistress?

TESMAN No thank you, Berta—you needn't. She said she would ring if she wanted anything.

BERTA. [*Going towards the right.*] Very well.

TESMAN But look here—take this portmanteau with you.

BERTA [*Taking it.*] I'll put it in the attic.

[*She goes out by the hall door.*]

TESMAN Fancy, Auntie—I had the whole of that portmanteau chock full of copies of documents. You wouldn't believe how much I have picked up from all the archives I have been examining—curious old details that no one has had any idea of . . .

MISS TESMAN Yes, you don't seem to have wasted your time on your wedding trip, George.

TESMAN No, that I haven't. But do take off your bonnet, Auntie. Look here! Let me untie the strings—eh?

MISS TESMAN [*While he does so.*] Well, well—this is just as if you were still at home with us.

TESMAN [*With the bonnet in his hand, looks at it from all sides.*] Why, what a gorgeous bonnet you've been investing in!

MISS TESMAN I bought it on Hedda's account.

TESMAN On Hedda's account? Eh?

MISS TESMAN Yes, so that Hedda needn't be ashamed of me if we happened to go out together.

TESMAN [*Patting her cheek.*] You always think of everything, Aunt Julia. [*Lays the bonnet on a chair beside the table.*] And now, look here—suppose we sit comfortably on the sofa and have a little chat, till Hedda comes. [*They seat themselves. She places her parasol in the corner of the sofa.*]

MISS TESMAN [*Takes both his hands and looks at him.*] What a delight it is to have you again, as large as life, before my very eyes, George! My George—my poor brother's own boy!

TESMAN And it's a delight for me, too, to see you again, Aunt Julia! You, who have been father and mother in one to me.

MISS TESMAN Oh yes, I know you will always keep a place in your heart for your old aunts.

TESMAN And what about Aunt Rina? No improvement—eh?

MISS TESMAN Oh no—we can scarcely look for any improvement in her case, poor thing. There she lies, helpless, as she has lain for all these years. But heaven grant I may not lose her yet awhile. For if I did, I don't know what I should make of my life, George—especially now that I haven't you to look after any more.

TESMAN [*Patting her back.*] There, there, there . . . !

MISS TESMAN [*Suddenly changing her tone.*] And to think that here you are a married man, George! And that you should be the one to carry off Hedda Gabler—the beautiful Hedda Gabler! Only think of it—she, that was so beset with admirers!

TESMAN [*Hums a little and smiles complacently.*] Yes, I fancy I have several good friends about town who would like to stand in my shoes—eh?

MISS TESMAN And then this fine long wedding tour you have had! More than five—nearly six months . . .

TESMAN Well, for me it has been a sort of tour of research as well. I have had to do so much grubbing among old records—and to read no end of books too, Auntie.

MISS TESMAN Oh yes, I suppose so. [*More confidentially, and lowering her voice a little.*] But listen now, George—have you nothing—nothing special to tell me?

TESMAN As to our journey?

MISS TESMAN Yes.

TESMAN No, I don't know of anything except what I have told you in my letters. I had a doctor's degree conferred on me—but that I told you yesterday.

MISS TESMAN Yes, yes, you did. But what I mean is—haven't you any—any—expectations . . . ?

TESMAN Expectations?

MISS TESMAN Why you know, George—I'm your old auntie!

TESMAN Why, of course I have expectations.

MISS TESMAN Ah!

TESMAN I have every expectation of being a professor one of these days.

MISS TESMAN Oh yes, a professor . . .

TESMAN Indeed, I may say I am certain of it. But my dear Auntie—you know all about that already!

MISS TESMAN [*Laughing to herself.*] Yes, of course I do. You are quite right there. [*Changing the subject.*] But we were talking about your journey. It must have cost a great deal of money, George?

TESMAN Well, you see—my handsome traveling scholarship went a good way.

MISS TESMAN But I can't understand how you can have made it go far enough for two.

TESMAN No, that's not so easy to understand—eh?

MISS TESMAN And especially traveling with a lady—they tell me that makes it ever so much more expensive.

TESMAN Yes, of course—it makes it a little more expensive. But Hedda had to have this trip, Auntie! She really had to. Nothing else would have done.

MISS TESMAN No, no, I suppose not. A wedding tour seems to be quite indispensable nowadays. But tell me now—have you gone thoroughly over the house yet.

TESMAN Yes, you may be sure I have. I have been afoot ever since daylight.

MISS TESMAN And what do you think of it all?

TESMAN I'm delighted! Quite delighted! Only I can't think

what we are to do with the two empty rooms between this inner parlor and Hedda's bedroom.

MISS TESMAN [*Laughing.*] Oh my dear George, I daresay you may find some use for them—in the course of time.

TESMAN Why of course you are quite right, Aunt Julia! You mean as my library increases—eh?

MISS TESMAN Yes, quite so, my dear boy. It was your library I was thinking of.

TESMAN I am specially pleased on Hedda's account. Often and often, before we were engaged, she said that she would never care to live anywhere but in Secretary Falk's villa.

MISS TESMAN Yes, it was lucky that this very house should come into the market, just after you had started.

TESMAN Yes, Aunt Julia, the luck was on our side, wasn't it—eh?

MISS TESMAN But the expense, my dear George! You will find it very expensive, all this.

TESMAN [*Looks at her, a little cast down.*] Yes, I suppose I shall, Aunt!

MISS TESMAN Oh, frightfully!

TESMAN How much do you think? In round numbers?—Eh?

MISS TESMAN Oh, I can't even guess until all the accounts come in.

TESMAN Well, fortunately, Judge Brack has secured the most favorable terms for me—so he said in a letter to Hedda.

MISS TESMAN Yes, don't be uneasy, my dear boy. Besides, I have given security for the furniture and all the carpets.

TESMAN Security? You? My dear Aunt Julia—what sort of security could you give?

MISS TESMAN I have given a mortgage on our annuity.

TESMAN [*Jumps up.*] What! On your—and Aunt Rina's annuity!

MISS TESMAN Yes, I knew of no other plan, you see.

TESMAN [*Placing himself before her.*] Have you gone out of your senses, Auntie! Your annuity—it's all that you and Aunt Rina have to live upon.

MISS TESMAN Well, well—don't get so excited about it. It's

only a matter of form you know—Judge Brack assured me of that. It was he that was kind enough to arrange the whole affair for me. A mere matter of form, he said.

TESMAN Yes, that may be all very well. But nevertheless . . .

MISS TESMAN You will have your own salary to depend upon now. And, good heavens, even if we did have to pay up a little . . . ! To eke things out a bit at the start . . . ! Why, it would be nothing but a pleasure to us.

TESMAN Oh Auntie—will you never be tired of making sacrifices for me!

MISS TESMAN [*Rises and lays her hands on his shoulders.*] Have I any other happiness in this world except to smooth your way for you, my dear boy? You, who have had neither father nor mother to depend on. And now we have reached the goal, George! Things have looked black enough for us, sometimes; but, thank heaven, now you have nothing to fear.

TESMAN Yes, it is really marvelous how everything has turned out for the best.

MISS TESMAN And the people who opposed you—who wanted to bar the way for you—now you have them at your feet. They have fallen, George. Your most dangerous rival—his fall was the worst. And now he has to lie on the bed he has made for himself —poor misguided creature.

TESMAN Have you heard anything of Eilert? Since I went away, I mean.

MISS TESMAN Only that he is said to have published a new book.

TESMAN What! Eilert Lövborg! Recently—eh?

MISS TESMAN Yes, so they say. Heaven knows whether it can be worth anything! Ah, when your new book appears—that will be another story, George! What is it to be about?

TESMAN It will deal with the domestic industries of Brabant during the Middle Ages.

MISS TESMAN Fancy—to be able to write on such a subject as that!

TESMAN However, it may be some time before the book is ready. I have all these collections to arrange first, you see.

MISS TESMAN Yes, collecting and arranging—no one can beat you at that. There you are my poor brother's own son.

TESMAN I am looking forward eagerly to setting to work at it; especially now that I have my own delightful home to work in.

MISS TESMAN And, most of all, now that you have got a wife of your heart, my dear George.

TESMAN [*Embracing her.*] Oh yes, yes, Aunt Julia. Hedda—she is the best part of it all! [*Looks towards the doorway.*] I believe I hear her coming—eh?

[HEDDA *enters from the left through the inner room. She is a woman of nine-and-twenty. Her face and figure show refinement and distinction. Her complexion is pale and opaque. Her steel-gray eyes express a cold, unruffled repose. Her hair is of an agreeable medium brown, but not particularly abundant. She is dressed in a tasteful, somewhat loose-fitting morning gown.*]

MISS TESMAN [*Going to meet* HEDDA.] Good morning, my dear Hedda! Good morning, and a hearty welcome!

HEDDA [*Holds out her hand.*] Good morning, dear Miss Tesman! So early a call! That is kind of you.

MISS TESMAN [*With some embarrassment.*] Well—has the bride slept well in her new home?

HEDDA Oh yes, thanks. Passably.

TESMAN [*Laughing.*] Passably! Come, that's good, Hedda! You were sleeping like a stone when I got up.

HEDDA Fortunately. Of course one has always to accustom one's self to new surroundings, Miss Tesman—little by little. [*Looking towards the left.*] Oh—there the servant has gone and opened the veranda door, and let in a whole flood of sunshine.

MISS TESMAN [*Going towards the door.*] Well, then we will shut it.

HEDDA No, no, not that! Tesman, please draw the curtains. That will give a softer light.

TESMAN [*At the door.*] All right—all right. There now, Hedda, now you have both shade and fresh air.

HEDDA Yes, fresh air we certainly must have, with all these stacks of flowers . . . But—won't you sit down, Miss Tesman?

MISS TESMAN No, thank you. Now that I have seen that

everything is all right here—thank heaven!—I must be getting home again. My sister is lying longing for me, poor thing.

TESMAN Give her my very best love, Auntie; and say I shall look in and see her later in the day.

MISS TESMAN Yes, yes, I'll be sure to tell her. But by the by, George—[*feeling in her dress pocket*]—I had almost forgotten—I have something for you here.

TESMAN What is it, Auntie? Eh?

MISS TESMAN [*Produces a flat parcel wrapped in newspaper and hands it to him.*] Look here, my dear boy.

TESMAN [*Opening the parcel.*] Well, I declare! Have you really saved them for me, Aunt Julia! Hedda! Isn't this touching—eh?

HEDDA [*Beside the whatnot on the right.*] Well, what is it?

TESMAN My old morning shoes! My slippers.

HEDDA Indeed. I remember you often spoke of them while we were abroad.

TESMAN Yes, I missed them terribly. [*Goes up to her.*] Now you shall see them, Hedda!

HEDDA [*Going towards the stove.*] Thanks, I really don't care about it.

TESMAN [*Following her.*] Only think—ill as she was, Aunt Rina embroidered these for me. Oh you can't think how many associations cling to them.

HEDDA [*At the table.*] Scarcely for me.

MISS TESMAN Of course not for Hedda, George.

TESMAN Well, but now that she belongs to the family, I thought . . .

HEDDA [*Interrupting.*] We shall never get on with this servant, Tesman.

MISS TESMAN Not get on with Berta?

TESMAN Why, dear, what puts that in your head? Eh?

HEDDA [*Pointing.*] Look there! She has left her old bonnet lying about on a chair.

TESMAN [*In consternation, drops the slippers on the floor.*] Why, Hedda . . .

HEDDA Just fancy, if any one should come in and see it!

TESMAN But Hedda—that's Aunt Julia's bonnet.

HEDDA Is it!

MISS TESMAN [*Taking up the bonnet.*] Yes, indeed it's mine. And, what's more, it's not old, Madam Hedda.

HEDDA I really did not look closely at it, Miss Tesman.

MISS TESMAN [*Trying on the bonnet.*] Let me tell you it's the first time I have worn it—the very first time.

TESMAN And a very nice bonnet it is too—quite a beauty!

MISS TESMAN Oh, it's no such great thing, George. [*Looks around her.*] My parasol . . . ? Ah, here. [*Takes it.*] For this is mine too—[*mutters*]—not Berta's.

TESMAN A new bonnet and a new parasol! Only think, Hedda!

HEDDA Very handsome indeed.

TESMAN Yes, isn't it? Eh? But Auntie, take a good look at Hedda before you go! See how handsome she is!

MISS TESMAN Oh, my dear boy, there's nothing new in that. Hedda was always lovely. [*She nods and goes towards the right.*]

TESMAN [*Following.*] Yes, but have you noticed what splendid condition she is in? How she has filled out on the journey?

HEDDA [*Crossing the room.*] Oh, do be quiet . . . !

MISS TESMAN [*Who has stopped and turned.*] Filled out?

TESMAN Of course you don't notice it so much now that she has that dress on. But I, who can see . . .

HEDDA [*At the glass door, impatiently.*] Oh, you can't see anything.

TESMAN It must be the mountain air in the Tyrol . . .

HEDDA [*Curtly, interrupting.*] I am exactly as I was when I started.

TESMAN So you insist; but I'm quite certain you are not. Don't you agree with me, Auntie?

MISS TESMAN [*Who has been gazing at her with folded hands.*] Hedda is lovely—lovely—lovely. [*Goes up to her, takes her head between both hands, draws it downwards, and kisses her hair.*] God bless and preserve Hedda Tesman—for George's sake.

HEDDA [*Gently freeing herself.*] Oh—! Let me go.

MISS TESMAN [*In quiet emotion.*] I shall not let a day pass without coming to see you.

TESMAN No you won't, will you, Auntie? Eh?

MISS TESMAN Good-bye—good-bye!

[*She goes out by the hall door.* TESMAN *accompanies her. The door remains half open.* TESMAN *can be heard repeating his message to* AUNT RINA *and his thanks for the slippers. In the meantime,* HEDDA *walks about the room, raising her arms and clenching her hands as if in desperation. Then she flings back the curtains from the glass door, and stands there looking out. Presently* TESMAN *returns and closes the door behind him.*]

TESMAN [*Picks up the slippers from the floor.*] What are you looking at, Hedda?

HEDDA [*Once more calm and mistress of herself.*] I am only looking at the leaves. They are so yellow—so withered.

TESMAN [*Wraps up the slippers and lays them on the table.*] Well you see, we are well into September now.

HEDDA [*Again restless.*] Yes, to think of it! Already in—in September.

TESMAN Don't you think Aunt Julia's manner was strange, dear? Almost solemn? Can you imagine what was the matter with her? Eh?

HEDDA I scarcely know her, you see. Is she not often like that?

TESMAN No, not as she was today.

HEDDA [*Leaving the glass door.*] Do you think she was annoyed about the bonnet?

TESMAN Oh, scarcely at all. Perhaps a little, just at the moment . . .

HEDDA But what an idea, to pitch her bonnet about in the drawing room! No one does that sort of thing.

TESMAN Well you may be sure Aunt Julia won't do it again.

HEDDA In any case, I shall manage to make my peace with her.

TESMAN Yes, my dear, good Hedda, if you only would.

HEDDA When you call this afternoon, you might invite her to spend the evening here.

TESMAN Yes, that I will. And there's one thing more you could do that would delight her heart.

HEDDA What is it?

TESMAN If you could only prevail on yourself to say *du*[1] to her. For my sake, Hedda? Eh?

HEDDA No, no, Tesman—you really mustn't ask that of me. I have told you so already. I shall try to call her "Aunt"; and you must be satisfied with that.

TESMAN Well, well. Only I think now that you belong to the family, you . . .

HEDDA H'm—I can't in the least see why . . . [*She goes up towards the middle doorway.*]

TESMAN [*After a pause.*] Is there anything the matter with you, Hedda? Eh?

HEDDA I'm only looking at my old piano. It doesn't go at all well with all the other things.

TESMAN The first time I draw my salary, we'll see about exchanging it.

HEDDA No, no—no exchanging. I don't want to part with it. Suppose we put it there in the inner room, and then get another here in its place. When it's convenient, I mean.

TESMAN [*A little taken aback.*] Yes—of course we could do that.

HEDDA [*Takes up the bouquet from the piano.*] These flowers were not here last night when we arrived.

TESMAN Aunt Julia must have brought them for you.

HEDDA [*Examining the bouquet.*] A visiting card. [*Takes it out and reads.*] "Shall return later in the day." Can you guess whose card it is?

TESMAN No. Whose? Eh?

HEDDA The name is "Mrs. Elvsted."

TESMAN Is it really? Sheriff Elvsted's wife? Miss Rysing that was.

HEDDA Exactly. The girl with the irritating hair, that she was always showing off. An old flame of yours I've been told.

TESMAN [*Laughing.*] Oh, that didn't last long; and it was before I knew you, Hedda. But fancy her being in town!

---

1. The familiar form of the pronoun, used only between persons who are on a footing of intimacy; hence its significance here and later.

HEDDA It's odd that she should call upon us. I have scarcely seen her since we left school.

TESMAN I haven't seen her either for—heaven knows how long. I wonder how she can endure to live in such an out-of-the-way hole—eh?

HEDDA [*After a moment's thought, says suddenly.*] Tell me, Tesman—isn't it somewhere near there that he—that—Eilert Lövborg is living?

TESMAN Yes, he is somewhere in that part of the country.

[BERTA *enters by the hall door.*]

BERTA That lady, ma'am, that brought some flowers a little while ago, is here again. [*Pointing.*] The flowers you have in your hand, ma'am.

HEDDA Ah, is she? Well, please show her in.

[BERTA *opens the door for* MRS. ELVSTED, *and goes out herself.* —MRS. ELVSTED *is a woman of fragile figure, with pretty, soft features. Her eyes are light blue, large, round, and somewhat prominent, with a startled, inquiring expression. Her hair is remarkably light, almost flaxen, and unusually abundant and wavy. She is a couple of years younger than* HEDDA. *She wears a dark visiting dress, tasteful, but not quite in the lastest fashion.*]

HEDDA [*Receives her warmly.*] How do you do, my dear Mrs. Elvsted? It's delightful to see you again.

MRS. ELVSTED [*Nervously, struggling for self-control.*] Yes, it's a very long time since we met.

TESMAN [*Gives her his hand.*] And we too—eh?

HEDDA Thanks for your lovely flowers . . .

MRS. ELVSTED Oh, not at all . . . I would have come straight here yesterday afternoon; but I heard that you were away . . .

TESMAN Have you just come to town? Eh?

MRS. ELVSTED I arrived yesterday, about midday. Oh, I was quite in despair when I heard that you were not at home.

HEDDA In despair! How so?

TESMAN Why, my dear Mrs. Rysing—I mean Mrs. Elvsted . . .

HEDDA I hope that you are not in any trouble?

MRS. ELVSTED Yes, I am. And I don't know another living creature here that I can turn to.

HEDDA [*Laying the bouquet on the table.*] Come—let us sit here on the sofa . . .

MRS. ELVSTED Oh, I am too restless to sit down.

HEDDA Oh no, you're not. Come here. [*She draws* MRS. ELVSTED *down upon the sofa and sits at her side.*]

TESMAN Well? What is it, Mrs. Elvsted . . . ?

HEDDA Has anything particular happened to you at home?

MRS. ELVSTED Yes—and no. Oh—I am so anxious you should not misunderstand me . . .

HEDDA Then your best plan is to tell us the whole story, Mrs. Elvsted.

TESMAN I suppose that's what you have come for—eh?

MRS. ELVSTED Yes, yes—of course it is. Well then, I must tell you, if you don't already know, that Eilert Lövborg is in town, too.

HEDDA Lövborg . . . !

TESMAN What! Has Eilert Lövborg come back? Fancy that, Hedda!

HEDDA Well, well—I hear it.

MRS. ELVSTED He has been here a week already. Just fancy—a whole week! In this terrible town, alone! With so many temptations on all sides.

HEDDA But, my dear Mrs. Elvsted—how does he concern you so much?

MRS. ELVSTED [*Looks at her with a startled air, and says rapidly*] He was the children's tutor.

HEDDA Your children's?

MRS. ELVSTED My husband's. I have none.

HEDDA Your stepchildren's, then?

MRS. ELVSTED Yes.

TESMAN [*Somewhat hesitatingly.*] Then was he—I don't know how to express it—was he—regular enough in his habits to be fit for the post? Eh?

MRS. ELVSTED For the last two years his conduct has been irreproachable.

TESMAN Has it indeed? Fancy that, Hedda!

HEDDA I hear it.

MRS. ELVSTED Perfectly irreproachable, I assure you! In every respect. But all the same—now that I know he is here—in this great town—and with a large sum of money in his hands—I can't help being in mortal fear for him.

TESMAN Why did he not remain where he was? With you and your husband? Eh?

MRS. ELVSTED After his book was published he was too restless and unsettled to remain with us.

TESMAN Yes, by the by, Aunt Julia told me he had published a new book.

MRS. ELVSTED Yes, a big book, dealing with the march of civilization—in broad outline, as it were. It came out about a fortnight ago. And since it has sold so well, and been so much read —and made such a sensation . . .

TESMAN Has it indeed? It must be something he has had lying by since his better days.

MRS. ELVSTED Long ago, you mean?

TESMAN Yes.

MRS. ELVSTED No, he has written it all since he has been with us—within the last year.

TESMAN Isn't that good news, Hedda? Think of that.

MRS. ELVSTED Ah yes, if only it would last!

HEDDA Have you seen him here in town?

MRS. ELVSTED No, not yet. I have had the greatest difficulty in finding out his address. But this morning I discovered it at last.

HEDDA [*Looks searchingly at her.*] Do you know, it seems to me a little odd of your husband—h'm . . .

MRS. ELVSTED [*Starting nervously.*] Of my husband! What?

HEDDA That he should send you to town on such an errand—that he does not come himself and look after his friend.

MRS. ELVSTED Oh no, no—my husband has no time. And besides, I—I had some shopping to do.

HEDDA [*With a slight smile.*] Ah, that is a different matter.

MRS. ELVSTED [*Rising quickly and uneasily.*] And now I beg and implore you, Mr. Tesman—receive Eilert Lövborg kindly if he comes to you! And that he is sure to do. You see you were such great friends in the old days. And then you are interested in the same studies—the same branch of science—so far as I can understand.

TESMAN We used to be, at any rate.

MRS. ELVSTED That is why I beg so earnestly that you—you too—will keep a sharp eye upon him. Oh, you will promise me that, Mr. Tesman— won't you?

TESMAN With the greatest of pleasure, Mrs. Rysing . . .

HEDDA Elvsted.

TESMAN I assure you I shall do all I possibly can for Eilert. You may rely upon me.

MRS. ELVSTED Oh, how very, very kind of you! [*Presses his hands.*] Thanks, thanks, thanks! [*Frightened.*] You see, my husband is so very fond of him!

HEDDA [*Rising.*] You ought to write to him, Tesman. Perhaps he may not care to come to you of his own accord.

TESMAN Well, perhaps it would be the right thing to do, Hedda? Eh?

HEDDA And the sooner the better. Why not at once?

MRS. ELVSTED [*Imploringly.*] Oh, if you only would!

TESMAN I'll write this moment. Have you his address, Mrs.—Mrs. Elvsted?

MRS. ELVSTED Yes. [*Takes a slip of paper from her pocket, and hands it to him.*] Here it is.

TESMAN Good, good. Then I'll go in . . . [*Looks about him.*] By the by—my slippers? Oh, here. [*Takes the packet, and is about to go.*]

HEDDA Be sure you write him a cordial, friendly letter. And a good long one too.

TESMAN Yes, I will.

MRS. ELVSTED But please, please don't say a word to show that I have suggested it.

TESMAN No, how could you think I would? Eh? [*He goes out to the right, through the inner room.*]

HEDDA [*Goes up to* MRS. ELVSTED, *smiles and says in a low voice.*] There! We have killed two birds with one stone.

MRS. ELVSTED What do you mean?

HEDDA Could you not see that I wanted him to go?

MRS. ELVSTED Yes, to write the letter . . .

HEDDA And that I might speak to you alone.

MRS. ELVSTED [*Confused.*] About the same thing?

HEDDA Precisely.

MRS. ELVSTED [*Apprehensively.*] But there is nothing more, Mrs. Tesman! Absolutely nothing!

HEDDA Oh yes, but there is. There is a great deal more—I can see that. Sit here—and we'll have a cozy, confidential chat. [*She forces* MRS. ELVSTED *to sit in the easy-chair beside the stove, and seats herself on one of the footstools.*]

MRS. ELVSTED [*Anxiously, looking at her watch.*] But, my dear Mrs. Tesman—I was really on the point of going.

HEDDA Oh, you can't be in such a hurry. Well? Now tell me something about your life at home.

MRS. ELVSTED Oh, that is just what I care least to speak about.

HEDDA But to me, dear . . . ? Why, weren't we schoolfellows?

MRS. ELVSTED Yes, but you were in the class above me. Oh, how dreadfully afraid of you I was then!

HEDDA Afraid of me?

MRS. ELVSTED Yes, dreadfully. For when we met on the stairs you used always to pull my hair.

HEDDA Did I, really?

MRS. ELVSTED Yes, and once you said you would burn it off my head.

HEDDA Oh, that was all nonsense, of course.

MRS. ELVSTED Yes, but I was so silly in those days. And since then, too—we have drifted so far—far apart from each other. Our circles have been so entirely different.

HEDDA Well then, we must try to drift together again. Now listen! At school we said *du*[2] to each other; and we called each other by our Christian names . . .

MRS. ELVSTED No, I am sure you must be mistaken.

HEDDA No, not at all! I can remember quite distinctly. So now

2. See note, p. 15.

we are going to renew our old friendship. [*Draws the footstool closer to* MRS. ELVSTED.] There now! [*Kisses her cheek.*] You must say *du* to me and call me Hedda.

MRS. ELVSTED [*Presses and pats her hands.*] Oh, how good and kind you are! I am not used to such kindness.

HEDDA There, there, there! And I shall say *du* to you, as in the old days, and call you my dear Thora.

MRS. ELVSTED My name is Thea.

HEDDA Why, of course! I meant Thea. [*Looks at her compassionately.*] So you are not accustomed to goodness and kindness, Thea? Not in your own home?

MRS. ELVSTED Oh, if I only had a home! But I haven't any; I have never had a home.

HEDDA [*Looks at her for a moment.*] I almost suspected as much.

MRS. ELVSTED [*Gazing helplessly before her.*] Yes—yes—yes.

HEDDA I don't quite remember—was it not as housekeeper that you first went to Mr. Elvsted's?

MRS. ELVSTED I really went as governess. But his wife—his late wife—was an invalid, and rarely left her room. So I had to look after the housekeeping as well.

HEDDA And then—at last—you became mistress of the house.

MRS. ELVSTED [*Sadly.*] Yes, I did.

HEDDA Let me see—about how long ago was that?

MRS. ELVSTED My marriage?

HEDDA Yes.

MRS. ELVSTED Five years ago.

HEDDA To be sure; it must be that.

MRS. ELVSTED Oh those five years . . . ! Or at all events the last two or three of them! Oh, if you[3] could only imagine . . .

HEDDA [*Giving her a little slap on the hand.*] *De?* Fie, Thea!

MRS. ELVSTED Yes, yes, I will try . . . Well, if—you could only imagine and understand . . .

HEDDA [*Lightly.*] Eilert Lövborg has been in your neighborhood about three years, hasn't he?

---

3. Instead of *du,* Mrs. Elvsted uses *De,* the formal pronoun. After being rebuked, she says *du.*

MRS. ELVSTED [*Looks at her doubtfully.*] Eilert Lövborg? Yes—he has.

HEDDA Had you known him before, in town here?

MRS. ELVSTED Scarcely at all. I mean—I knew him by name of course.

HEDDA But you saw a good deal of him in the country?

MRS. ELVSTED Yes, he came to us every day. You see, he gave the children lessons; for in the long run I couldn't manage it all myself.

HEDDA No, that's clear. And your husband . . . ? I suppose he is often away from home?

MRS. ELVSTED Yes. Being sheriff, you know, he has to travel about a good deal in his district.

HEDDA [*Leaning against the arm of the chair.*] Thea—my poor, sweet Thea—now you must tell me everything—exactly as it stands.

MRS. ELVSTED Well then, you must question me.

HEDDA What sort of a man is your husband, Thea? I mean—you know—in everyday life. Is he kind to you?

MRS. ELVSTED [*Evasively.*] I am sure he means well in everything.

HEDDA I should think he must be altogether too old for you. There is at least twenty years' difference between you, is there not?

MRS. ELVSTED [*Irritably.*] Yes, that is true, too. Everything about him is repellent to me! We have not a thought in common. We have no single point of sympathy—he and I.

HEDDA But is he not fond of you all the same? In his own way?

MRS. ELVSTED Oh I really don't know. I think he regards me simply as a useful property. And then it doesn't cost much to keep me. I am not expensive.

HEDDA That is stupid of you.

MRS. ELVSTED [*Shakes her head.*] It cannot be otherwise—not with him. I don't think he really cares for any one but himself—and perhaps a little for the children.

HEDDA And for Eilert Lövborg, Thea.

MRS. ELVSTED [*Looking at her.*] For Eilert Lövborg? What puts that into your head?

HEDDA Well, my dear—I should say, when he sends you after him all the way to town . . . [*Smiling almost imperceptibly.*] And besides, you said so yourself, to Tesman.

MRS. ELVSTED [*With a little nervous twitch.*] Did I? Yes, I suppose I did. [*Vehemently, but not loudly.*] No—I may just as well make a clean breast of it at once! For it must all come out in any case.

HEDDA Why, my dear Thea . . . ?

MRS. ELVSTED Well, to make a long story short: My husband did not know that I was coming.

HEDDA What! Your husband didn't know it!

MRS. ELVSTED No, of course not. For that matter, he was away from home himself—he was traveling. Oh, I could bear it no longer, Hedda! I couldn't indeed—so utterly alone as I should have been in future.

HEDDA Well? And then?

MRS. ELVSTED So I put together some of my things—what I needed most—as quietly as possible. And then I left the house.

HEDDA Without a word?

MRS. ELVSTED Yes—and took the train straight to town.

HEDDA Why, my dear, good Thea—to think of you daring to do it!

MRS. ELVSTED [*Rises and moves about the room.*] What else could I possibly do?

HEDDA But what do you think your husband will say when you go home again?

MRS. ELVSTED [*At the table, looks at her.*] Back to him?

HEDDA Of course.

MRS. ELVSTED I shall never go back to him again.

HEDDA [*Rising and going towards her.*] Then you have left your home—for good and all?

MRS. ELVSTED Yes. There was nothing else to be done.

HEDDA But then—to take flight so openly.

MRS. ELVSTED Oh, it's impossible to keep things of that sort secret.

HEDDA But what do you think people will say of you, Thea?

MRS. ELVSTED They may say what they like, for aught *I* care.

[*Seats herself wearily and sadly on the sofa.*] I have done nothing but what I had to do.

HEDDA [*After a short silence.*] And what are your plans now? What do you think of doing?

MRS. ELVSTED I don't know yet. I only know this, that I must live here, where Eilert Lövborg is—if I am to live at all.

HEDDA [*Takes a chair from the table, seats herself beside her, and strokes her hands.*] My dear Thea—how did this—this friendship—between you and Eilert Lövborg come about?

MRS. ELVSTED Oh it grew up gradually. I gained a sort of influence over him.

HEDDA Indeed?

MRS. ELVSTED He gave up his old habits. Not because I asked him to, for I never dared do that. But of course he saw how repulsive they were to me; and so he dropped them.

HEDDA [*Concealing an involuntary smile of scorn.*] Then you have reclaimed him—as the saying goes—my little Thea.

MRS. ELVSTED So he says himself, at any rate. And he, on his side, has made a real human being of me—taught me to think, and to understand so many things.

HEDDA Did he give you lessons too, then?

MRS. ELVSTED No, not exactly lessons. But he talked to me—talked about such an infinity of things. And then came the lovely, happy time when I began to share in his work—when he allowed me to help him!

HEDDA Oh he did, did he?

MRS. ELVSTED Yes! He never wrote anything without my assistance.

HEDDA You were two good comrades, in fact?

MRS. ELVSTED [*Eagerly.*] Comrades! Yes, fancy, Hedda—that is the very word he used! Oh, I ought to feel perfectly happy; and yet I cannot; for I don't know how long it will last.

HEDDA Are you no surer of him than that?

MRS. ELVSTED [*Gloomily.*] A woman's shadow stands between Eilert Lövborg and me.

HEDDA [*Looks at her anxiously.*] Who can that be?

MRS. ELVSTED I don't know. Some one he knew in his—in his past. Some one he has never been able wholly to forget.

HEDDA What has he told you—about this?

MRS. ELVSTED He has only once—quite vaguely—alluded to it.

HEDDA Well! And what did he say?

MRS. ELVSTED He said that when they parted, she threatened to shoot him with a pistol.

HEDDA [*With cold composure.*] Oh, nonsense! No one does that sort of thing here.

MRS. ELVSTED No. And that is why I think it must have been that red-haired singing woman whom he once . . .

HEDDA Yes, very likely.

MRS. ELVSTED For I remember they used to say of her that she carried loaded firearms.

HEDDA Oh— then of course it must have been she.

MRS. ELVSTED [*Wringing her hands.*] And now just fancy, Hedda—I hear that this singing woman—that she is in town again! Oh, I don't know what to do . . .

HEDDA [*Glancing towards the inner room.*] Hush! Here comes Tesman. [*Rises and whispers.*] Thea—all this must remain between you and me.

MRS. ELVSTED [*Springing up.*] Oh yes—yes! For heaven's sake . . . !

[GEORGE TESMAN, *with a letter in his hand, comes from the right through the inner room.*]

TESMAN There now—the epistle is finished.

HEDDA That's right. And now Mrs. Elvsted is just going. Wait a moment—I'll go with you to the garden gate.

TESMAN Do you think Berta could post the letter, Hedda dear?

HEDDA [*Takes it.*] I will tell her to.

[BERTA *enters from the hall.*]

BERTA Judge Brack wishes to know if Mrs. Tesman will receive him.

HEDDA Yes, ask Judge Brack to come in. And look here—put this letter in the post.

BERTA [*Taking the letter.*] Yes, ma'am.

[*She opens the door for* JUDGE BRACK *and goes out herself.* BRACK *is a man of forty-five; thickset, but well built and elastic in his movements. His face is roundish with an aristocratic profile. His hair is short, still almost black, and carefully dressed. His eyes are lively and sparkling. His eyebrows thick. His mustaches are also thick, with short-cut ends. He wears a well-cut walking suit, a little too youthful for his age. He uses an eyeglass, which he now and then lets drop.*]

JUDGE BRACK [*With his hat in his hand, bowing.*] May one venture to call so early in the day?

HEDDA Of course one may.

TESMAN [*Presses his hand.*] You are welcome at any time. [*Introducing him.*] Judge Brack—Miss Rysing . . .

HEDDA Oh . . . !

BRACK [*Bowing.*] Ah—delighted . . .

HEDDA [*Looks at him and laughs.*] It's nice to have a look at you by daylight, Judge!

BRACK Do you find me—altered?

HEDDA A little younger, I think.

BRACK Thank you so much.

TESMAN But what do you think of Hedda—eh? Doesn't she look flourishing? She has actually . . .

HEDDA Oh, do leave me alone. You haven't thanked Judge Brack for all the trouble he has taken . . .

BRACK Oh, nonsense—it was a pleasure to me . . .

HEDDA Yes, you are a friend indeed. But here stands Thea all impatience to be off—so *au revoir,* Judge. I shall be back again presently.

[*Mutual salutations.* MRS. ELVSTED *and* HEDDA *go out by the hall door.*]

BRACK Well, is your wife tolerably satisfied . . .

TESMAN Yes, we can't thank you sufficiently. Of course she talks of a little rearrangement here and there; and one or two things are still wanting. We shall have to buy some additional trifles.

BRACK Indeed!

TESMAN But we won't trouble you about these things. Hedda says she herself will look after what is wanting. Shan't we sit down? Eh?

BRACK Thanks, for a moment. [*Seats himself beside the table.*] There is something I wanted to speak to you about, my dear Tesman.

TESMAN Indeed? Ah, I understand! [*Seating himself.*] I suppose it's the serious part of the frolic that is coming now. Eh?

BRACK Oh, the money question is not so very pressing; though, for that matter, I wish we had gone a little more economically to work.

TESMAN But that would never have done, you know! Think of Hedda, my dear fellow! You, who know her so well . . . I couldn't possibly ask her to put up with a shabby style of living!

BRACK No, no—that is just the difficulty.

TESMAN And then—fortunately—it can't be long before I receive my appointment.[4]

BRACK Well, you see—such things are often apt to hang fire for a time.

TESMAN Have you heard anything definite? Eh?

BRACK Nothing exactly definite . . . [*Interrupting himself.*] But by the by—I have one piece of news for you.

TESMAN Well?

BRACK Your old friend, Eilert Lövborg, has returned to town.

TESMAN I know that already.

BRACK Indeed! How did you learn it?

TESMAN From that lady who went out with Hedda.

BRACK Really? What was her name? I didn't quite catch it.

TESMAN Mrs. Elvsted.

BRACK Aha—Sheriff Elvsted's wife? Of course—he has been living up in their regions.

TESMAN And fancy—I'm delighted to hear that he is quite a reformed character!

BRACK So they say.

TESMAN And then he has published a new book—eh?

BRACK Yes, indeed he has.

4. As professor.

TESMAN And I hear it has made some sensation!

BRACK Quite an unusual sensation.

TESMAN Fancy—isn't that good news! A man of such extraordinary talents . . . I felt so grieved to think that he had gone irretrievably to ruin.

BRACK That was what everybody thought.

TESMAN But I cannot imagine what he will take to now! How in the world will he be able to make his living? Eh?

[*During the last words,* HEDDA *has entered by the hall door.*]

HEDDA [*To* BRACK, *laughing with a touch of scorn.*] Tesman is for ever worrying about how people are to make their living.

TESMAN Well you see, dear—we were talking about poor Eilert Lövborg.

HEDDA [*Glancing at him rapidly.*] Oh, indeed? [*Seats herself in the armchair beside the stove and asks indifferently.*] What is the matter with him?

TESMAN Well—no doubt he has run through all his property long ago; and he can scarcely write a new book every year—eh? So I really can't see what is to become of him.

BRACK Perhaps I can give you some information on that point.

TESMAN Indeed!

BRACK You must remember that his relations have a good deal of influence.

TESMAN Oh, his relations, unfortunately, have entirely washed their hands of him.

BRACK At one time they called him the hope of the family.

TESMAN At one time, yes! But he has put an end to all that.

HEDDA Who knows? [*With a slight smile.*] I hear they have reclaimed him up at Sheriff Elvsted's . . .

BRACK And then this book that he has published . . .

TESMAN Well, well, I hope to goodness they may find something for him to do. I have just written to him. I asked him to come and see us this evening, Hedda dear.

BRACK But my dear fellow, you are booked for my bachelors' party this evening. You promised on the pier last night.

HEDDA Had you forgotten, Tesman?

TESMAN Yes, I had utterly forgotten.

BRACK But it doesn't matter, for you may be sure he won't come.

TESMAN What makes you think that? Eh?

BRACK [*With a little hesitation, rising and resting his hands on the back of his chair.*] My dear Tesman—and you too, Mrs. Tesman—I think I ought not to keep you in the dark about something that—that . . .

TESMAN That concerns Eilert . . . ?

BRACK Both you and him.

TESMAN Well, my dear Judge, out with it.

BRACK You must be prepared to find your appointment deferred longer than you desired or expected.

TESMAN [*Jumping up uneasily.*] Is there some hitch about it? Eh?

BRACK The nomination may perhaps be made conditional on the result of a competition . . .

TESMAN Competition! Think of that, Hedda!

HEDDA [*Leans further back in the chair.*] Aha—aha!

TESMAN But who can my competitor be? Surely not . . . ?

BRACK Yes, precisely—Eilert Lövborg.

TESMAN [*Clasping his hands.*] No, no—it's quite inconceivable! Quite impossible! Eh?

BRACK H'm—that is what it may come to, all the same.

TESMAN Well but, Judge Brack—it would show the most incredible lack of consideration for me. [*Gesticulates with his arms.*] For—just think—I'm a married man! We have married on the strength of these prospects, Hedda and I; and run deep into debt; and borrowed money from Aunt Julia too. Good heavens, they had as good as promised me the appointment. Eh?

BRACK Well, well, well—no doubt you will get it in the end; only after a contest.

HEDDA [*Immovable in her armchair.*] Fancy, Tesman, there will be a sort of sporting interest in that.

TESMAN Why, my dearest Hedda, how can you be so indifferent about it?

HEDDA [*As before.*] I am not at all indifferent. I am most eager to see who wins.

BRACK In any case, Mrs. Tesman, it is best that you should know how matters stand. I mean—before you set about the little purchases I hear you are threatening.

HEDDA This can make no difference.

BRACK Indeed! Then I have no more to say. Good-bye! [*To* TESMAN.] I shall look in on my way back from my afternoon walk, and take you home with me.

TESMAN Oh yes, yes—your news has quite upset me.

HEDDA [*Reclining, holds out her hand.*] Good-bye, Judge; and be sure you call in the afternoon.

BRACK Many thanks. Good-bye, good-bye!

TESMAN [*Accompanying him to the door.*] Good-bye, my dear Judge! You must really excuse me . . .

[JUDGE BRACK *goes out by the hall door.*]

TESMAN [*Crosses the room.*] Oh Hedda—one should never rush into adventures. Eh?

HEDDA [*Looks at him, smiling.*] Do you do that?

TESMAN Yes, dear—there is no denying—it was adventurous to go and marry and set up house upon mere expectations.

HEDDA Perhaps you are right there.

TESMAN Well—at all events, we have our delightful home, Hedda! Fancy, the home we both dreamed of—the home we were in love with, I may almost say. Eh?

HEDDA [*Rising slowly and wearily.*] It was part of our compact that we were to go into society—to keep open house.

TESMAN Yes, if you only knew how I had been looking forward to it! Fancy—to see you as hostess—in a select circle! Eh? Well, well, well—for the present we shall have to get on without society, Hedda—only to invite Aunt Julia now and then. Oh, I intended you to lead such an utterly different life, dear . . . !

HEDDA Of course I cannot have my man in livery just yet.

TESMAN Oh no, unfortunately. It would be out of the question for us to keep a footman, you know.

HEDDA And the saddle horse I was to have had . . .

TESMAN [*Aghast.*] The saddle horse!

HEDDA . . . I suppose I must not think of that now.

TESMAN Good heavens, no!—that's as clear as daylight.

HEDDA [*Goes up the room.*] Well, I shall have one thing at least to kill time with in the meanwhile.

TESMAN [*Beaming.*] Oh thank heaven for that! What is it, Hedda? Eh?

HEDDA [*In the middle doorway, looks at him with covert scorn.*] My pistols, George.

TESMAN [*In alarm.*] Your pistols!

HEDDA [*With cold eyes.*] General Gabler's pistols. [*She goes out through the inner room, to the left.*]

TESMAN [*Rushes up to the middle doorway and calls after her.*] No, for heaven's sake, Hedda darling—don't touch those dangerous things! For my sake, Hedda! Eh?

ACT II

SCENE: *The room at the* TESMANS' *as in the first act, except that the piano has been removed, and an elegant little writing table with bookshelves put in its place. A smaller table stands near the sofa on the left. Most of the bouquets have been taken away.* MRS. ELVSTED'S *bouquet is upon the large table in front. It is afternoon.* HEDDA, *dressed to receive callers, is alone in the room. She stands by the open glass door, loading a revolver. The fellow to it lies in an open pistol case on the writing table.*

HEDDA [*Looks down the garden, and calls.*] So you are here again, Judge!

BRACK [*Is heard calling from a distance.*] As you see, Mrs. Tesman!

HEDDA [*Raises the pistol and points.*] Now I'll shoot you, Judge Brack!

BRACK [*Calling unseen.*] No, no, no! Don't stand aiming at me!

HEDDA This is what comes of sneaking in by the back way. [*She fires.*]

BRACK [*Nearer.*] Are you out of your senses! . . .

HEDDA Dear me—did I happen to hit you?

BRACK [*Still outside.*] I wish you would let these pranks alone!

HEDDA Come in then, Judge.

[JUDGE BRACK, *dressed as though for a men's party, enters by the glass door. He carries a light overcoat over his arm.*]

BRACK What the deuce—haven't you tired of that sport, yet? What are you shooting at?

HEDDA Oh, I am only firing in the air.

BRACK [*Gently takes the pistol out of her hand.*] Allow me, Madam! [*Looks at it.*] Ah—I know this pistol well! [*Looks around.*] Where is the case? Ah, here it is. [*Lays the pistol in it, and shuts it.*] Now we won't play at that game any more today.

HEDDA Then what in heaven's name would you have me do with myself?

BRACK Have you had no visitors?

HEDDA [*Closing the glass door.*] Not one. I suppose all our set are still out of town.

BRACK And is Tesman not at home either?

HEDDA [*At the writing table, putting the pistol case in a drawer which she shuts.*] No. He rushed off to his aunts' directly after lunch; he didn't expect you so early.

BRACK H'm—how stupid of me not to have thought of that!

HEDDA [*Turning her head to look at him.*] Why stupid?

BRACK Because if I had thought of it I should have come a little—earlier.

HEDDA [*Crossing the room.*] Then you would have found no one to receive you; for I have been in my room changing my dress ever since lunch.

BRACK And is there no sort of little chink that we could hold a parley through?

HEDDA You have forgotten to arrange one.

BRACK That was another piece of stupidity.

HEDDA Well, we must just settle down here—and wait. Tesman is not likely to be back for some time yet.

BRACK Never mind; I shall not be impatient.

[HEDDA *seats herself in the corner of the sofa.* BRACK *lays his overcoat over the back of the nearest chair, and sits down, but keeps his hat in his hand. A short silence. They look at each other.*]

HEDDA Well?

BRACK [*In the same tone.*] Well?

HEDDA I spoke first.

BRACK [*Bending a little forward.*] Come, let us have a cozy little chat, Mrs. Hedda.

HEDDA [*Leaning further back in the sofa.*] Does it not seem like a whole eternity since our last talk? Of course I don't count those few words yesterday evening and this morning.

BRACK You mean since our last confidential talk? Our last *tête-à-tête?*

HEDDA Well, yes—since you put it so.

BRACK Not a day has passed but I have wished that you were home again.

HEDDA And I have done nothing but wish the same thing.

BRACK You? Really, Mrs. Hedda? And I thought you had been enjoying your tour so much!

HEDDA Oh, yes, you may be sure of that!

BRACK But Tesman's letters spoke of nothing but happiness.

HEDDA Oh, Tesman! You see, he thinks nothing so delightful as grubbing in libraries and making copies of old parchments, or whatever you call them.

BRACK [*With a spice of malice.*] Well, that is his vocation in life—or part of it at any rate.

HEDDA Yes, of course; and no doubt when it's your vocation . . . But *I!* Oh, my dear Mr. Brack, how mortally bored I have been.

BRACK [*Sympathetically.*] Do you really say so? In downright earnest?

HEDDA Yes, you can surely understand it . . . ! To go for six whole months without meeting a soul that knew anything of our circle, or could talk about the things we are interested in.

BRACK Yes, yes—I, too, should feel that a deprivation.

HEDDA And then, what I found most intolerable of all . . .

BRACK Well?

HEDDA . . . was being everlastingly in the company of—one and the same person . . .

BRACK [*With a nod of assent.*] Morning, noon, and night, yes—at all possible times and seasons.

HEDDA I said "everlastingly."

BRACK Just so. But I should have thought, with our excellent Tesman, one could . . .

HEDDA Tesman is—a specialist, my dear Judge.

BRACK Undeniably.

HEDDA And specialists are not at all amusing to travel with. Not in the long run at any rate.

BRACK Not even—the specialist one happens to love?

HEDDA Faugh—don't use that sickening word!

BRACK [*Taken aback.*] What do you say, Mrs. Hedda?

HEDDA [*Half laughingly, half irritated.*] You should just try it! To hear of nothing but the history of civilization morning, noon, and night . . .

BRACK Everlastingly.

HEDDA Yes, yes, yes! And then all this about the domestic industry of the Middle Ages . . . ! That's the most disgusting part of it!

BRACK [*Looks searchingly at her.*] But tell me—in that case, how am I to understand your . . . ? H'm . . .

HEDDA My accepting George Tesman, you mean?

BRACK Well, let us put it so.

HEDDA Good heavens, do you see anything so wonderful in that?

BRACK Yes and no—Mrs. Hedda.

HEDDA I had positively danced myself tired, my dear Judge. My day was done . . . [*With a slight shudder.*] Oh, no—I won't say that; nor think it, either!

BRACK You have assuredly no reason to.

HEDDA Oh, reasons . . . [*Watching him closely.*] And George Tesman—after all, you must admit that he is correctness itself.

BRACK His correctness and respectability are beyond all question.

HEDDA And I don't see anything absolutely ridiculous about him. Do you?

BRACK Ridiculous? N—no—I shouldn't exactly say so . . .

HEDDA Well—and his powers of research, at all events, are untiring. I see no reason why he should not one day come to the front, after all.

BRACK [*Looks at her hesitatingly.*] I thought that you, like every one else, expected him to attain the highest distinction.

HEDDA [*With an expression of fatigue.*] Yes, so I did—And then, since he was bent, at all hazards, on being allowed to provide for me—I really don't know why I should not have accepted his offer.

BRACK No—if you look at it in that light . . .

HEDDA It was more than my other adorers were prepared to do for me, my dear Judge.

BRACK [*Laughing.*] Well, I can't answer for all the rest; but as for myself, you know quite well that I have always entertained a—a certain respect for the marriage tie—for marriage as an institution, Mrs. Hedda.

HEDDA [*Jestingly.*] Oh, I assure you I have never cherished any hopes with respect to you.

BRACK All I require is a pleasant and intimate interior, where I can make myself useful in every way, and am free to come and go as—as a trusted friend . . .

HEDDA Of the master of the house, do you mean?

BRACK [*Bowing.*] Frankly—of the mistress first of all; but, of course, of the master, too, in the second place. Such a triangular friendship—if I may call it so—is really a great convenience for all parties, let me tell you.

HEDDA Yes, I have many a time longed for some one to make a third on our travels. Oh—those railway-carriage *tête-à-têtes* . . . !

BRACK Fortunately your wedding journey is over now.

HEDDA [*Shaking her head.*] Not by a long—long way. I have only arrived at a station on the line.

BRACK Well, then the passengers jump out and move about a little, Mrs. Hedda.

HEDDA I never jump out.

BRACK Really?

HEDDA No—because there is always some one standing by to . . .

BRACK [*Laughing.*] To look at your legs, do you mean?

HEDDA Precisely.

BRACK Well, but, dear me . . .

HEDDA [*With a gesture of repulsion.*] I won't have it. I would rather keep my seat where I happen to be—and continue the *tête-à-tête.*

BRACK But suppose a third person were to jump in and join the couple.

HEDDA Ah—that is quite another matter!

BRACK A trusted, sympathetic friend . . .

HEDDA . . . with a fund of conversation on all sorts of lively topics . . .

BRACK . . . and not the least bit of a specialist!

HEDDA [*With an audible sigh.*] Yes, that would be a relief, indeed.

BRACK [*Hears the front door open, and glances in that direction.*] The triangle is completed.

HEDDA [*Half aloud.*] And on goes the train.

[GEORGE TESMAN, *in a gray walking suit, with a soft felt hat, enters from the hall. He has a number of unbound books under his arm and in his pockets.*]

TESMAN [*Goes up to the table beside the corner settee.*] Ouf—what a load for a warm day—all these books. [*Lays them on the table.*] I'm positively perspiring, Hedda. Hallo—are you there already, my dear Judge? Eh? Berta didn't tell me.

BRACK [*Rising.*] I came in through the garden.

HEDDA What books have you got there?

TESMAN [*Stands looking them through.*] Some new books on my special subjects—quite indispensable to me.

HEDDA Your special subjects?

BRACK Yes, books on his special subjects, Mrs. Tesman.

[BRACK *and* HEDDA *exchange a confidential smile.*]

HEDDA Do you need still more books on your special subjects?

TESMAN Yes, my dear Hedda, one can never have too many of them. Of course, one must keep up with all that is written and published.

HEDDA Yes, I suppose one must.

TESMAN [*Searching among his books.*] And look here—I have got hold of Eilert Lövborg's new book, too. [*Offering it to her.*] Perhaps you would like to glance through it, Hedda? Eh?

HEDDA No, thank you. Or rather—afterwards perhaps.

TESMAN I looked into it a little on the way home.

BRACK Well, what do you think of it—as a specialist?

TESMAN I think it shows quite remarkable soundness of judgment. He never wrote like that before. [*Putting the books together.*] Now I shall take all these into my study. I'm longing to cut the leaves . . . ! And then I must change my clothes. [*To* BRACK.] I suppose we needn't start just yet? Eh?

BRACK Oh, dear, no—there is not the slightest hurry.

TESMAN Well, then, I will take my time. [*Is going with his books, but stops in the doorway and turns.*] By the by, Hedda—Aunt Julia is not coming this evening.

HEDDA Not coming? Is it that affair of the bonnet that keeps her away?

TESMAN Oh, not at all. How could you think such a thing of Aunt Julia? Just fancy . . . ! The fact is, Aunt Rina is very ill.

HEDDA She always is.

TESMAN Yes, but today she is much worse than usual, poor dear.

HEDDA Oh, then it's only natural that her sister should remain with her. I must bear my disappointment.

TESMAN And you can't imagine, dear, how delighted Aunt Julia seemed to be—because you had come home looking so flourishing!

HEDDA [*Half aloud, rising.*] Oh, those everlasting aunts!

TESMAN What?

HEDDA [*Going to the glass door.*] Nothing.

TESMAN Oh, all right. [*He goes through the inner room, out to the right.*]

BRACK What bonnet were you talking about?

HEDDA Oh, it was a little episode with Miss Tesman this morning. She had laid down her bonnet on the chair there—[*looks at him and smiles*]—and I pretended to think it was the servant's.

BRACK [*Shaking his head.*] Now, my dear Mrs. Hedda, how could you do such a thing? To that excellent old lady, too!

HEDDA [*Nervously crossing the room.*] Well, you see—these impulses come over me all of a sudden; and I cannot resist them. [*Throws herself down in the easy-chair by the stove.*] Oh, I don't know how to explain it.

BRACK [*Behind the easy-chair.*] You are not really happy—that is at the bottom of it.

HEDDA [*Looking straight before her.*] I know of no reason why I should be—happy. Perhaps you can give me one?

BRACK Well—amongst other things, because you have got exactly the home you had set your heart on.

HEDDA [*Looks up at him and laughs.*] Do you, too, believe in that legend?

BRACK Is there nothing in it, then?

HEDDA Oh, yes, there is something in it.

BRACK Well?

HEDDA There is this in it, that I made use of Tesman to see me home from evening parties last summer . . .

BRACK I, unfortunately, had to go quite a different way.

HEDDA That's true. I know you were going a different way last summer.

BRACK [*Laughing.*] Oh fie, Mrs. Hedda! Well, then—you and Tesman . . . ?

HEDDA Well, we happened to pass here one evening; Tesman, poor fellow, was writhing in the agony of having to find conversation; so I took pity on the learned man . . .

BRACK [*Smiles doubtfully.*] You took pity? H'm . . .

HEDDA Yes, I really did. And so—to help him out of his torment—I happened to say, in pure thoughtlessness, that I should like to live in this villa.

BRACK No more than that?

HEDDA Not that evening.

BRACK But afterwards?

HEDDA Yes, my thoughtlessness had consequences, my dear Judge.

BRACK Unfortunately that too often happens, Mrs. Hedda.

HEDDA Thanks! So you see it was this enthusiasm for Secretary Falk's villa that first constituted a bond of sympathy between George Tesman and me. From that came our engagement and our marriage, and our wedding journey, and all the rest of it. Well, well, my dear Judge—as you make your bed so you must lie, I could almost say.

BRACK This is exquisite! And you really cared not a rap about it all the time?

HEDDA No, heaven knows I didn't.

BRACK But now? Now that we have made it so homelike for you?

HEDDA Ugh—the rooms all seem to smell of lavender and dried roseleaves. But perhaps it's Aunt Julia that has brought that scent with her.

BRACK [*Laughing.*] No, I think it must be a legacy from the late Mrs. Secretary Falk.

HEDDA Yes, there is an odor of mortality about it. It reminds me of a bouquet—the day after the ball. [*Clasps her hands behind her head, leans back in her chair and looks at him.*] Oh, my dear Judge—you cannot imagine how horribly I shall bore myself here.

BRACK Why should not you, too, find some sort of vocation in life, Mrs. Hedda?

HEDDA A vocation—that should attract me?

BRACK If possible, of course.

HEDDA Heaven knows what sort of a vocation that could be. I often wonder whether . . . [*Breaking off.*] But that would never do, either.

BRACK Who can tell? Let me hear what it is.

HEDDA Whether I might not get Tesman to go into politics, I mean.

BRACK [*Laughing.*] Tesman? No, really now, political life is not the thing for him—not at all in his line.

HEDDA No, I daresay not. But if I could get him into it all the same?

BRACK Why—what satisfaction could you find in that? If he is not fitted for that sort of thing, why should you want to drive him into it?

HEDDA Because I am bored, I tell you! [*After a pause.*] So you think it quite out of the question that Tesman should ever get into the ministry?

BRACK H'm—you see, my dear Mrs. Hedda—to get into the ministry, he would have to be a tolerably rich man.

HEDDA [*Rising impatiently.*] Yes, there we have it! It is this genteel poverty I have managed to drop into . . . ! [*Crosses the room.*] That is what makes life so pitiable! So utterly ludicrous! —For that's what it is.

BRACK Now *I* should say the fault lay elsewhere.

HEDDA Where, then?

BRACK You have never gone through any really stimulating experience.

HEDDA Anything serious, you mean?

BRACK Yes, you may call it so. But now you may perhaps have one in store.

HEDDA [*Tossing her head.*] Oh, you're thinking of the annoyances about this wretched professorship! But that must be Tesman's own affair. I assure you I shall not waste a thought upon it.

BRACK No, no, I daresay not. But suppose now that what people call—in elegant language—a solemn responsibility were to come upon you? [*Smiling.*] A new responsibility, Mrs. Hedda?

HEDDA [*Angrily.*] Be quiet! Nothing of that sort will ever happen!

BRACK [*Warily.*] We will speak of this again a year hence—at the very outside.

HEDDA [*Curtly.*] I have no turn for anything of the sort, Judge Brack. No responsibilities for me!

BRACK Are you so unlike the generality of women as to have no turn for duties which . . . ?

HEDDA [*Beside the glass door.*] Oh, be quiet, I tell you! I often think there is only one thing in the world I have any turn for.

BRACK [*Drawing near to her.*] And what is that, if I may ask?

HEDDA [*Stands looking out.*] Boring myself to death. Now you know it. [*Turns, looks towards the inner room, and laughs.*] Yes, as I thought! Here comes the Professor.

BRACK [*Softly, in a tone of warning.*] Come, come, come, Mrs. Hedda!

[GEORGE TESMAN, *dressed for the party, with his gloves and hat in his hand, enters from the right through the inner room.*]

TESMAN Hedda, has no message come from Eilert Lövborg? Eh?

HEDDA No.

TESMAN Then you'll see he'll be here presently.

BRACK Do you really think he will come?

TESMAN Yes, I am almost sure of it. For what you were telling us this morning must have been a mere floating rumor.

BRACK You think so?

TESMAN At any rate, Aunt Julia said she did not believe for a moment that he would ever stand in my way again. Fancy that!

BRACK Well, then, that's all right.

TESMAN [*Placing his hat and gloves on a chair on the right.*] Yes, but you must really let me wait for him as long as possible.

BRACK We have plenty of time yet. None of my guests will arrive before seven or half-past.

TESMAN Then meanwhile we can keep Hedda company, and see what happens. Eh?

HEDDA [*Placing* BRACK'S *hat and overcoat upon the corner settee.*] And at the worst Mr. Lövborg can remain here with me.

BRACK [*Offering to take his things.*] Oh, allow me, Mrs. Tesman! What do you mean by "at the worst"?

HEDDA If he won't go with you and Tesman.

TESMAN [*Looks dubiously at her.*] But, Hedda, dear—do you think it would quite do for him to remain with you? Eh? Remember, Aunt Julia can't come.

HEDDA No, but Mrs. Elvsted is coming. We three can have a cup of tea together.

TESMAN Oh, yes, that will be all right.

BRACK [*Smiling.*] And that would perhaps be the safest plan for him.

HEDDA Why so?

BRACK Well, you know, Mrs. Tesman, how you used to jeer at my little bachelor parties. You declared they were adapted only for men of the strictest principles.

HEDDA But no doubt Mr. Lövborg's principles are strict enough now. A converted sinner . . .

[BERTA *appears at the hall door.*]

BERTA There's a gentleman asking if you are at home, ma'am . . .

HEDDA Well, show him in.

TESMAN [*Softly.*] I'm sure it is he! Fancy that!

[EILERT LÖVBORG *enters from the hall. He is slim and lean; of the same age as* TESMAN, *but looks older and somewhat worn-out. His hair and beard are of a blackish brown, his face long and pale, but with patches of color on the cheekbones. He is dressed in a well-cut black visiting suit, quite new. He has dark gloves and a silk hat. He stops near the door, and makes a rapid bow, seeming somewhat embarrassed.*]

TESMAN [*Goes up to him and shakes him warmly by the hand.*] Well, my dear Eilert—so at last we meet again!

EILERT LÖVBORG [*Speaks in a subdued voice.*] Thanks for your letter, Tesman. [*Approaching* HEDDA.] Will you, too, shake hands with me, Mrs. Tesman?

HEDDA [*Taking his hand.*] I am glad to see you, Mr. Lövborg. [*With a motion of her hand.*] I don't know whether you two gentlemen . . . ?

LÖVBORG [*Bowing slightly.*] Judge Brack, I think.

BRACK [*Doing likewise.*] Oh, yes—in the old days . . .

TESMAN [*To* LÖVBORG, *with his hands on his shoulders.*] And now you must make yourself entirely at home, Eilert! Mustn't he, Hedda?—For I hear you are going to settle in town again? Eh?

LÖVBORG Yes, I am.

TESMAN Quite right, quite right. Let me tell you, I have got hold of your new book; but I haven't had time to read it yet.

LÖVBORG You may spare yourself the trouble.

TESMAN Why so?

LÖVBORG Because there is very little in it.

TESMAN Just fancy—how can you say so?

BRACK But it has been very much praised, I hear.

LÖVBORG That was what I wanted; so I put nothing into the book but what every one would agree with.

BRACK Very wise of you.

TESMAN Well, but, my dear Eilert . . . !

LÖVBORG For now I mean to win myself a position again—to make a fresh start.

TESMAN [*A little embarrassed.*] Ah, that is what you wish to do? Eh?

LÖVBORG [*Smiling, lays down his hat, and draws a packet, wrapped in paper, from his coat pocket.*] But when this one appears, George Tesman, you will have to read it. For this is the real book—the book I have put my true self into.

TESMAN Indeed? And what is it?

LÖVBORG It is the continuation.

TESMAN The continuation? Of what?

LÖVBORG Of the book.

TESMAN Of the new book?

LÖVBORG Of course.

TESMAN Why, my dear Eilert—does it not come down to our own days?

LÖVBORG Yes, it does; and this one deals with the future.

TESMAN With the future! But, good heavens, we know nothing of the future!

LÖVBORG No; but there is a thing or two to be said about it all the same. [*Opens the packet.*] Look here . . .

TESMAN Why, that's not your handwriting.

LÖVBORG I dictated it. [*Turning over the pages.*] It falls into two sections. The first deals with the civilizing forces of the future. And here is the second—[*running through the pages towards the end*]—forecasting the probable line of development.

TESMAN How odd now! I should never have thought of writing anything of that sort.

HEDDA [*At the glass door, drumming on the pane.*] H'm . . . I daresay not.

LÖVBORG [*Replacing the manuscript in its paper and laying the packet on the table.*] I brought it, thinking I might read you a little of it this evening.

TESMAN That was very good of you, Eilert. But this evening . . . ? [*Looking at* BRACK.] I don't quite see how we can manage it . . .

LÖVBORG Well, then, some other time. There is no hurry.

BRACK I must tell you, Mr. Lövborg—there is a little gathering at my house this evening—mainly in honor of Tesman, you know . . .

LÖVBORG [*Looking for his hat.*] Oh—then I won't detain you . . .

BRACK No, but listen—will you not do me the favor of joining us?

LÖVBORG [*Curtly and decidedly.*] No, I can't—thank you very much.

BRACK Oh, nonsense—do! We shall be quite a select little circle. And I assure you we shall have a "lively time," as Mrs. Hed—as Mrs. Tesman says.

LÖVBORG I have no doubt of it. But nevertheless . . .

BRACK And then you might bring your manuscript with you, and read it to Tesman at my house. I could give you a room to yourselves.

TESMAN Yes, think of that, Eilert—why shouldn't you? Eh?

HEDDA [*Interposing.*] But, Tesman, if Mr. Lövborg would really rather not! I am sure Mr. Lövborg is much more inclined to remain here and have supper with me.

LÖVBORG [*Looking at her.*] With you, Mrs. Tesman?

HEDDA And with Mrs. Elvsted.

LÖVBORG Ah . . . [*Lightly.*] I saw her for a moment this morning.

HEDDA Did you? Well, she is coming this evening. So you see you are almost bound to remain, Mr. Lövborg, or she will have no one to see her home.

LÖVBORG That's true. Many thanks, Mrs. Tesman—in that case I will remain.

HEDDA Then I have one or two orders to give the servant . . .

[*She goes to the hall door and rings.* BERTA *enters.* HEDDA *talks to her in a whisper, and points towards the inner room.* BERTA *nods and goes out again.*]

TESMAN [*At the same time, to* LÖVBORG.] Tell me, Eilert—is it this new subject—the future—that you are going to lecture about?

LÖVBORG Yes.

TESMAN They told me at the bookseller's that you are going to deliver a course of lectures this autumn.

LÖVBORG That is my intention. I hope you won't take it ill, Tesman.

TESMAN Oh no, not in the least! But . . . ?

LÖVBORG I can quite understand that it must be disagreeable to you.

TESMAN [*Cast down.*] Oh, I can't expect you, out of consideration for me, to . . .

LÖVBORG But I shall wait till you have received your appointment.

TESMAN Will you wait? Yes, but—yes, but—are you not going to compete with me? Eh?

LÖVBORG No; it is only the moral victory I care for.

TESMAN Why, bless me—then Aunt Julia was right after all! Oh, yes—I knew it! Hedda! Just fancy—Eilert Lövborg is not going to stand in our way!

HEDDA [*Curtly.*] Our way? Pray leave me out of the question.

[*She goes up towards the inner room, where* BERTA *is placing a tray with decanters and glasses on the table.* HEDDA *nods approval, and comes forward again.* BERTA *goes out.*]

TESMAN [*At the same time.*] And you, Judge Brack—what do you say to this? Eh?

BRACK Well, I say that a moral victory—h'm—may be all very fine . . .

TESMAN Yes, certainly. But all the same . . .

HEDDA [*Looking at* TESMAN *with a cold smile.*] You stand there looking as if you were thunderstruck . . .

TESMAN Yes—so I am—I almost think . . .

BRACK Don't you see, Mrs. Tesman, a thunderstorm has just passed over?

HEDDA [*Pointing towards the inner room.*] Will you not take a glass of cold punch, gentlemen?

BRACK [*Looking at his watch.*] A stirrup cup? Yes, it wouldn't come amiss.

TESMAN A capital idea, Hedda! Just the thing! Now that the weight has been taken off my mind . . .

HEDDA Will you not join them, Mr. Lövborg?

LÖVBORG [*With a gesture of refusal.*] No, thank you. Nothing for me.

BRACK Why bless me—cold punch is surely not poison.

LÖVBORG Perhaps not for every one.

HEDDA I will keep Mr. Lövborg company in the meantime.

TESMAN Yes, yes, Hedda dear, do.

[*He and* BRACK *go into the inner room, seat themselves, drink punch, smoke cigarettes, and carry on a lively conversation during what follows.* EILERT LÖVBORG *remains standing beside the stove.* HEDDA *goes to the writing table.*]

HEDDA [*Raising her voice a little.*] Do you care to look at some photographs, Mr. Lövborg? You know Tesman and I made a tour in the Tyrol on our way home?

[*She takes up an album, and places it on the table beside the sofa, in the further corner of which she seats herself.* EILERT LÖVBORG *approaches, stops, and looks at her. Then he takes a chair and seats himself to her left, with his back towards the inner room.*]

HEDDA [*Opening the album.*] Do you see this range of mountains, Mr. Lövborg? It's the Ortler group. Tesman has written the name underneath. Here it is: "The Ortler group near Meram."

LÖVBORG [*Who has never taken his eyes off her, says softly and slowly.*] Hedda—Gabler!

HEDDA [*Glancing hastily at him.*] Ah! Hush!

LÖVBORG [*Repeats softly.*] Hedda Gabler!

HEDDA [*Looking at the album.*] That was my name in the old days—when we two knew each other.

LÖVBORG And I must teach myself never to say Hedda Gabler again—never, as long as I live.

HEDDA [*Still turning over the pages.*] Yes, you must. And I think you ought to practice in time. The sooner the better, I should say.

LÖVBORG [*In a tone of indignation.*] Hedda Gabler married? And married to—George Tesman!

HEDDA Yes—so the world goes.

LÖVBORG Oh, Hedda, Hedda—how could you[5] throw yourself away!

HEDDA [*Looks sharply at him.*] What? I can't allow this!

LÖVBORG What do you mean?

[TESMAN *comes into the room and goes towards the sofa.*]

HEDDA [*Hears him coming and says in an indifferent tone.*] And this is a view from the Val d'Ampezzo, Mr. Lövborg. Just look at these peaks! [*Looks affectionately up at* TESMAN.] What's the name of these curious peaks, dear?

TESMAN Let me see. Oh, those are the Dolomites.

HEDDA Yes, that's it! Those are the Dolomites, Mr. Lövborg.

TESMAN Hedda, dear, I only wanted to ask whether I shouldn't bring you a little punch after all? For yourself, at any rate—eh?

HEDDA Yes, do, please; and perhaps a few biscuits.

TESMAN No cigarettes?

HEDDA No.

TESMAN Very well.

[*He goes into the inner room and out to the right.* BRACK *sits in the inner room, and keeps an eye from time to time on* HEDDA *and* LÖVBORG.]

---

5. Lövborg uses the familiar *du.*

LÖVBORG [*Softly, as before.*] Answer me, Hedda—how could you go and do this?

HEDDA [*Apparently absorbed in the album.*] If you continue to say *du* to me I won't talk to you.

LÖVBORG May I not say *du* even when we are alone?

HEDDA No. You may think it; but you mustn't say it.

LÖVBORG Ah, I understand. It is an offense against George Tesman, whom you[6] love.

HEDDA [*Glances at him and smiles.*] Love? What an idea!

LÖVBORG You don't love him then!

HEDDA But I won't hear of any sort of unfaithfulness! Remember that.

LÖVBORG Hedda—answer me one thing . . .

HEDDA Hush!

[TESMAN *enters with a small tray from the inner room.*]

TESMAN Here you are! Isn't this tempting?

[*He puts the tray on the table.*]

HEDDA Why do you bring it yourself?

TESMAN [*Filling the glasses.*] Because I think it's such fun to wait upon you, Hedda.

HEDDA But you have poured out two glasses. Mr. Lövborg said he wouldn't have any . . .

TESMAN No, but Mrs. Elvsted will soon be here, won't she?

HEDDA Yes, by the by—Mrs. Elvsted . . .

TESMAN Had you forgotten her? Eh?

HEDDA We were so absorbed in these photographs. [*Shows him a picture.*] Do you remember this little village?

TESMAN Oh, it's that one just below the Brenner Pass. It was there we passed the night . . .

HEDDA . . . and met that lively party of tourists.

TESMAN Yes, that was the place. Fancy—if we could only have had you with us, Eilert! Eh?

[*He returns to the inner room and sits beside* BRACK.]

LÖVBORG Answer me this one thing, Hedda . . .

HEDDA Well?

---

6. From here on Lövborg uses the formal *De.*

LÖVBORG Was there no love in your friendship for me, either? Not a spark—not a tinge of love in it?

HEDDA I wonder if there was? To me it seems as though we were two good comrades—two thoroughly intimate friends. [*Smilingly.*] You especially were frankness itself.

LÖVBORG It was you that made me so.

HEDDA As I look back upon it all, I think there was really something beautiful, something fascinating—something daring—in—in that secret intimacy—that comradeship which no living creature so much as dreamed of.

LÖVBORG Yes, yes, Hedda! Was there not?—When I used to come to your father's in the afternoon—and the General sat over at the window reading his papers—with his back towards us . . .

HEDDA And we two on the corner sofa . . .

LÖVBORG Always with the same illustrated paper before us . . .

HEDDA For want of an album, yes.

LÖVBORG Yes, Hedda, and when I made my confessions to you—told you about myself, things that at that time no one else knew! There I would sit and tell you of my escapades—my days and nights of devilment. Oh, Hedda—what was the power in you that forced me to confess these things?

HEDDA Do you think it was any power in me?

LÖVBORG How else can I explain it? And all those—those roundabout questions you used to put to me . . .

HEDDA Which you understood so particularly well . . .

LÖVBORG How could you sit and question me like that? Question me quite frankly . . .

HEDDA In roundabout terms, please observe.

LÖVBORG Yes, but frankly nevertheless. Cross-question me about—all that sort of thing?

HEDDA And how could you answer, Mr. Lövborg?

LÖVBORG Yes, that is just what I can't understand—in looking back upon it. But tell me now, Hedda—was there not love at the bottom of our friendship? On your side, did you not feel as though you might purge my stains away—if I made you my confessor? Was it not so?

HEDDA No, not quite.

LÖVBORG What was your motive, then?

HEDDA Do you think it quite incomprehensible that a young girl—when it can be done—without any one knowing . . .

LÖVBORG Well?

HEDDA . . . should be glad to have a peep, now and then, into a world which . . .

LÖVBORG Which . . . ?

HEDDA . . . which she is forbidden to know anything about?

LÖVBORG So that was it?

HEDDA Partly. Partly—I almost think.

LÖVBORG Comradeship is the thirst for life. But why should not that, at any rate, have continued?

HEDDA The fault was yours.

LÖVBORG It was you that broke with me.

HEDDA Yes, when our friendship threatened to develop into something more serious. Shame upon you, Eilert Lövborg! How could you think of wronging your—your frank comrade?

LÖVBORG [*Clenching his hands.*] Oh, why did you not carry out your threat? Why did you not shoot me down?

HEDDA Because I have such a dread of scandal.

LÖVBORG Yes, Hedda, you are a coward at heart.

HEDDA A terrible coward. [*Changing her tone.*] But it was a lucky thing for you. And now you have found ample consolation at the Elvsteds'.

LÖVBORG I know what Thea has confided to you.

HEDDA And perhaps you have confided to her something about us?

LÖVBORG Not a word. She is too stupid to understand anything of that sort.

HEDDA Stupid?

LÖVBORG She is stupid about matters of that sort.

HEDDA And I am cowardly. [*Bends over towards him, without looking him in the face, and says more softly.*] But now I will confide something to you.

LÖVBORG [*Eagerly.*] Well?

HEDDA The fact that I dared not shoot you down . . .

LÖVBORG Yes!

HEDDA . . . that was not my most arrant cowardice—that evening.

LÖVBORG [*Looks at her a moment, understands and whispers passionately.*] Oh, Hedda! Hedda Gabler! Now I begin to see a hidden reason beneath our comradeship! You[7] and I . . . ! After all, then, it was your craving for life . . .

HEDDA [*Softly, with a sharp glance.*] Take care! Believe nothing of the sort!

[*Twilight has begun to fall. The hall door is opened from without by* BERTA.]

HEDDA [*Closes the album with a bang and calls smilingly.*] Ah, at last! My darling Thea—come along!

[MRS. ELVSTED *enters from the hall. She is in evening dress. The door is closed behind her.*]

HEDDA [*On the sofa, stretches out her arms towards her.*] My sweet Thea—you can't think how I have been longing for you!

[MRS. ELVSTED, *in passing, exchanges slight salutations with the gentlemen in the inner room, then goes up to the table and gives* HEDDA *her hand.* EILERT LÖVBORG *has risen. He and* MRS. ELVSTED *greet each other with a silent nod.*]

MRS. ELVSTED Ought I to go in and talk to your husband for a moment?

HEDDA Oh, not at all. Leave those two alone. They will soon be going.

MRS. ELVSTED Are they going out?

HEDDA Yes, to a supper party.

MRS. ELVSTED [*Quickly, to* LÖVBORG.] Not you?

LÖVBORG No.

HEDDA Mr. Lövborg remains with us.

MRS. ELVSTED [*Takes a chair and is about to seat herself at his side.*] Oh, how nice it is here!

HEDDA No, thank you, my little Thea! Not there! You'll be good enough to come over here to me. I will sit between you.

MRS. ELVSTED Yes, just as you please.

7. *Du* once more. Hedda uses *De* consistently.

[*She goes round the table and seats herself on the sofa on* HEDDA'S *right.* LÖVBORG *reseats himself on his chair.*]

LÖVBORG [*After a short pause, to* HEDDA.] Is not she lovely to look at?

HEDDA [*Lightly stroking her hair.*] Only to look at?

LÖVBORG Yes. For we two—she and I—we are two real comrades. We have absolute faith in each other; so we can sit and talk with perfect frankness . . .

HEDDA Not roundabout, Mr. Lövborg?

LÖVBORG Well . . .

MRS. ELVSTED [*Softly clinging close to* HEDDA.] Oh, how happy I am, Hedda! For, only think, he says I have inspired him, too.

HEDDA [*Looks at her with a smile.*] Ah! Does he say that, dear?

LÖVBORG And then she is so brave, Mrs. Tesman!

MRS. ELVSTED Good heavens—am I brave?

LÖVBORG Exceedingly—where your comrade is concerned.

HEDDA Ah, yes—courage! If one only had that!

LÖVBORG What then? What do you mean?

HEDDA Then life would perhaps be livable, after all. [*With a sudden change of tone.*] But now, my dearest Thea, you really must have a glass of cold punch.

MRS. ELVSTED No, thanks—I never take anything of that kind.

HEDDA Well, then, you, Mr. Lövborg.

LÖVBORG Nor I, thank you.

MRS. ELVSTED No, he doesn't, either.

HEDDA [*Looks fixedly at him.*] But if I say you shall?

LÖVBORG It would be no use.

HEDDA [*Laughing.*] Then I, poor creature, have no sort of power over you?

LÖVBORG Not in that respect.

HEDDA But seriously, I think you ought to—for your own sake.

MRS. ELVSTED Why, Hedda . . . !

LÖVBORG How so?

HEDDA Or rather on account of other people.

LÖVBORG Indeed?

HEDDA Otherwise people might be apt to suspect that—in your heart of hearts—you did not feel quite secure—quite confident in yourself.

MRS. ELVSTED [*Softly.*] Oh, please, Hedda . . . !

LÖVBORG People may suspect what they like—for the present.

MRS. ELVSTED [*Joyfully.*] Yes, let them!

HEDDA I saw it plainly in Judge Brack's face a moment ago.

LÖVBORG What did you see?

HEDDA His contemptuous smile, when you dared not go with them into the inner room.

LÖVBORG Dared not? Of course I preferred to stop here and talk to you.

MRS. ELVSTED What could be more natural, Hedda?

HEDDA But the Judge could not guess that. And I saw, too, the way he smiled and glanced at Tesman when you dared not accept his invitation to this wretched little supper party of his.

LÖVBORG Dared not? Do you say I dared not?

HEDDA *I* don't say so. But that was how Judge Brack understood it.

LÖVBORG Well, let him.

HEDDA Then you are not going with them?

LÖVBORG I will stay here with you and Thea.

MRS. ELVSTED Yes, Hedda—how can you doubt that?

HEDDA [*Smiles and nods approvingly to* LÖVBORG.] Firm as a rock! Faithful to your principles, now and forever! Ah, that is how a man should be! [*Turns to* MRS. ELVSTED *and caresses her.*] Well, now, what did I tell you, when you came to us this morning in such a state of distraction . . .

LÖVBORG [*Surprised.*] Distraction!

MRS. ELVSTED [*Terrified.*] Hedda—oh, Hedda . . . !

HEDDA You can see for yourself! You haven't the slightest reason to be in such mortal terror . . . [*Interrupting herself.*] There! Now we can all three enjoy ourselves!

LÖVBORG [*Who has given a start.*] Ah—what is all this, Mrs. Tesman?

MRS. ELVSTED Oh, my God, Hedda! What are you saying? What are you doing?

HEDDA Don't get excited! That horrid Judge Brack is sitting watching you.

LÖVBORG So she was in mortal terror! On my account!

MRS. ELVSTED [*Softly and piteously.*] Oh, Hedda—now you have ruined everything!

LÖVBORG [*Looks fixedly at her for a moment. His face is distorted.*] So that was my comrade's frank confidence in me?

MRS. ELVSTED [*Imploringly.*] Oh, my dearest friend—only let me tell you . . .

LÖVBORG [*Takes one of the glasses of punch, raises it to his lips, and says in a low, husky voice.*] Your health, Thea!

[*He empties the glass, puts it down, and takes the second.*]

MRS. ELVSTED [*Softly.*] Oh, Hedda, Hedda—how could you do this?

HEDDA *I* do it? *I*? Are you crazy?

LÖVBORG Here's to your health, too, Mrs. Tesman. Thanks for the truth. Hurrah for the truth!

[*He empties the glass and is about to refill it.*]

HEDDA [*Lays her hand on his arm.*] Come, come—no more for the present. Remember you are going out to supper.

MRS. ELVSTED No, no, no!

HEDDA Hush! They are sitting watching you.

LÖVBORG [*Putting down the glass.*] Now, Thea—tell me the truth . . .

MRS. ELVSTED Yes.

LÖVBORG Did your husband know that you had come after me?

MRS. ELVSTED [*Wringing her hands.*] Oh, Hedda—do you hear what he is asking?

LÖVBORG Was it arranged between you and him that you were to come to town and look after me? Perhaps it was the Sheriff himself that urged you to come? Aha, my dear—no doubt he wanted my help in his office. Or was it at the card table that he missed me?

MRS. ELVSTED [*Softly, in agony.*] Oh, Lövborg, Lövborg . . . !

LÖVBORG [*Seizes a glass and is on the point of filling it.*] Here's a glass for the old Sheriff, too!

HEDDA [*Preventing him.*] No more just now. Remember, you have to read your manuscript to Tesman.

LÖVBORG [*Calmly, putting down the glass.*] It was stupid of me all this, Thea—to take it in this way, I mean. Don't be angry with me, my dear, dear comrade. You shall see—both you and the others—that if I was fallen once—now I have risen again! Thanks to you, Thea.

MRS. ELVSTED [*Radiant with joy.*] Oh, heaven be praised . . . !

[BRACK *has in the meantime looked at his watch. He and* TESMAN *rise and come into the drawing room.*]

BRACK [*Takes his hat and overcoat.*] Well, Mrs. Tesman, our time has come.

HEDDA I suppose it has.

LÖVBORG [*Rising.*] Mine too, Judge Brack.

MRS. ELVSTED [*Softly and imploringly.*] Oh, Lövborg, don't do it!

HEDDA [*Pinching her arm.*] They can hear you!

MRS. ELVSTED [*With a suppressed shriek.*] Ow!

LÖVBORG [*To* BRACK.] You were good enough to invite me.

BRACK Well, are you coming after all?

LÖVBORG Yes, many thanks.

BRACK I'm delighted . . .

LÖVBORG [*To* TESMAN, *putting the parcel of MS. in his pocket.*] I should like to show you one or two things before I send it to the printers.

TESMAN Fancy—that will be delightful. But, Hedda dear, how is Mrs. Elvsted to get home? Eh?

HEDDA Oh, that can be managed somehow.

LÖVBORG [*Looking towards the ladies.*] Mrs. Elvsted? Of course, I'll come again and fetch her. [*Approaching.*] At ten or thereabouts, Mrs. Tesman? Will that do?

HEDDA Certainly. That will do capitally.

TESMAN Well, then, that's all right. But you must not expect me so early, Hedda.

HEDDA Oh, you may stop as long—as long as ever you please.

MRS. ELVSTED [*Trying to conceal her anxiety.*] Well, then, Mr. Lövborg—I shall remain here until you come.

LÖVBORG [*With his hat in his hand.*] Pray do, Mrs. Elvsted.

BRACK And now off goes the excursion train, gentlemen! I hope we shall have a lively time, as a certain fair lady puts it.

HEDDA Ah, if only the fair lady could be present unseen . . . !

BRACK Why unseen?

HEDDA In order to hear a little of your liveliness at first hand, Judge Brack.

BRACK [*Laughing.*] I should not advise the fair lady to try it.

TESMAN [*Also laughing.*] Come, you're a nice one, Hedda! Fancy that!

BRACK Well, good-bye, good-bye, ladies.

LÖVBORG [*Bowing.*] About ten o'clock, then.

[BRACK, LÖVBORG, *and* TESMAN *go out by the hall door. At the same time,* BERTA *enters from the inner room with a lighted lamp, which she places on the drawing room table; she goes out by the way she came.*]

MRS. ELVSTED [*Who has risen and is wandering restlessly about the room.*] Hedda—Hedda—what will come of all this?

HEDDA At ten o'clock—he will be here. I can see him already —with vine leaves[8] in his hair—flushed and fearless . . .

MRS. ELVSTED Oh, I hope he may.

HEDDA And then, you see—then he will have regained control over himself. Then he will be a free man for all his days.

MRS. ELVSTED Oh, God!—if he would only come as you see him now!

HEDDA He will come as I see him—so, and not otherwise! [*Rises and approaches* THEA]. You may doubt him as long as you please; *I* believe in him. And now we will try . . .

MRS. ELVSTED You have some hidden motive in this, Hedda!

HEDDA Yes, I have. I want for once in my life to have power to mold a human destiny.

MRS. ELVSTED Have you not the power?

---

8. Bacchus (Greek god of wine) wore vine leaves in his hair. For Hedda, the vine leaves symbolize triumphantly courageous unconventionality.

HEDDA I have not—and have never had it.

MRS. ELVSTED Not your husband's?

HEDDA Do you think that is worth the trouble? Oh, if you could only understand how poor I am. And fate has made you so rich! [*Clasps her passionately in her arms.*] I think I must burn your hair off, after all.

MRS. ELVSTED Let me go! Let me go! I am afraid of you, Hedda!

BERTA [*In the middle doorway.*] Tea is laid in the dining room, ma'am.

HEDDA Very well. We are coming.

MRS. ELVSTED No, no, no! I would rather go home alone! At once!

HEDDA Nonsense! First you shall have a cup of tea, you little stupid. And then—at ten o'clock—Eilert Lövborg will be here—with vine leaves in his hair.

[*She drags* MRS. ELVSTED *almost by force towards the middle doorway.*]

ACT III

SCENE: *The room at the* TESMANS'. *The curtains are drawn over the middle doorway, and also over the glass door. The lamp, half turned down, and with a shade over it, is burning on the table. In the stove, the door of which stands open, there has been a fire, which is now nearly burnt out.* MRS. ELVSTED, *wrapped in a large shawl, and with her feet upon a footrest, sits close to the stove, sunk back in the armchair.* HEDDA, *fully dressed, lies sleeping upon the sofa, with a sofa-blanket over her.*

MRS. ELVSTED [*After a pause, suddenly sits up in her chair, and listens eagerly. Then she sinks back again wearily, moaning to herself.*] Not yet! Oh, God—oh, God—not yet!

[BERTA *slips cautiously in by the hall door. She has a letter in her hand.*]

MRS. ELVSTED [*Turns and whispers eagerly.*] Well—has any one come?

BERTA [*Softly.*] Yes, a girl has just brought this letter.

MRS. ELVSTED [*Quickly, holding out her hand.*] A letter! Give it to me!

BERTA No, it's for Dr. Tesman, ma'am.

MRS. ELVSTED Oh, indeed.

BERTA It was Miss Tesman's servant that brought it. I'll lay it here on the table.

MRS. ELVSTED Yes, do.

BERTA [*Laying down the letter.*] I think I had better put out the lamp. It's smoking.

MRS. ELVSTED Yes, put it out. It must soon be daylight now.

BERTA [*Putting out the lamp.*] It is daylight already, ma'am.

MRS. ELVSTED Yes, broad day! And no one come back yet . . . !

BERTA Lord bless you, ma'am—I guessed how it would be.

MRS. ELVSTED You guessed?

BERTA Yes, when I saw that a certain person had come back to town—and that he went off with them. For we've heard enough about that gentleman before now.

MRS. ELVSTED Don't speak so loud. You will waken Mrs. Tesman.

BERTA [*Looks towards the sofa and sighs.*] No, no—let her sleep, poor thing. Shan't I put some wood on the fire?

MRS. ELVSTED Thanks, not for me.

BERTA Oh, very well.

[*She goes softly out by the hall door.*]

HEDDA [*Is awakened by the shutting of the door, and looks up.*] What's that . . . ?

MRS. ELVSTED It was only the servant . . .

HEDDA [*Looking about her.*] Oh, we're here . . . ! Yes, now I remember. [*Sits erect upon the sofa, stretches herself, and rubs her eyes.*] What o'clock is it, Thea?

MRS. ELVSTED [*Looks at her watch.*] It's past seven.

HEDDA When did Tesman come home?

MRS. ELVSTED He has not come.

HEDDA Not come home yet?

MRS. ELVSTED [*Rising.*] No one has come.

HEDDA Think of our watching and waiting here till four in the morning . . .

MRS. ELVSTED [*Wringing her hands.*] And how I watched and waited for him!

HEDDA [*Yawns, and says with her hand before her mouth.*] Well, well—we might have spared ourselves the trouble.

MRS. ELVSTED Did you get a little sleep?

HEDDA Oh, yes; I believe I have slept pretty well. Have you not?

MRS. ELVSTED Not for a moment. I couldn't, Hedda!—not to save my life.

HEDDA [*Rises and goes towards her.*] There, there, there! There's nothing to be so alarmed about. I understand quite well what has happened.

MRS. ELVSTED Well, what do you think? Won't you tell me?

HEDDA Why, of course, it has been a very late affair at Judge Brack's . . .

MRS. ELVSTED Yes, yes—that is clear enough. But all the same . . .

HEDDA And then, you see, Tesman hasn't cared to come home and ring us up in the middle of the night. [*Laughing.*] Perhaps he wasn't inclined to show himself either—immediately after a jollification.

MRS. ELVSTED But in that case—where can he have gone?

HEDDA Of course, he has gone to his aunts' and slept there. They have his old room ready for him.

MRS. ELVSTED No, he can't be with them; for a letter has just come for him from Miss Tesman. There it lies.

HEDDA Indeed? [*Looks at the address.*] Why, yes, it's addressed in Aunt Julia's own hand. Well, then, he has remained at Judge Brack's. And as for Eilert Lövborg—he is sitting, with vine leaves in his hair, reading his manuscript.

MRS. ELVSTED Oh, Hedda, you are just saying things you don't believe a bit.

HEDDA You really are a little blockhead, Thea.

MRS. ELVSTED Oh, yes, I suppose I am.

HEDDA And how mortally tired you look.

MRS. ELVSTED Yes, I am mortally tired.

HEDDA Well, then, you must do as I tell you. You must go into my room and lie down for a little while.

MRS. ELVSTED Oh, no, no—I shouldn't be able to sleep.

HEDDA I am sure you would.

MRS. ELVSTED Well, but your husband is certain to come soon now; and then I want to know at once . . .

HEDDA I shall take care to let you know when he comes.

MRS. ELVSTED Do you promise me, Hedda?

HEDDA Yes, rely upon me. Just you go in and have a sleep in the meantime.

MRS. ELVSTED Thanks; then I'll try to.

[*She goes off through the inner room.* HEDDA *goes up to the glass door and draws back the curtains. The broad daylight streams into the room. Then she takes a little hand glass from the writing table, looks at herself in it and arranges her hair. Next she goes to the hall door and presses the bell button.* BERTA *presently appears at the hall door.*]

BERTA Did you want anything, ma'am?

HEDDA Yes; you must put some more wood in the stove. I am shivering.

BERTA Bless me—I'll make up the fire at once. [*She rakes the embers together and lays a piece of wood upon them; then stops and listens.*] That was a ring at the front door, ma'am.

HEDDA Then go to the door. I will look after the fire.

BERTA It'll soon burn up.

[*She goes out by the hall door.* HEDDA *kneels on the footrest and lays some more pieces of wood in the stove. After a short pause,* GEORGE TESMAN *enters from the hall. He looks tired and rather serious. He steals on tiptoe towards the middle doorway and is about to slip through the curtains.*]

HEDDA [*At the stove, without looking up.*] Good morning.

TESMAN [*Turns.*] Hedda! [*Approaching her.*] Good heavens—are you up so early? Eh?

HEDDA Yes, I am up very early this morning.

TESMAN And I never doubted you were still sound asleep! Fancy that, Hedda!

HEDDA Don't speak so loud. Mrs. Elvsted is resting in my room.

TESMAN Has Mrs. Elvsted been here all night?

HEDDA Yes, since no one came to fetch her.

TESMAN Ah, to be sure.

HEDDA [*Closes the door of the stove and rises.*] Well, did you enjoy yourselves at Judge Brack's?

TESMAN Have you been anxious about me? Eh?

HEDDA No, I should never think of being anxious. But I asked if you had enjoyed yourself.

TESMAN Oh, yes—for once in a way. Especially the beginning of the evening; for then Eilert read me part of his book. We arrived more than an hour too early—fancy that! And Brack had all sorts of arrangements to make—so Eilert read to me.

HEDDA [*Seating herself by the table on the right.*] Well? Tell me, then . . .

TESMAN [*Sitting on a footstool near the stove.*] Oh, Hedda, you can't conceive what a book that is going to be! I believe it is one of the most remarkable things that have ever been written. Fancy that!

HEDDA Yes, yes; I don't care about that . . .

TESMAN I must make a confession to you, Hedda. When he had finished reading—a horrid feeling came over me.

HEDDA A horrid feeling?

TESMAN I felt jealous of Eilert for having had it in him to write such a book. Only think, Hedda!

HEDDA Yes, yes, I am thinking!

TESMAN And then how pitiful to think that he—with all his gifts—should be irreclaimable, after all.

HEDDA I suppose you mean that he has more courage than the rest?

TESMAN No, not at all—I mean that he is incapable of taking his pleasures in moderation.

HEDDA And what came of it all—in the end?

TESMAN Well, to tell the truth, I think it might best be described as an orgy, Hedda.

HEDDA Had he vine leaves in his hair?

TESMAN Vine leaves? No, I saw nothing of the sort. But he made a long, rambling speech in honor of the woman who had inspired him in his work—that was the phrase he used.

HEDDA Did he name her?

TESMAN No, he didn't; but I can't help thinking he meant Mrs. Elvsted. You may be sure he did.

HEDDA Well—where did you part from him?

TESMAN On the way to town. We broke up—the last of us at any rate—all together; and Brack came with us to get a breath of fresh air. And then, you see, we agreed to take Eilert home; for he had had far more than was good for him.

HEDDA I daresay.

TESMAN But now comes the strange part of it, Hedda; or, I should rather say, the melancholy part of it. I declare I am almost ashamed—on Eilert's account—to tell you . . .

HEDDA Oh, go on . . . !

TESMAN Well, as we were getting near town, you see, I happened to drop a little behind the others. Only for a minute or two—fancy that!

HEDDA Yes, yes, yes, but . . . ?

TESMAN And then, as I hurried after them—what do you think I found by the wayside? Eh?

HEDDA Oh, how should I know!

TESMAN You mustn't speak of it to a soul, Hedda! Do you hear? Promise me, for Eilert's sake. [*Draws a parcel, wrapped in paper, from his coat pocket.*] Fancy, dear—I found this.

HEDDA Is not that the parcel he had with him yesterday?

TESMAN Yes, it is the whole of his precious, irreplaceable manuscript! And he had gone and lost it, and knew nothing about it. Only fancy, Hedda! So deplorably . . .

HEDDA But why did you not give him back the parcel at once?

TESMAN I didn't dare to—in the state he was then in . . .

HEDDA Did you not tell any of the others that you had found it?

TESMAN Oh, far from it! You can surely understand that, for Eilert's sake, I wouldn't do that.

HEDDA So no one knows that Eilert Lövborg's manuscript is in your possession?

TESMAN No. And no one must know it.

HEDDA Then what did you say to him afterwards?

TESMAN I didn't talk to him again at all; for when we got in among the streets, he and two or three of the others gave us the slip and disappeared. Fancy that!

HEDDA Indeed! They must have taken him home then.

TESMAN Yes, so it would appear. And Brack, too, left us.

HEDDA And what have you been doing with yourself since?

TESMAN Well, I and some of the others went home with one of the party, a jolly fellow, and took our morning coffee with him; or perhaps I should rather call it our night coffee—eh? But now, when I have rested a little, and given Eilert, poor fellow, time to have his sleep out, I must take this back to him.

HEDDA [*Holds out her hand for the packet.*] No—don't give it to him! Not in such a hurry, I mean. Let me read it first.

TESMAN No, my dearest Hedda, I mustn't, I really mustn't.

HEDDA You must not?

TESMAN No—for you can imagine what a state of despair he will be in when he wakens and misses the manuscript. He has no copy of it, you must know! He told me so.

HEDDA [*Looking searchingly at him.*] Can such a thing not be reproduced? Written over again?

TESMAN No, I don't think that would be possible. For the inspiration, you see . . .

HEDDA Yes, yes—I suppose it depends on that . . . [*Lightly.*] But, by the by—here is a letter for you.

TESMAN Fancy . . . !

HEDDA [*Handing it to him.*] It came early this morning.

TESMAN It's from Aunt Julia! What can it be? [*He lays the packet on the other footstool, opens the letter, runs his eye through it, and jumps up.*] Oh, Hedda—she says that poor Aunt Rina is dying!

HEDDA Well, we were prepared for that.

TESMAN And that if I want to see her again, I must make haste. I'll run in to them at once.

HEDDA [*Suppressing a smile.*] Will you run?

TESMAN Oh, my dearest Hedda—if you could only make up your mind to come with me! Just think!

HEDDA [*Rises and says wearily, repelling the idea.*] No, no, don't ask me. I will not look upon sickness and death. I loathe all sorts of ugliness.

TESMAN Well, well, then . . . ! [*Bustling around.*] My hat . . . ? My overcoat . . . ? Oh, in the hall . . . I do hope I mayn't come too late, Hedda! Eh?

HEDDA Oh, if you run . . .

[BERTA *appears at the hall door.*]

BERTA Judge Brack is at the door, and wishes to know if he may come in.

TESMAN At this time! No, I can't possibly see him.

HEDDA But I can. [*To* BERTA.] Ask Judge Brack to come in.

[BERTA *goes out.*]

HEDDA [*Quickly, whispering.*] The parcel, Tesman!

[*She snatches it up from the stool.*]

TESMAN Yes, give it to me!

HEDDA No, no, I will keep it till you come back.

[*She goes to the writing table and places it in the bookcase.* TESMAN *stands in a flurry of haste, and cannot get his gloves on.* JUDGE BRACK *enters from the hall.*]

HEDDA [*Nodding to him.*] You are an early bird, I must say.

BRACK Yes, don't you think so? [*To* TESMAN.] Are you on the move, too?

TESMAN Yes, I must rush off to my aunts'. Fancy—the invalid one is lying at death's door, poor creature.

BRACK Dear me, is she indeed? Then on no account let me detain you. At such a critical moment . . .

TESMAN Yes, I must really rush . . . Good-bye! Good-bye!

[*He hastens out by the hall door.*]

HEDDA [*Approaching.*] You seem to have made a particularly lively night of it at your rooms, Judge Brack.

BRACK I assure you I have not had my clothes off, Mrs. Hedda.

HEDDA Not you, either?

BRACK No, as you may see. But what has Tesman been telling you of the night's adventures?

HEDDA Oh, some tiresome story. Only that they went and had coffee somewhere or other.

BRACK I have heard about that coffee party already. Eilert Lövborg was not with them, I fancy?

HEDDA No, they had taken him home before that.

BRACK Tesman too?

HEDDA No, but some of the others, he said.

BRACK [*Smiling.*] George Tesman is really an ingenuous creature, Mrs. Hedda.

HEDDA Yes, heaven knows he is. Then is there something behind all this?

BRACK Yes, perhaps there may be.

HEDDA Well then, sit down, my dear Judge, and tell your story in comfort.

[*She seats herself to the left of the table.* BRACK *sits near her, at the long side of the table.*]

HEDDA Now then?

BRACK I had special reasons for keeping track of my guests—or rather of some of my guests—last night.

HEDDA Of Eilert Lövborg among the rest, perhaps?

BRACK Frankly—yes.

HEDDA Now you make me really curious . . .

BRACK Do you know where he and one or two of the others finished the night, Mrs. Hedda?

HEDDA If it is not quite unmentionable, tell me.

BRACK Oh no, it's not at all unmentionable. Well, they put in an appearance at a particularly animated *soirée.*

HEDDA Of the lively kind?

BRACK Of the very liveliest . . .

HEDDA Tell me more of this, Judge Brack . . .

BRACK Lövborg, as well as the others, had been invited in advance. I knew all about it. But he had declined the invitation; for now, as you know, he has become a new man.

HEDDA Up at the Elvsteds', yes. But he went after all, then?

BRACK Well, you see, Mrs. Hedda—unhappily the spirit moved him at my rooms last evening . . .

HEDDA Yes, I hear he found inspiration.

BRACK Pretty violent inspiration. Well, I fancy that altered his purpose; for we menfolk are unfortunately not always so firm in our principles as we ought to be.

HEDDA Oh, I am sure you are an exception, Judge Brack. But as to Lövborg . . . ?

BRACK To make a long story short—he landed at last in Mademoiselle Diana's rooms.

HEDDA Mademoiselle Diana's?

BRACK It was Mademoiselle Diana that was giving the *soirée*, to a select circle of her admirers and her lady friends.

HEDDA Is she a red-haired woman?

BRACK Precisely.

HEDDA A sort of a—singer?

BRACK Oh yes—in her leisure moments. And moreover a mighty huntress—of men—Mrs. Hedda. You have no doubt heard of her. Eilert Lövborg was one of her most enthusiastic protectors—in the days of his glory.

HEDDA And how did all this end?

BRACK Far from amicably, it appears. After a most tender meeting, they seem to have come to blows . . .

HEDDA Lövborg and she?

BRACK Yes. He accused her or her friends of having robbed him. He declared that his pocketbook had disappeared—and other things as well. In short, he seems to have made a furious disturbance.

HEDDA And what came of it all?

BRACK It came to a general scrimmage, in which the ladies as well as the gentlemen took part. Fortunately the police at last appeared on the scene.

HEDDA The police too?

BRACK Yes. I fancy it will prove a costly frolic for Eilert Lövborg, crazy being that he is.

HEDDA How so?

BRACK He seems to have made a violent resistance—to have hit one of the constables on the head and torn the coat off his back. So they had to march him off to the police station with the rest.

HEDDA How have you learnt all this?

BRACK From the police themselves.

HEDDA [*Gazing straight before her.*] So that is what happened. Then he had no vine leaves in his hair.

BRACK Vine leaves, Mrs. Hedda?

HEDDA [*Changing her tone.*] But tell me now, Judge—what is your real reason for tracking out Eilert Lövborg's movements so carefully?

BRACK In the first place, it could not be entirely indifferent to me if it should appear in the police court that he came straight from my house.

HEDDA Will the matter come into court then?

BRACK Of course. However, I should scarcely have troubled so much about that. But I thought that, as a friend of the family, it was my duty to supply you and Tesman with a full account of his nocturnal exploits.

HEDDA Why so, Judge Brack?

BRACK Why, because I have a shrewd suspicion that he intends to use you as a sort of blind.

HEDDA Oh, how can you think such a thing!

BRACK Good heavens, Mrs. Hedda—we have eyes in our head. Mark my words! This Mrs. Elvsted will be in no hurry to leave town again.

HEDDA Well, even if there should be anything between them, I suppose there are plenty of other places where they could meet.

BRACK Not a single home. Henceforth, as before, every respectable house will be closed against Eilert Lövborg.

HEDDA And so ought mine to be, you mean?

BRACK Yes. I confess it would be more than painful to me if this personage were to be made free of your house. How superfluous, how intrusive, he would be, if he were to force his way into . . .

HEDDA . . . into the triangle?

BRACK Precisely. It would simply mean that I should find myself homeless.

HEDDA [*Looks at him with a smile.*] So you want to be the one cock in the basket[9]—that is your aim.

BRACK [*Nods slowly and lowers his voice.*] Yes, that is my aim. And for that I will fight—with every weapon I can command.

HEDDA [*Her smile vanishing.*] I see you are a dangerous person—when it comes to the point.

BRACK Do you think so?

HEDDA I am beginning to think so. And I am exceedingly glad to think—that you have no sort of hold over me.

BRACK [*Laughing equivocally.*] Well, well, Mrs. Hedda—perhaps you are right there. If I had, who knows what I might be capable of?

HEDDA Come, come now, Judge Brack! That sounds almost like a threat.

BRACK [*Rising.*] Oh, not at all! The triangle, you know, ought, if possible, to be spontaneously constructed.

HEDDA There I agree with you.

BRACK Well, now I have said all I had to say; and I had better be getting back to town. Good-bye, Mrs. Hedda. [*He goes towards the glass door.*]

HEDDA [*Rising.*] Are you going through the garden?

BRACK Yes, it's a short cut for me.

HEDDA And then it is a back way, too.

BRACK Quite so. I have no objection to back ways. They may be piquant enough at times.

HEDDA When there is shooting practice going on, you mean?

BRACK [*In the doorway, laughing to her.*] Oh, people don't shoot their tame poultry, I fancy.

HEDDA [*Also laughing.*] Oh no, when there is only one cock in the basket . . .

[*They exchange laughing nods of farewell. He goes. She closes the door behind him.* HEDDA, *who has become quite serious, stands*

---

9. A proverbial saying in Norway.

for a moment looking out. Presently she goes and peeps through the curtain over the middle doorway. Then she goes to the writing table, takes LÖVBORG'S *packet out of the bookcase, and is on the point of looking through its contents.* BERTA *is heard speaking loudly in the hall.* HEDDA *turns and listens. Then she hastily locks up the packet in the drawer, and lays the key on the inkstand.* EILERT LÖVBORG, *with his greatcoat on and his hat in his hand, tears open the hall door. He looks somewhat confused and irritated.*]

LÖVBORG [*Looking towards the hall.*] And I tell you I must and will come in! There!

[*He closes the door, turns, sees* HEDDA, *at once regains his self-control, and bows.*]

HEDDA [*At the writing table.*] Well, Mr. Lövborg, this is rather a late hour to call for Thea.

LÖVBORG You mean rather an early hour to call on you. Pray pardon me.

HEDDA How do you know that she is still here?

LÖVBORG They told me at her lodgings that she had been out all night.

HEDDA [*Going to the oval table.*] Did you notice anything about the people of the house when they said that?

LÖVBORG [*Looks inquiringly at her.*] Notice anything about them?

HEDDA I mean, did they seem to think it odd?

LÖVBORG [*Suddenly understanding.*] Oh yes, of course! I am dragging her down with me! However, I didn't notice anything.—I suppose Tesman is not up yet?

HEDDA No—I think not . . .

LÖVBORG When did he come home?

HEDDA Very late.

LÖVBORG Did he tell you anything?

HEDDA Yes, I gathered that you had had an exceedingly jolly evening at Judge Brack's.

LÖVBORG Nothing more?

HEDDA I don't think so. However, I was so dreadfully sleepy . . .

[MRS. ELVSTED *enters through the curtains of the middle doorway.*]

MRS. ELVSTED [*Going towards him.*] Ah, Lövborg! At last . . . !

LÖVBORG Yes, at last. And too late!

MRS. ELVSTED [*Looks anxiously at him.*] What is too late?

LÖVBORG Everything is too late now. It is all over with me.

MRS. ELVSTED Oh no, no—don't say that!

LÖVBORG You will say the same when you hear . . .

MRS. ELVSTED I won't hear anything!

HEDDA Perhaps you would prefer to talk to her alone? If so, I will leave you.

LÖVBORG No, stay—you too. I beg you to stay.

MRS. ELVSTED Yes, but I won't hear anything, I tell you.

LÖVBORG It is not last night's adventures that I want to talk about.

MRS. ELVSTED What is it then . . . ?

LÖVBORG I want to say that now our ways must part.

MRS. ELVSTED Part!

HEDDA [*Involuntarily.*] I knew it!

LÖVBORG You can be of no more service to me, Thea.

MRS. ELVSTED How can you stand there and say that! No more service to you! Am I not to help you now, as before? Are we not to go on working together?

LÖVBORG Henceforward I shall do no work.

MRS. ELVSTED [*Despairingly.*] Then what am I to do with my life?

LÖVBORG You must try to live your life as if you had never known me.

MRS. ELVSTED But you know I cannot do that!

LÖVBORG Try if you cannot, Thea. You must go home again . . .

MRS. ELVSTED [*In vehement protest.*] Never in this world! Where you are, there will I be also! I will not let myself be driven away like this! I will remain here! I will be with you when the book appears.

HEDDA [*Half aloud, in suspense.*] Ah yes—the book!

LÖVBORG [*Looks at her.*] My book and Thea's; for that is what it is.

MRS. ELVSTED Yes, I feel that it is. And that is why I have a right to be with you when it appears! I will see with my own eyes how respect and honor pour in upon you afresh. And the happiness—the happiness—oh, I must share it with you!

LÖVBORG Thea—our book will never appear.

HEDDA Ah!

MRS. ELVSTED Never appear!

LÖVBORG Can never appear.

MRS. ELVSTED [*In agonized foreboding.*] Lövborg—what have you done with the manuscript?

HEDDA [*Looks anxiously at him.*] Yes, the manuscript . . .

MRS. ELVSTED Where is it?

LÖVBORG Oh Thea—don't ask me about it!

MRS. ELVSTED Yes, yes, I will know. I demand to be told at once.

LÖVBORG The manuscript . . . Well then—I have torn the manuscript into a thousand pieces.

MRS. ELVSTED [*Shrieks.*] Oh no, no . . . !

HEDDA [*Involuntarily.*] But that's not . . .

LÖVBORG [*Looks at her.*] Not true, you think?

HEDDA [*Collecting herself.*] Oh well, of course—since you say so. But it sounded so improbable . . .

LÖVBORG It is true, all the same.

MRS. ELVSTED [*Wringing her hands.*] Oh God—oh God, Hedda—torn his own work to pieces!

LÖVBORG I have torn my own life to pieces. So why should I not tear my lifework too . . . ?

MRS. ELVSTED And you did this last night?

LÖVBORG Yes, I tell you! Tore it into a thousand pieces—and scattered them on the fjord—far out. There there is cool sea water at any rate—let them drift upon it—drift with the current and the wind. And then presently they will sink—deeper and deeper—as I shall, Thea.

MRS. ELVSTED Do you know, Lövborg, that what you have

done with the book—I shall think of it to my dying day as though you had killed a little child.

LÖVBORG Yes, you are right. It is a sort of child murder.

MRS. ELVSTED How could you, then . . . ! Did not the child belong to me too?

HEDDA [*Almost inaudibly.*] Ah, the child . . .

MRS. ELVSTED [*Breathing heavily.*] It is all over then. Well, well, now I will go, Hedda.

HEDDA But you are not going away from town?

MRS. ELVSTED Oh, I don't know what I shall do. I see nothing but darkness before me. [*She goes out by the hall door.*]

HEDDA [*Stands waiting for a moment.*] So you are not going to see her home, Mr. Lövborg?

LÖVBORG I? Through the streets? Would you have people see her walking with me?

HEDDA Of course I don't know what else may have happened last night. But is it so utterly irretrievable?

LÖVBORG It will not end with last night—I know that perfectly well. And the thing is that now I have no taste for that sort of life either. I won't begin it anew. She has broken my courage and my power of braving life out.

HEDDA [*Looking straight before her.*] So that pretty little fool has had her fingers in a man's destiny. [*Looks at him.*] But all the same, how could you treat her so heartlessly?

LÖVBORG Oh, don't say that it was heartless!

HEDDA To go and destroy what has filled her whole soul for months and years! You do not call that heartless!

LÖVBORG To you I can tell the truth, Hedda.

HEDDA The truth?

LÖVBORG First promise me—give me your word—that what I now confide to you Thea shall never know.

HEDDA I give you my word.

LÖVBORG Good. Then let me tell you that what I said just now was untrue.

HEDDA About the manuscript?

LÖVBORG Yes. I have not torn it to pieces—nor thrown it into the fjord.

HEDDA No, no . . . But—where is it then?

LÖVBORG I have destroyed it none the less—utterly destroyed it, Hedda!

HEDDA I don't understand.

LÖVBORG Thea said that what I had done seemed to her like a child murder.

HEDDA Yes, so she said.

LÖVBORG But to kill his child—that is not the worst thing a father can do to it.

HEDDA Not the worst?

LÖVBORG No. I wanted to spare Thea from hearing the worst.

HEDDA Then what is the worst?

LÖVBORG Suppose now, Hedda, that a man—in the small hours of the morning—came home to his child's mother after a night of riot and debauchery, and said: "Listen—I have been here and there—in this place and in that. And I have taken our child with me—to this place and to that. And I have lost the child—utterly lost it. The devil knows into what hands it may have fallen—who may have had their clutches on it."

HEDDA Well—but when all is said and done, you know—this was only a book . . .

LÖVBORG Thea's pure soul was in that book.

HEDDA Yes, so I understand.

LÖVBORG And you can understand, too, that for her and me together no future is possible.

HEDDA What path do you mean to take then?

LÖVBORG None. I will only try to make an end of it all—the sooner the better.

HEDDA [*A step nearer him.*] Eilert Lövborg—listen to me. Will you not try to—to do it beautifully?

LÖVBORG Beautifully? [*Smiling.*] With vine leaves in my hair, as you used to dream in the old days . . . ?

HEDDA No, no. I have lost my faith in the vine leaves. But beautifully nevertheless! For once in a way! Good-bye! You must go now—and do not come here any more.

LÖVBORG Good-bye, Mrs. Tesman. And give George Tesman my love. [*He is on the point of going.*]

HEDDA No, wait! I must give you a memento to take with you.

[*She goes to the writing table and opens the drawer and the pistol case; then returns to* LÖVBORG *with one of the pistols.*]

LÖVBORG [*Looks at her.*] This? Is this the memento?

HEDDA [*Nodding slowly.*] Do you recognize it? It was aimed at you once.

LÖVBORG You should have used it then.

HEDDA Take it—and do you use it now.

LÖVBORG [*Puts the pistol in his breast pocket.*] Thanks!

HEDDA And beautifully, Eilert Lövborg. Promise me that!

LÖVBORG Good-bye, Hedda Gabler.

[*He goes out by the hall door.* HEDDA *listens for a moment at the door. Then she goes up to the writing table, takes out the packet of manuscript, peeps under the cover, draws a few of the sheets half out, and looks at them. Next she goes over and seats herself in the armchair beside the stove, with the packet in her lap. Presently she opens the stove door, and then the packet.*]

HEDDA [*Throws one of the quires into the fire and whispers to herself.*] Now I am burning your child, Thea!—Burning it, curly-locks! [*Throwing one or two more quires into the stove.*] Your child and Eilert Lövborg's. [*Throws the rest in.*] I am burning—I am burning your child.

ACT IV

SCENE: *The same rooms at the* TESMANS'. *It is evening. The drawing room is in darkness. The back room is lighted by the hanging lamp over the table. The curtains over the glass door are drawn close.* HEDDA, *dressed in black, walks to and fro in the dark room. Then she goes into the back room and disappears for a moment to the left. She is heard to strike a few chords on the piano. Presently she comes in sight again, and returns to the drawing room.* BERTA *enters from the right, through the inner room, with a lighted lamp, which she places on the table in front of the corner settee in the drawing room. Her eyes are red with weeping, and she has black ribbons in her cap. She goes quietly and circumspectly out to the right.* HEDDA *goes up to the glass door, lifts the curtain a little aside, and looks out into the darkness. Shortly afterwards,* MISS TESMAN, *in mourning, with a bonnet and veil on, comes in from the hall.* HEDDA *goes towards her and holds out her hand.*

MISS TESMAN Yes, Hedda, here I am, in mourning and forlorn; for now my poor sister has at last found peace.

HEDDA I have heard the news already, as you see. Tesman sent me a card.

MISS TESMAN Yes, he promised me he would. But nevertheless I thought that to Hedda—here in the house of life—I ought myself to bring the tidings of death.

HEDDA That was very kind of you.

MISS TESMAN Ah, Rina ought not to have left us just now. This is not the time for Hedda's house to be a house of mourning.

HEDDA [*Changing the subject.*] She died quite peacefully, did she not, Miss Tesman?

MISS TESMAN Oh, her end was so calm, so beautiful. And then she had the unspeakable happiness of seeing George once more—and bidding him good-bye. Has he not come home yet?

HEDDA No. He wrote that he might be detained. But won't you sit down?

MISS TESMAN No thank you, my dear, dear Hedda. I should like to, but I have so much to do. I must prepare my dear one for her rest as well as I can. She shall go to her grave looking her best.

HEDDA Can I not help you in any way?

MISS TESMAN Oh, you must not think of it! Hedda Tesman must have no hand in such mournful work. Nor let her thoughts dwell on it either—not at this time.

HEDDA One is not always mistress of one's thoughts . . .

MISS TESMAN [*Continuing.*] Ah yes, it is the way of the world. At home we shall be sewing a shroud; and here there will soon be sewing too, I suppose—but of another sort, thank God!

[GEORGE TESMAN *enters by the hall door.*]

HEDDA Ah, you have come at last!

TESMAN You here, Aunt Julia? With Hedda? Fancy that!

MISS TESMAN I was just going, my dear boy. Well, have you done all you promised?

TESMAN No; I'm really afraid I have forgotten half of it. I must come to you again tomorrow. Today my brain is all in a whirl. I can't keep my thoughts together.

MISS TESMAN Why, my dear George, you mustn't take it in this way.

TESMAN Mustn't . . . ? How do you mean?

MISS TESMAN Even in your sorrow you must rejoice, as I do—rejoice that she is at rest.

TESMAN Oh yes, yes—you are thinking of Aunt Rina.

HEDDA You will feel lonely now, Miss Tesman.

MISS TESMAN Just at first, yes. But that will not last very long, I hope. I daresay I shall soon find an occupant for poor Rina's little room.

TESMAN Indeed? Who do you think will take it? Eh?

MISS TESMAN Oh, there's always some poor invalid or other in want of nursing, unfortunately.

HEDDA Would you really take such a burden upon you again?

MISS TESMAN A burden! Heaven forgive you, child—it has been no burden to me.

HEDDA But suppose you had a total stranger on your hands . . .

MISS TESMAN Oh, one soon makes friends with sick folk; and it's such an absolute necessity for me to have some one to live for. Well, heaven be praised, there may soon be something in *this* house, too, to keep an old aunt busy.

HEDDA Oh, don't trouble about anything here.

TESMAN Yes, just fancy what a nice time we three might have together, if . . . ?

HEDDA If . . . ?

TESMAN [*Uneasily.*] Oh, nothing. It will all come right. Let us hope so—eh?

MISS TESMAN Well, well, I daresay you two want to talk to

each other. [*Smiling.*] And perhaps Hedda may have something to tell you too, George. Good-bye! I must go home to Rina. [*Turning at the door.*] How strange it is to think that now Rina is with me and with my poor brother as well!

TESMAN Yes, fancy that, Aunt Julia! Eh? [MISS TESMAN *goes out by the hall door.*]

HEDDA [*Follows* TESMAN *coldly and searchingly with her eyes.*] I almost believe your Aunt Rina's death affects you more than it does your Aunt Julia.

TESMAN Oh, it's not that alone. It's Eilert I am so terribly uneasy about.

HEDDA [*Quickly.*] Is there anything new about him?

TESMAN I looked in at his rooms this afternoon, intending to tell him the manuscript was in safe keeping.

HEDDA Well, did you not find him?

TESMAN No. He wasn't at home. But afterwards I met Mrs. Elvsted, and she told me that he had been here early this morning.

HEDDA Yes, directly after you had gone.

TESMAN And he said that he had torn his manuscript to pieces—eh?

HEDDA Yes, so he declared.

TESMAN Why, good heavens, he must have been completely out of his mind! And I suppose you thought it best not to give it back to him, Hedda?

HEDDA No, he did not get it.

TESMAN But of course you told him that we had it?

HEDDA No. [*Quickly.*] Did you tell Mrs. Elvsted?

TESMAN No; I thought I had better not. But you ought to have told him. Fancy, if, in desperation, he should go and do himself some injury! Let me have the manuscript, Hedda! I will take it to him at once. Where is it?

HEDDA [*Cold and immovable, leaning on the armchair.*] I have not got it.

TESMAN Have not got it? What in the world do you mean?

HEDDA I have burnt it—every line of it.

TESMAN [*With a violent movement of terror.*] Burnt! Burnt Eilert's manuscript!

HEDDA Don't scream so. The servant might hear you.

TESMAN Burnt! Why, good God . . . ! No, no, no! It's impossible!

HEDDA It is so, nevertheless.

TESMAN Do you know what you have done, Hedda? It's unlawful appropriation of lost property. Fancy that! Just ask Judge Brack, and he'll tell you what it is.

HEDDA I advise you not to speak of it—either to Judge Brack, or to any one else.

TESMAN But how could you do anything so unheard of? What put it into your head? What possessed you? Answer me that —eh?

HEDDA [*Suppressing an almost imperceptible smile.*] I did it for your sake, George.

TESMAN For my sake!

HEDDA This morning, when you told me about what he had read to you . . .

TESMAN Yes, yes—what then?

HEDDA You acknowledged that you envied him his work.

TESMAN Oh, of course I didn't mean that literally.

HEDDA No matter—I could not bear the idea that any one should throw you into the shade.

TESMAN [*In an outburst of mingled doubt and joy.*] Hedda! Oh, is this true? But—but—I never knew you to show your love like that before. Fancy that!

HEDDA Well, I may as well tell you that—just at this time . . . [*Impatiently, breaking off.*] No, no; you can ask Aunt Julia. She will tell you, fast enough.

TESMAN Oh, I almost think I understand you, Hedda! [*Clasps his hands together.*] Great heavens! do you really mean it? Eh?

HEDDA Don't shout so. The servant might hear.

TESMAN [*Laughing in irrepressible glee.*] The servant! Why, how absurd you are, Hedda. It's only my old Berta! Why, I'll tell Berta myself.

HEDDA [*Clenching her hands together in desperation.*] Oh, it is killing me—it is killing me, all this!

TESMAN What is, Hedda? Eh?

HEDDA [*Coldly, controlling herself.*] All this—absurdity—George.

TESMAN Absurdity! Do you see anything absurd in my being overjoyed at the news! But after all—perhaps I had better not say anything to Berta.

HEDDA Oh . . . why not that too?

TESMAN No, no, not yet! But I must certainly tell Aunt Julia. And then that you have begun to call me George too! Fancy that! Oh, Aunt Julia will be so happy—so happy!

HEDDA When she hears that I have burnt Eilert Lövborg's manuscript—for your sake?

TESMAN No, by the by—that affair of the manuscript—of course nobody must know about that. But that you love me so much, Hedda—Aunt Julia must really share my joy in that! I wonder, now, whether this sort of thing is usual in young wives? Eh?

HEDDA I think you had better ask Aunt Julia that question too.

TESMAN I will indeed, some time or other. [*Looks uneasy and downcast again.*] And yet the manuscript—the manuscript! Good God! It is terrible to think what will become of poor Eilert now.

[MRS. ELVSTED, *dressed as in the first act, with hat and cloak, enters by the hall door.*]

MRS. ELVSTED [*Greets them hurriedly, and says in evident agitation.*] Oh, dear Hedda, forgive my coming again.

HEDDA What is the matter with you, Thea?

TESMAN Something about Eilert Lövborg again—eh?

MRS. ELVSTED Yes! I am dreadfully afraid some misfortune has happened to him.

HEDDA [*Seizes her arm.*] Ah—do you think so?

TESMAN Why, good Lord—what makes you think that, Mrs. Elvsted?

MRS. ELVSTED I heard them talking at my boardinghouse just as I came in. Oh, the most incredible rumors are afloat about him today.

TESMAN Yes, fancy, so I heard too! And I can bear witness that he went straight home to bed last night. Fancy that!

HEDDA Well, what did they say at the boardinghouse?

MRS. ELVSTED Oh, I couldn't make out anything clearly. Either they knew nothing definite, or else . . . They stopped talking when they saw me; and I did not dare to ask.

TESMAN [*Moving about uneasily.*] We must hope—we must hope that you misunderstood them, Mrs. Elvsted.

MRS. ELVSTED No, no; I am sure it was of him they were talking. And I heard something about the hospital or . . .

TESMAN The hospital?

HEDDA No—surely that cannot be!

MRS. ELVSTED Oh, I was in such mortal terror! I went to his lodgings and asked for him there.

HEDDA You could make up your mind to that, Thea!

MRS. ELVSTED What else could I do? I really could bear the suspense no longer.

TESMAN But you didn't find him either—eh?

MRS. ELVSTED No. And the people knew nothing about him. He hadn't been home since yesterday afternoon, they said.

TESMAN Yesterday! Fancy, how could they say that?

MRS. ELVSTED Oh, I am sure something terrible must have happened to him.

TESMAN Hedda dear—how would it be if I were to go and make inquiries . . . ?

HEDDA No, no—don't mix yourself up in this affair.

[JUDGE BRACK, *with his hat in his hand, enters by the hall door, which* BERTA *opens, and closes behind him. He looks grave and bows in silence.*]

TESMAN Oh, is that you, my dear Judge? Eh?

BRACK Yes. It was imperative I should see you this evening.

TESMAN I can see you have heard the news about Aunt Rina?

BRACK Yes, that among other things.

TESMAN Isn't it sad—eh?

BRACK Well, my dear Tesman, that depends on how you look at it.

TESMAN [*Looks doubtfully at him.*] Has anything else happened?

BRACK Yes.

HEDDA [*In suspense.*] Anything sad, Judge Brack?

BRACK That, too, depends on how you look at it, Mrs. Tesman.

MRS. ELVSTED [*Unable to restrain her anxiety.*] Oh! it is something about Eilert Lövborg!

BRACK [*With a glance at her.*] What makes you think that, Madam? Perhaps you have already heard something . . . ?

MRS. ELVSTED [*In confusion.*] No, nothing at all, but . . .

TESMAN Oh, for heaven's sake, tell us!

BRACK [*Shrugging his shoulders.*] Well, I regret to say Eilert Lövborg has been taken to the hospital. He is lying at the point of death.

MRS. ELVSTED [*Shrieks.*] Oh God! oh God . . . !

TESMAN To the hospital! And at the point of death!

HEDDA [*Involuntarily.*] So soon then . . .

MRS. ELVSTED [*Wailing.*] And we parted in anger, Hedda!

HEDDA [*Whispers.*] Thea—Thea—be careful!

MRS. ELVSTED [*Not heeding her.*] I must go to him! I must see him alive!

BRACK It is useless, Madam. No one will be admitted.

MRS. ELVSTED Oh, at least tell me what has happened to him? What is it?

TESMAN You don't mean to say that he has himself . . . Eh?

HEDDA Yes, I am sure he has.

TESMAN Hedda, how can you . . . ?

BRACK [*Keeping his eyes fixed upon her.*] Unfortunately you have guessed quite correctly, Mrs. Tesman.

MRS. ELVSTED Oh, how horrible!

TESMAN Himself, then! Fancy that!

HEDDA Shot himself!

BRACK Rightly guessed again, Mrs. Tesman.

MRS. ELVSTED [*With an effort at self-control.*] When did it happen, Mr. Brack?

BRACK This afternoon between three and four.

TESMAN But, good Lord, where did he do it? Eh?

BRACK [*With some hesitation.*] Where? Well—I suppose at his lodgings.

MRS. ELVSTED No, that cannot be; for I was there between six and seven.

BRACK Well then, somewhere else. I don't know exactly. I only know that he was found . . . He had shot himself—in the breast.

MRS. ELVSTED Oh, how terrible! That he should die like that!

HEDDA [*To* BRACK.] Was it in the breast?

BRACK Yes—as I told you.

HEDDA Not in the temple?

BRACK In the breast, Mrs. Tesman.

HEDDA Well, well—the breast is a good place, too.

BRACK How do you mean, Mrs. Tesman?

HEDDA [*Evasively.*] Oh, nothing—nothing.

TESMAN And the wound is dangerous, you say—eh?

BRACK Absolutely mortal. The end has probably come by this time.

MRS. ELVSTED Yes, yes, I feel it. The end! The end! Oh, Hedda . . . !

TESMAN But tell me, how have you learnt all this?

BRACK [*Curtly.*] Through one of the police. A man I had some business with.

HEDDA [*In a clear voice.*] At last a deed worth doing!

TESMAN [*Terrified.*] Good heavens, Hedda! what are you saying?

HEDDA I say there is beauty in this.

BRACK H'm, Mrs. Tesman . . .

TESMAN Beauty! Fancy that!

MRS. ELVSTED Oh, Hedda, how can you talk of beauty in such an act!

HEDDA Eilert Lövborg has himself made up his account with life. He has had the courage to do—the one right thing.

MRS. ELVSTED No, you must never think that was how it happened! It must have been in delirium that he did it.

TESMAN In despair!

HEDDA That he did not. I am certain of that.

MRS. ELVSTED Yes, yes! In delirium! Just as when he tore up our manuscript.

BRACK [*Starting.*] The manuscript? Has he torn that up?

MRS. ELVSTED Yes, last night.

TESMAN [*Whispers softly.*] Oh, Hedda, we shall never get over this.

BRACK H'm, very extraordinary.

TESMAN [*Moving about the room.*] To think of Eilert going out of the world in this way! And not leaving behind him the book that would have immortalized his name . . .

MRS. ELVSTED Oh, if only it could be put together again!

TESMAN Yes, if it only could! I don't know what I would not give . . .

MRS. ELVSTED Perhaps it can, Mr. Tesman.

TESMAN What do you mean?

MRS. ELVSTED [*Searches in the pocket of her dress.*] Look here. I have kept all the loose notes he used to dictate from.

HEDDA [*A step forward.*] Ah . . . !

TESMAN You have kept them, Mrs. Elvsted! Eh?

MRS. ELVSTED Yes, I have them here. I put them in my pocket when I left home. Here they still are . . .

TESMAN Oh, do let me see them!

MRS. ELVSTED [*Hands him a bundle of papers.*] But they are in such disorder—all mixed up.

TESMAN Fancy, if we could make something out of them, after all! Perhaps if we two put our heads together . . .

MRS. ELVSTED Oh yes, at least let us try . . .

TESMAN We will manage it! We must! I will dedicate my life to this task.

HEDDA You, George? Your life?

TESMAN Yes, or rather all the time I can spare. My own collections must wait in the meantime. Hedda—you understand, eh? I owe this to Eilert's memory.

HEDDA Perhaps.

TESMAN And so, my dear Mrs. Elvsted, we will give our whole minds to it. There is no use in brooding over what can't be undone—eh? We must try to control our grief as much as possible, and . . .

MRS. ELVSTED Yes, yes, Mr. Tesman, I will do the best I can.

TESMAN Well then, come here. I can't rest until we have looked through the notes. Where shall we sit? Here? No, in there, in the back room. Excuse me, my dear Judge. Come with me, Mrs. Elvsted.

MRS. ELVSTED Oh, if only it were possible!

[TESMAN *and* MRS. ELVSTED *go into the back room. She takes off her hat and cloak. They both sit at the table under the hanging lamp, and are soon deep in an eager examination of the papers.* HEDDA *crosses to the stove and sits in the armchair. Presently* BRACK *goes up to her.*]

HEDDA [*In a low voice.*] Oh, what a sense of freedom it gives one, this act of Eilert Lövborg's.

BRACK Freedom, Mrs. Hedda? Well, of course, it is a release for him . . .

HEDDA I mean for me. It gives me a sense of freedom to know that a deed of deliberate courage is still possible in this world—a deed of spontaneous beauty.

BRACK [*Smiling.*] H'm—my dear Mrs. Hedda . . .

HEDDA Oh, I know what you are going to say. For you are a kind of specialist, too, like—you know!

BRACK [*Looking hard at her.*] Eilert Lövborg was more to you than perhaps you are willing to admit to yourself. Am I wrong?

HEDDA I don't answer such questions. I only know that Eilert Lövborg has had the courage to live his life after his own fashion. And then—the last great act, with its beauty! Ah! that he should have the will and the strength to turn away from the banquet of life—so early.

BRACK I am sorry, Mrs. Hedda, but I fear I must dispel an amiable illusion.

HEDDA Illusion?

BRACK Which could not have lasted long in any case.

HEDDA What do you mean?

BRACK Eilert Lövborg did not shoot himself—voluntarily.

HEDDA Not voluntarily!

BRACK No. The thing did not happen exactly as I told it.

HEDDA [*In suspense.*] Have you concealed something? What is it?

BRACK For poor Mrs. Elvsted's sake I idealized the facts a little.

HEDDA What are the facts?

BRACK First, that he is already dead.

HEDDA At the hospital?

BRACK Yes—without regaining consciousness.

HEDDA What more have you concealed?

BRACK This—the event did not happen at his lodgings.

HEDDA Oh, that can make no difference.

BRACK Perhaps it may. For I must tell you—Eilert Lövborg was found shot in—in Mademoiselle Diana's boudoir.

HEDDA [*Makes a motion as if to rise, but sinks back again.*] That is impossible, Judge Brack! He cannot have been there again today.

BRACK He was there this afternoon. He went there, he said, to demand the return of something which they had taken from him. Talked wildly about a lost child . . .

HEDDA Ah—so that was why . . .

BRACK I thought probably he meant his manuscript; but now I hear he destroyed that himself. So I suppose it must have been his pocketbook.

HEDDA Yes, no doubt. And there—there he was found?

BRACK Yes, there. With a pistol in his breast pocket, discharged. The ball had lodged in a vital part.

HEDDA In the breast—yes.

BRACK No—in the bowels.

HEDDA [*Looks up at him with an expression of loathing.*] That, too! Oh, what curse is it that makes everything I touch turn ludicrous and mean?

BRACK There is one point more, Mrs. Hedda—another disagreeable feature in the affair.

HEDDA And what is that?

BRACK The pistol he carried . . .

HEDDA [*Breathless.*] Well? What of it?

BRACK He must have stolen it.

HEDDA [*Leaps up.*] Stolen it! That is not true! He did not steal it!

BRACK No other explanation is possible. He must have stolen it . . . Hush!

[TESMAN *and* MRS. ELVSTED *have risen from the table in the back room, and come into the drawing room.*]

TESMAN [*With the papers in both his hands.*] Hedda, dear, it is almost impossible to see under that lamp. Think of that!

HEDDA Yes, I am thinking.

TESMAN Would you mind our sitting at your writing table —eh?

HEDDA If you like. [*Quickly.*] No, wait! Let me clear it first!

TESMAN Oh, you needn't trouble, Hedda. There is plenty of room.

HEDDA No, no, let me clear it, I say! I will take these things in and put them on the piano. There!

[*She has drawn out an object, covered with sheet music, from under the bookcase, places several other pieces of music upon it, and carries the whole into the inner room, to the left.* TESMAN *lays the scraps of paper on the writing table, and moves the lamp there from the corner table. He and* MRS. ELVSTED *sit down and proceed with their work.* HEDDA *returns.*]

HEDDA [*Behind* MRS. ELVSTED'S *chair, gently ruffing her hair.*] Well, my sweet Thea, how goes it with Eilert Lövborg's monument?

MRS. ELVSTED [*Looks dispiritedly up at her.*] Oh, it will be terribly hard to put in order.

TESMAN We must manage it. I am determined. And arranging other people's papers is just the work for me.

[HEDDA *goes over to the stove, and seats herself on one of the footstools.* BRACK *stands over her, leaning on the armchair.*]

HEDDA [*Whispers.*] What did you say about the pistol?

BRACK [*Softly.*] That he must have stolen it.

HEDDA Why stolen it?

BRACK Because every other explanation ought to be impossible, Mrs. Hedda.

HEDDA Indeed?

BRACK [*Glances at her.*] Of course, Eilert Lövborg was here this morning. Was he not?

HEDDA Yes.

BRACK Were you alone with him?

HEDDA Part of the time.

BRACK Did you not leave the room whilst he was here?

HEDDA No.

BRACK Try to recollect. Were you not out of the room a moment?

HEDDA Yes, perhaps just a moment—out in the hall.

BRACK And where was your pistol case during that time?

HEDDA I had it locked up in . . .

BRACK Well, Mrs. Hedda?

HEDDA The case stood there on the writing table.

BRACK Have you looked since, to see whether both the pistols are there?

HEDDA No.

BRACK Well, you need not. I saw the pistol found in Lövborg's pocket, and I knew it at once as the one I had seen yesterday—and before, too.

HEDDA Have you it with you?

BRACK No, the police have it.

HEDDA What will the police do with it?

BRACK Search till they find the owner.

HEDDA Do you think they will succeed?

BRACK [*Bends over her and whispers.*] No, Hedda Gabler—not so long as I say nothing.

HEDDA [*Looks frightened at him.*] And if you do not say nothing—what then?

BRACK [*Shrugs his shoulders.*] There is always the possibility that pistol was stolen.

HEDDA [*Firmly.*] Death rather than that.

BRACK [*Smiling.*] People say such things—but they don't do them.

HEDDA [*Without replying.*] And supposing the pistol was not stolen, and the owner is discovered? What then?

BRACK Well, Hedda—then comes the scandal.

HEDDA The scandal!

BRACK Yes, the scandal—of which you are so mortally afraid. You will, of course, be brought before the court—both you and Mademoiselle Diana. She will have to explain how the thing happened—whether it was an accidental shot or murder. Did the pistol go off as he was trying to take it out of his pocket, to threaten her with? Or did she tear the pistol out of his hand, shoot him, and push it back into his pocket? That would be quite like her; for she is an able-bodied young person, this same Mademoiselle Diana.

HEDDA But *I* have nothing to do with all this repulsive business.

BRACK No. But you will have to answer the question: Why did you give Eilert Lövborg the pistol? And what conclusions will people draw from the fact that you did give it to him?

HEDDA [*Lets her head sink.*] That is true. I did not think of that.

BRACK Well, fortunately, there is no danger, so long as I say nothing.

HEDDA [*Looks up at him.*] So I am in your power, Judge Brack. You have me at your beck and call, from this time forward.

BRACK [*Whispers softly.*] Dearest Hedda—believe me—I shall not abuse my advantage.

HEDDA I am in your power none the less. Subject to your will and your demands. A slave, a slave then! [*Rises impetuously.*] No, I cannot endure the thought of that! Never!

BRACK [*Looks half-mockingly at her.*] People generally get used to the inevitable.

HEDDA [*Returns his look.*] Yes, perhaps. [*She crosses to the writing table. Suppressing an involuntary smile, she imitates* TESMAN'S *intonations.*] Well? Are you getting on, George? Eh?

TESMAN Heaven knows, dear. In any case it will be the work of months.

HEDDA [*As before.*] Fancy that! [*Passes her hands softly through* MRS. ELVSTED'S *hair.*] Doesn't it seem strange to you, Thea? Here are you sitting with Tesman—just as you used to sit with Eilert Lövborg?

MRS. ELVSTED Ah, if I could only inspire your husband in the same way!

HEDDA Oh, that will come, too—in time.

TESMAN Yes, do you know, Hedda—I really think I begin to

feel something of the sort. But won't you go and sit with Brack again?

HEDDA Is there nothing I can do to help you two?

TESMAN No, nothing in the world. [*Turning his head.*] I trust to you to keep Hedda company, my dear Brack.

BRACK [*With a glance at* HEDDA.] With the very greatest of pleasure.

HEDDA Thanks. But I am tired this evening. I will go in and lie down a little on the sofa.

TESMAN Yes, do, dear—eh?

[HEDDA *goes into the back room and draws the curtains. A short pause. Suddenly she is heard playing a wild dance on the piano.*]

MRS. ELVSTED [*Starts from her chair.*] Oh—what is that?

TESMAN [*Runs to the doorway.*] Why, my dearest Hedda—don't play dance music tonight! Just think of Aunt Rina! And of Eilert, too!

HEDDA [*Puts her head out between the curtains.*] And of Aunt Julia. And of all the rest of them. After this, I will be quiet. [*Closes the curtains again.*]

TESMAN [*At the writing table.*] It's not good for her to see us at this distressing work. I'll tell you what, Mrs. Elvsted—you shall take the empty room at Aunt Julia's, and then I will come over in the evenings, and we can sit and work there—eh?

HEDDA [*In the inner room.*] I hear what you are saying, Tesman. But how am *I* to get through the evenings out here?

TESMAN [*Turning over the papers.*] Oh, I daresay Judge Brack will be so kind as to look in now and then, even though I am out.

BRACK [*In the armchair, calls out gaily.*] Every blessed evening, with all the pleasure in life, Mrs. Tesman! We shall get on capitally together, we two!

HEDDA [*Speaking loud and clear.*] Yes, don't you flatter yourself we will, Judge Brack? Now that you are the one cock in the basket . . .

[*A shot is heard within.* TESMAN, MRS. ELVSTED, *and* BRACK *leap to their feet.*]

TESMAN Oh, now she is playing with those pistols again.

[*He throws back the curtains and runs in, followed by* MRS. ELVSTED. HEDDA *lies stretched on the sofa, lifeless. Confusion and cries.* BERTA *enters in alarm from the right.*]

TESMAN [*Shrieks to* BRACK.] Shot herself! Shot herself in the temple! Fancy that!

BRACK [*Half-fainting in the armchair.*] Good God!—people don't do such things.

BERNARD SHAW

Pygmalion

Headmaster of the Universe
Satan, Saint, and Superman

CAST

HENRY HIGGINS

COLONEL PICKERING

FREDDY EYNSFORD HILL

ALFRED DOOLITTLE

A BYSTANDER

ANOTHER ONE

ELIZA DOOLITTLE

MRS EYNSFORD HILL

MISS EYNSFORD HILL

MRS HIGGINS

MRS PEARCE

PARLORMAID

When Eliza realizes she can't have Higgins, she senses that she will always be secondary p194

SCENE: *London.*

PREFACE TO PYGMALION

A PROFESSOR OF PHONETICS

As will be seen later on, Pygmalion needs, not a preface, but a sequel, which I have supplied in its due place.

The English have no respect for their language, and will not teach their children to speak it. They cannot spell it because they have nothing to spell it with but an old foreign alphabet of which only the consonants—and not all of them—have any agreed speech value. Consequently no man can teach himself what it should sound like from reading it; and it is impossible for an Englishman to open his mouth without making some other Englishman despise him. Most European languages are now accessible in black and white to foreigners: English and French are not thus accessible even to Englishmen and Frenchmen. The reformer we need most today is an energetic enthusiast: that is why I have made such a one the hero of a popular play.

There have been heroes of that kind crying in the wilderness for many years past. When I became interested in the subject towards the end of the eighteen-seventies, the illustrious Alexander Melville Bell, the inventor of Visible Speech, had emigrated to Canada, where his son invented the telephone; but Alexander J. Ellis was still a London Patriarch, with an impressive head always covered by a velvet skull cap, for which he would apologize to public meetings in a very courtly manner. He and Tito Pagliardini, another phonetic veteran, were men whom it was impossible to dislike. Henry Sweet, then a young man, lacked their sweetness of character: he was about as conciliatory to conventional mortals as Ibsen or Samuel Butler. His great ability as a phonetician (he was, I think, the best of them all at his job) would have entitled him to high official recognition, and perhaps enabled him to popularize his subject, but for his Satanic contempt for all academic dignitaries and persons in general who thought more of Greek than of phonetics. Once, in the days when the Imperial Institute rose in South Kensington, and Joseph Chamberlain was booming the Empire, I induced the editor of a leading monthly review to commission an article from Sweet on the imperial importance of his subject. When it arrived, it contained nothing but a savagely derisive attack on a professor of language and literature whose chair Sweet regarded as proper to a phonetic expert only. The article, being libellous, had to be returned as impossible; and I had to renounce my dream of dragging its author into the limelight. When I met him afterwards, for the first time for many years, I found to my astonishment that he, who had been a quite tolerably presentable young man, had actually managed by sheer scorn to alter his personal appearance until he had become a sort of walking repudiation of Oxford and all its traditions. It must have been largely in his own despite that he was squeezed into something called a Readership of phonetics there. The future of phonetics rests probably with his pupils who all swore by him; but nothing could bring the man himself into any sort of compliance with the university to which he nevertheless clung by divine right in an intensely Oxonian way. I daresay his papers, if he has left any, include some satires that may be published without too destructive results fifty years hence. He was, I believe, not in the least an ill-natured man: very much the opposite, I should say; but he would not suffer fools gladly; and to him all scholars who were not rabid phoneticians were fools.

Those who knew him will recognize in my third act the allusion to the Current Shorthand in which he used to write postcards. It may be acquired from a four and sixpenny manual published by the Clarendon Press. The postcards which Mrs Higgins describes are such as I have received from Sweet. I would decipher a sound which a cockney would represent by *zerr,* and a Frenchman by *seu,* and then write demanding with some heat what on earth it meant. Sweet, with boundless contempt for my stupidity, would reply that it not only meant but obviously was the word Result, as no other word containing that sound, and capable of making sense with the context, existed in any language spoken on earth. That less expert mortals should require fuller indications was beyond Sweet's patience. Therefore, though the whole point of his Current Shorthand is that it can express every sound in the language perfectly, vowels as well as consonants, and that your hand has to make no stroke except the easy and current ones with which you write m, n, and u, l, p, and q, scribbling them at whatever angle comes easiest to you, his unfortunate determination to make this remarkable and quite legible script serve also as a shorthand reduced it in his own practice to the most inscrutable of cryptograms. His true objective was the provision of a full, accurate, legible script for our language; but he was led past that by his contempt for the popular Pitman system of shorthand, which he called the Pitfall system. The triumph of Pitman was a triumph of business organization: there was a weekly paper to persuade you to learn Pitman: there were cheap textbooks and exercise books and transcripts of speeches for you to copy, and schools where experienced teachers coached you up to the necessary proficiency. Sweet could not organize his market in that fashion. He might as well have been the Sybil who tore up the leaves of prophecy that nobody would attend to. The four and sixpenny manual, mostly in his lithographed handwriting, that was never vulgarly advertised, may perhaps some day be taken up by a syndicate and pushed upon the public as *The Times* pushed the *Encyclopædia Britannica;* but until then it will certainly not prevail against Pitman. I have bought three copies of it during my lifetime; and I am informed by the publishers that its cloistered existence is still a steady and healthy one. I actually learned the system two several times; and yet the shorthand in which I am writing these lines is Pitman's. And the reason is, that my secretary cannot transcribe Sweet, having been perforce taught in the schools of Pitman. In America I could use the commercially organized Gregg shorthand, which has taken a hint from Sweet by making its letters writable (current, Sweet would have called them) instead of having to be geometrically drawn like Pitman's; but all these systems, including Sweet's, are spoilt by making them available for verbatim reporting, in which complete and exact spelling and word division are impossible. A complete and exact phonetic script is neither practicable nor necessary for ordinary use; but if we enlarge our alphabet to the Russian size, and make our spelling as phonetic as Spanish, the advance will be prodigious.

Pygmalion Higgins is not a portrait of Sweet, to whom the adventure of Eliza Doolittle would have been impossible; still, as will be seen, there are touches of Sweet in the play. With Higgins's physique and temperament Sweet might have set the Thames on fire. As it was, he impressed himself professionally on Europe to an extent that made his comparative personal obscurity, and the failure of Oxford to do justice to his eminence, a puzzle to foreign specialists in his subject. I do not blame Oxford, because I think Oxford is quite right in demanding a certain social amenity from its nurslings (heaven knows it is not exorbitant in its requirement!); for although I well know how hard it is for a man of genius with a seriously underrated subject to maintain serene and kindly relations with the men who underrate it, and who keep all the best places for less important subjects which they profess without originality and sometimes without much capacity for them, still, if he overwhelms them with wrath and disdain, he cannot expect them to heap honors on him.

Of the later generations of phoneticians I know little. Among them towered Robert Bridges, to whom perhaps Higgins may owe his Miltonic sympathies, though here again I must disclaim all portraiture. But if the play makes the public aware that there are such people as phoneticians, and that they are among the most important people in England at present, it will serve its turn.

I wish to boast that Pygmalion has been an extremely successful play, both on stage and screen, all over Europe and North America as well as at home. It is so intensely and deliberately didactic, and its subject is esteemed so dry, that I delight in throwing at the heads of the wiseacres who repeat the parrot cry that art should never be didactic. It goes to prove my contention that great art can never be anything else.

Finally, and for the encouragement of people troubled with accents that cut them off from all high employment, I may add that the change wrought by Professor Higgins in the flower girl is neither impossible nor uncommon. The modern concierge's daughter who fulfills her ambition by playing the Queen of Spain in *Ruy Blas* at the Théâtre Français is only one of the many thousands of men and women who have sloughed off their native dialects and acquired a new tongue. Our West End shop assistants and domestic servants are bilingual. But the thing has to be done scientifically, or the last state of the aspirant may be worse than the first. An honest slum dialect is more tolerable than the attempts of phonetically untaught persons to imitate the plutocracy. Ambitious flower girls who read this play must not imagine that they can pass themselves off as fine ladies by untutored imitation. They must learn their alphabet over again, and differently, from a phonetic expert. Imitation will only make them ridiculous.

Note for Technicians: A complete representation of the play as printed in this edition is technically possible only on the cinema screen or on stages furnished with exceptionally elaborate machinery. For ordinary theatrical use the scenes separated by rows of asterisks are to be omitted.

In the dialogue an e upside down indicates the indefinite vowel, sometimes called obscure or neutral, for which, though it is one of the commonest sounds in English speech, our wretched alphabet has no letter.

Shavian as adj - more than Shaw -
brilliant, unorthodox

ACT I

SCENE: *London at 11:15 p.m. Torrents of heavy summer rain. Cab whistles blowing frantically in all directions. Pedestrians running for shelter into the portico of St Paul's church (not Wren's cathedral but Inigo Jones's church in Covent Garden vegetable market), among them a lady and her daughter in evening dress. All are peering out gloomily at the rain, except one man with his back turned to the rest, wholly preoccupied with a notebook in which he is writing.*

The church clock strikes the first quarter.

THE DAUGHTER [*In the space between the central pillars, close to the one on her left.*] I'm getting chilled to the bone. What can Freddy be doing all this time? He's been gone twenty minutes.

THE MOTHER [*On her daughter's right.*] Not so long. But he ought to have got us a cab by this.

A BYSTANDER [*On the lady's right.*] He wont get no cab not until half-past eleven, missus, when they come back after dropping their theatre fares.

THE MOTHER But we must have a cab. We cant stand here until half-past eleven. It's too bad.

THE BYSTANDER Well, it aint my fault, missus.

THE DAUGHTER If Freddy had a bit of gumption, he would have got one at the theatre door.

THE MOTHER What could he have done, poor boy?

THE DAUGHTER Other people got cabs. Why couldnt he?

[*Freddy rushes in out of the rain from Southampton Street side, and comes between them closing a dripping umbrella. He is a young man of twenty, in evening dress, very wet round the ankles.*]

THE DAUGHTER Well, havnt you got a cab?

FREDDY Theres not one to be had for love or money.

THE MOTHER Oh, Freddy, there must be one. You cant have tried.

THE DAUGHTER It's too tiresome. Do you expect us to go and get one ourselves?

FREDDY I tell you theyre all engaged. The rain was so sudden: nobody was prepared; and everybody had to take a cab. Ive been to Charing Cross one way and nearly to Ludgate Circus the other; and they were all engaged.

THE MOTHER Did you try Trafalgar Square?

FREDDY There wasnt one at Trafalgar Square.

THE DAUGHTER Did you try?

FREDDY I tried as far as Charing Cross Station. Did you expect me to walk to Hammersmith?

THE DAUGHTER You havnt tried at all.

THE MOTHER You really are very helpless, Freddy. Go again; and dont come back until you have found a cab.

FREDDY I shall simply get soaked for nothing.

THE DAUGHTER And what about us? Are we to stay here all night in this draught, with next to nothing on? You selfish pig . . .

FREDDY Oh, very well: I'll go, I'll go. [*He opens his umbrella and dashes off Strandwards, but comes into collision with a flower girl who is hurrying in for shelter, knocking her basket out of her hands. A blinding flash of lightning, followed instantly by a rattling peal of thunder, orchestrates the incident.*]

THE FLOWER GIRL Nah then, Freddy: look wh' y' gowin, deah.

FREDDY Sorry. [*He rushes off.*]

THE FLOWER GIRL [*Picking up her scattered flowers and replacing them in the basket.*] Theres menners f' yer! Tə-oo banches o voylets trod into the mad. [*She sits down on the plinth of the column, sorting her flowers, on the lady's right. She is not at all a romantic figure. She is perhaps eighteen, perhaps twenty, hardly older. She wears a little sailor hat of black straw that has long been exposed to the dust and soot of London and has seldom if ever been brushed. Her hair needs washing rather badly: its mousy color can hardly be natural. She wears a shoddy black coat that reaches nearly to her knees and is shaped to her waist. She has a brown skirt with a coarse apron. Her boots are much the worse for wear. She is no doubt as clean as she can afford to be; but compared to the ladies she is very dirty. Her features are no worse than theirs; but their condition leaves something to be desired; and she needs the services of a dentist.*]

THE MOTHER How do you know that my son's name is Freddy, pray?

THE FLOWER GIRL Ow, eez yə-ooa san, is e? Wal, fewd dan y' də-ooty bawmz a mather should, eed now bettern to spawl a pore gel's flahrzn than ran awy athaht pyin. Will ye-oo py me f'them? [*Here, with apologies, this desperate attempt to represent her dialect without a phonetic alphabet must be abandoned as unintelligible outside London.*]

THE DAUGHTER Do nothing of the sort, mother. The idea!

THE MOTHER Please allow me, Clara. Have you any pennies?

THE DAUGHTER No. Ive nothing smaller than sixpence.

THE FLOWER GIRL [*Hopefully.*] I can give you change for a tanner, kind lady.

THE MOTHER [*To* CLARA.] Give it to me. [CLARA *parts reluctantly.*] Now [*to the girl*] this is for your flowers.

THE FLOWER GIRL Thank you kindly, lady.

THE DAUGHTER Make her give you the change. These things are only a penny a bunch.

THE MOTHER Do hold your tongue, Clara. [*To the girl.*] You can keep the change.

THE FLOWER GIRL Oh, thank you, lady.

THE MOTHER Now tell me how you know that young gentleman's name.

THE FLOWER GIRL I didnt.

THE MOTHER I heard you call him by it. Dont try to deceive me.

THE FLOWER GIRL [*Protesting.*] Who's trying to deceive you? I called him Freddy or Charlie same as you might yourself if you was talking to a stranger and wished to be pleasant.

THE DAUGHTER Sixpence thrown away! Really, mamma, you might have spared Freddy that. [*She retreats in disgust behind the pillar.*]

[*An elderly gentleman of the amiable military type rushes into the shelter, and closes a dripping umbrella. He is in the same plight as* FREDDY, *very wet about the ankles. He is in evening dress, with a light overcoat. He takes the place left vacant by the daughter.*]

THE GENTLEMAN Phew!

THE MOTHER [*To the gentleman.*] Oh, sir, is there any sign of its stopping?

THE GENTLEMAN I'm afraid not. It started worse than ever about two minutes ago. [*He goes to the plinth beside the flower girl; puts up his foot on it; and stoops to turn down his trouser ends.*]

THE MOTHER Oh dear! [*She retires sadly and joins her daughter.*]

THE FLOWER GIRL [*Taking advantage of the military gentleman's proximity to establish friendly relations with him.*] If it's worse, it's a sign it's nearly over. So cheer up, Captain; and buy a flower off a poor girl.

THE GENTLEMAN I'm sorry. I havnt any change.

THE FLOWER GIRL I can give you change, Captain.

THE GENTLEMAN For a sovereign? Ive nothing less.

THE FLOWER GIRL Garn! Oh do buy a flower off me, Captain. I can change a half-a-crown. Take this for tuppence.

THE GENTLEMAN Now dont be troublesome: theres a good girl. [*Trying his pockets.*] I really havnt any change—Stop: heres three hapence, if thats any use to you. [*He retreats to the other pillar.*]

THE FLOWER GIRL [*Disappointed, but thinking three half-pence better than nothing.*] Thank you, sir.

THE BYSTANDER [*To the girl.*] You be careful: give him a flower for it. Theres a bloke here behind taking down every blessed word youre saying. [*All turn to the man who is taking notes.*]

THE FLOWER GIRL [*Springing up terrified.*] I aint done nothing wrong by speaking to the gentleman. Ive a right to sell flowers if I keep off the kerb. [*Hysterically.*] I'm a respectable girl: so help me, I never spoke to him except to ask him to buy a flower off me.

General hubbub, mostly sympathetic to the flower girl, but deprecating her excessive sensibility. Cries of Dont start hollerin. Who's hurting you? Nobody's going to touch you. Whats the good of fussing? Steady on. Easy easy, etc., *come from the elderly staid spectators, who pat her comfortingly. Less patient ones bid her shut her head, or ask her roughly what is wrong with her. A remoter group, not knowing what the matter is, crowd in and increase the noise with question and answer: Whats the row?* What-she do? Where is he? A tec taking her down. What! him? Yes: him over there: Took money off the gentleman, etc.

THE FLOWER GIRL [*Breaking through them to the gentleman, crying wildly.*] Oh, sir, dont let him charge me. You dunno what it means to me. Theyll take away my character and drive me on the streets for speaking to gentlemen. They . . .

THE NOTE TAKER [*Coming forward on her right, the rest crowding after him.*] There! there! there! there! who's hurting you, you silly girl? What do you take me for?

THE BYSTANDER It's aw rawt: e's a gentleman: look at his bə-oots. [*Explaining to the note taker.*] She thought you was a copper's nark, sir.

THE NOTE TAKER [*With quick interest.*] Whats a copper's nark?

THE BYSTANDER [*Inapt at definition.*] It's a—well, it's a copper's nark, as you might say. What else would you call it? A sort of informer.

THE FLOWER GIRL [*Still hysterical.*] I take my Bible oath I never said a word . . .

THE NOTE TAKER [*Overbearing but good-humored.*] Oh, shut up, shut up. Do I look like a policeman?

THE FLOWER GIRL [*Far from reassured.*] Then what did you take down my words for? How do I know whether you took me down right? You just show me what youve wrote about me. [*The note taker opens his book and holds it steadily under her nose, though the pressure of the mob trying to read it over his shoulders would upset a weaker man.*] Whats that? That aint proper writing. I cant read that.

THE NOTE TAKER I can. [*Reads, reproducing her pronunciation exactly.*] "Cheer ap, Keptin; n' baw ya flahr orf a pore gel."

THE FLOWER GIRL [*Much distressed.*] It's because I called him Captain. I meant no harm. [*To the gentleman.*] Oh, sir, dont let him lay a charge agen me for a word like that. You . . .

THE GENTLEMAN Charge! I make no charge. [*To the note taker.*] Really, sir, if you are a detective, you need not begin protecting me against molestation by young women until I ask you. Anybody could see that the girl meant no harm.

THE BYSTANDERS GENERALLY [*Demonstrating against police espionage.*] Course they could. What business is it of yours? You mind your own affairs. He wants a promotion, he does. Taking down people's words! Girl never said a word to him. What harm if she did? Nice thing a girl cant shelter from the rain without being insulted, etc., etc., etc. [*She is conducted by the more sympathetic demonstrators back to her plinth, where she resumes her seat and struggles with her emotion.*]

THE BYSTANDER He aint a tec. He's a bloming busybody: thats what he is. I tell you, look at his bə-oots.

THE NOTE TAKER [*Turning on him genially.*] And how are all your people down at Selsey?

THE BYSTANDER [*Suspiciously.*] Who told you my people come from Selsey?

THE NOTE TAKER Never you mind. They did. [*To the girl.*] How do you come to be up so far east? You were born in Lisson Grove.

THE FLOWER GIRL [*Appalled.*] Oh, what harm is there in my leaving Lisson Grove? It wasn't fit for a pig to live in; and I had to pay four-and-six a week. [*In tears.*] Oh, boo—hoo—oo—

THE NOTE TAKER Live where you like; but stop that noise.

THE GENTLEMAN [*To the girl.*] Come, come! he cant touch you: you have a right to live where you please.

A SARCASTIC BYSTANDER [*Thrusting himself between the note

taker and the gentleman.] Park Lane, for instance. I'd like to go into the Housing Question with you, I would.

THE FLOWER GIRL [*Subsiding into a brooding melancholy over her basket, and talking very low-spiritedly to herself.*] I'm a good girl, I am.

THE SARCASTIC BYSTANDER [*Not attending to her.*] Do you know where *I* come from?

THE NOTE TAKER [*promptly.*] Hoxton.

[*Titterings. Popular interest in the note taker's performance increases.*]

THE SARCASTIC ONE [*Amazed.*] Well, who said I didnt? Bly me! you know everything, you do.

THE FLOWER GIRL [*Still nursing her sense of injury.*] Aint no call to meddle with me, he aint.

THE BYSTANDER [*To her.*] Of course he aint. Dont you stand it from him. [*To the note taker.*] See here: what call have you to know about people what never offered to meddle with you?

THE FLOWER GIRL Let him say what he likes. I dont want to have no truck with him.

THE BYSTANDER You take us for dirt under your feet, dont you? Catch you taking liberties with a gentleman!

THE SARCASTIC BYSTANDER Yes: tell him where he come from if you want to go fortune-telling.

THE NOTE TAKER Cheltenham, Harrow, Cambridge, and India.

THE GENTLEMAN Quite right.

Great laughter. Reaction in the note taker's favor. Exclamations of He knows all about it. Told him proper. Hear him tell the toff where he come from? etc.

THE GENTLEMAN May I ask, sir, do you do this for your living at a music hall?

THE NOTE TAKER Ive thought of that. Perhaps I shall some day.

[*The rain has stopped; and the persons on the outside of the crowd begin to drop off.*]

THE FLOWER GIRL [*Resenting the reaction.*] He's no gentleman, he aint, to interfere with a poor girl.

THE DAUGHTER [*Out of patience, pushing her way rudely to the front and displacing the gentleman, who politely retires to the other side of the pillar.*] What on earth is Freddy doing? I shall get pneumownia if I stay in this draught any longer.

THE NOTE TAKER [*To himself, hastily making a note of her pronunciation of "monia".*] Earlscourt.

THE DAUGHTER [*Violently.*] Will you please keep your impertinent remarks to yourself.

THE NOTE TAKER Did I say that out loud? I didnt mean to. I beg your pardon. Your mother's Epsom, unmistakably.

THE MOTHER [*Advancing between the daughter and the note taker.*] How very curious! I was brought up in Largelady Park, near Epsom.

THE NOTE TAKER [*Uproariously amused.*] Ha! Ha! What a devil of a name! Excuse me. [*To the daughter.*] You want a cab, do you?

THE DAUGHTER Dont dare speak to me.

THE MOTHER Oh please, please, Clara. [*Her daughter repudiates her with an angry shrug and retires haughtily.*] We should be so grateful to you, sir, if you found us a cab. [*The note taker produces a whistle.*] Oh, thank you. [*She joins her daughter.*]

[*The note taker blows a piercing blast.*]

THE SARCASTIC BYSTANDER There! I knowed he was a plainclothes copper.

THE BYSTANDER That aint a police whistle: thats a sporting whistle.

THE FLOWER GIRL [*Still preoccupied with her wounded feelings.*] He's no right to take away my character. My character is the same to me as any lady's.

THE NOTE TAKER I dont know whether youve noticed it; but the rain stopped about two minutes ago.

THE BYSTANDER So it has. Why didnt you say so before? and us losing our time listening to your silliness! [*He walks off towards the Strand.*]

THE SARCASTIC BYSTANDER I can tell where you come from. You come from Anwell. Go back there.

THE NOTE TAKER [*Helpfully.*] Hanwell.

THE SARCASTIC BYSTANDER [*Affecting great distinction of speech.*] Thenk you, teacher. Haw haw! So long. [*He touches his hat with mock respect and strolls off.*]

THE FLOWER GIRL Frightening people like that! How would he like it himself?

THE MOTHER It's quite fine now, Clara. We can walk to a motor bus. Come. [*She gathers her skirts above her ankles and hurries off towards the Strand.*]

THE DAUGHTER But the cab . . . [*Her mother is out of hearing.*] Oh, how tiresome! [*She follows angrily.*]

[*All the rest have gone except the note taker, the gentleman, and the flower girl, who sits arranging her basket, and still pitying herself in murmurs.*]

THE FLOWER GIRL Poor girl! Hard enough for her to live without being worrited and chivied.

THE GENTLEMAN [*Returning to his former place on the note taker's left.*] How do you do it, if I may ask?

THE NOTE TAKER Simply phonetics. The science of speech. Thats my profession: also my hobby. Happy is the man who can make a living by his hobby! You can spot an Irishman or a Yorkshireman by his brogue. *I* can place any man within six miles. I can place him within two miles in London. Sometimes within two streets.

THE FLOWER GIRL Ought to be ashamed of himself, unmanly coward!

THE GENTLEMAN But is there a living in that?

THE NOTE TAKER Oh yes. Quite a fat one. This is an age of upstarts. Men begin in Kentish Town with £80 a year, and end in Park Lane with a hundred thousand. They want to drop Kentish Town; but they give themselves away every time they open their mouths. Now I can teach them . . .

THE FLOWER GIRL Let him mind his own business and leave a poor girl . . .

THE NOTE TAKER [*Explosively.*] Woman: cease this detestable boohooing instantly; or else seek the shelter of some other place of worship.

THE FLOWER GIRL [*With feeble defiance.*] Ive a right to be here if I like, same as you.

THE NOTE TAKER A woman who utters such depressing and disgusting sounds has no right to be anywhere—no right to live. Remember that you are a human being with a soul and the divine gift of articulate speech: that your native language is the language of Shakespear and Milton and The Bible; and dont sit there crooning like a bilious pigeon.

THE FLOWER GIRL [*Quite overwhelmed, looking up at him in mingled wonder and deprecation without daring to raise her head.*] Ah-ah-ah-ow-ow-ow-oo!

THE NOTE TAKER [*Whipping out his book.*] Heavens! what a sound! [*He writes; then holds out the book and reads, reproducing her vowels exactly.*] Ah-ah-ah-ow-ow-ow-oo!

THE FLOWER GIRL [*Tickled by the performance, and laughing in spite of herself.*] Garn!

THE NOTE TAKER You see this creature with her kerbstone English: the English that will keep her in the gutter to the end of her days. Well, sir, in three months I could pass that girl off as a duchess at an ambassador's garden party. I could even get her a place as lady's maid or shop assistant, which requires better English.

THE FLOWER GIRL Whats that you say?

THE NOTE TAKER Yes, you squashed cabbage leaf, you disgrace to the noble architecture of these columns, you incarnate insult to the English language: I could pass you off as the Queen of Sheba. [*To the gentleman.*] Can you believe that?

THE GENTLEMAN Of course I can. I am myself a student of Indian dialects; and . . .

THE NOTE TAKER [*Eagerly.*] Are you? Do you know Colonel Pickering, the author of Spoken Sanscrit?

THE GENTLEMAN I am Colonel Pickering. Who are you?

THE NOTE TAKER Henry Higgins, author of Higgins's Universal Alphabet.

PICKERING [*With enthusiasm.*] I came from India to meet you.

HIGGINS I was going to India to meet you.

PICKERING Where do you live?

HIGGINS 27A Wimpole Street. Come and see me tomorrow.

PICKERING I'm at the Carlton. Come with me now and lets have a jaw over some supper.

HIGGINS Right you are.

THE FLOWER GIRL [*To* PICKERING, *as he passes her.*] Buy a flower, kind gentleman. I'm short for my lodging.

PICKERING I really havnt any change. I'm sorry. [*He goes away.*]

HIGGINS [*Shocked at the girl's mendacity.*] Liar. You said you could change half-a-crown.

THE FLOWER GIRL [*Rising in desperation.*] You ought to be stuffed with nails, you ought. [*Flinging the basket at his feet.*] Take the whole blooming basket for sixpence.

[*The church clock strikes the second quarter.*]

HIGGINS [*Hearing in it the voice of God, rebuking him for his Pharisaic want of charity to the poor girl.*] A reminder. [*He raises his hat solemnly; then throws a handful of money into the basket and follows* PICKERING.]

THE FLOWER GIRL [*Picking up a half-crown.*] Ah-ow-ooh! [*Picking up a couple of florins.*] Aaah-ow-ooh! [*Picking up several coins.*] Aaaaah-ow-ooh! [*Picking up a half-sovereign.*] Aaaaaaaaaaaa-ow-ooh!!!

FREDDY [*Springing out of a taxicab.*] Got one at last. Hallo! [*To the girl.*] Where are the two ladies that were here?

THE FLOWER GIRL They walked to the bus when the rain stopped.

FREDDY And left me with a cab on my hands! Damnation!

THE FLOWER GIRL [*With grandeur.*] Never mind, young man. I'm going home in a taxi. [*She sails off to the cab. The driver puts his hand behind him and holds the door firmly shut against her. Quite understanding his mistrust, she shows him her handful of money.*] A taxi fare aint no object to me, Charlie. [*He grins and opens the door.*] Here. What about the basket?

THE TAXIMAN Give it here. Tuppence extra.

LIZA No: I dont want nobody to see it. [*She crushes it into the cab and gets in, continuing the conversation through the window.*] Goodbye, Freddy.

FREDDY [*Dazedly raising his hat.*] Goodbye.

TAXIMAN Where to?

LIZA Bucknam Pellis [Buckingham Palace].

TAXIMAN What d'ye mean—Bucknam Pellis?

LIZA Dont you know where it is? In the Green Park, where the King lives. Goodbye, Freddy. Dont let me keep you standing there. Goodbye.

FREDDY Goodbye. [*He goes.*]

TAXIMAN Here? Whats this about Bucknam Pellis? What business have you at Bucknam Pellis?

LIZA Of course I havnt none. But I wasnt going to let him know that. You drive me home.

TAXIMAN And wheres home?

LIZA Angel Court, Drury Lane, next Meiklejohn's oil shop.

TAXIMAN That sounds more like it, Judy. [*He drives off.*]

* * * * * *

Let us follow the taxi to the entrance to Angel Court, a narrow little archway between two shops, one of them Meiklejohn's oil shop. When it stops there, Eliza gets out, dragging her basket with her.

LIZA How much?

TAXIMAN [*Indicating the taximeter.*] Cant you read? A shilling.

LIZA A shilling for two minutes!!

TAXIMAN Two minutes or ten: it's all the same.

LIZA Well, I dont call it right.

TAXIMAN Ever been in a taxi before?

LIZA [*With dignity.*] Hundreds and thousands of times, young man.

TAXIMAN [*Laughing at her.*] Good for you, Judy. Keep the shilling, darling, with best love from all at home. Good luck! [*He drives off.*]

LIZA [*Humiliated.*] Impidence!

[*She picks up the basket and trudges up the alley with it to her lodging: a small room with very old wall paper hanging loose in the damp places. A broken pane in the window is mended with paper. A portrait of a popular actor and a fashion plate of ladies' dresses, all wildly beyond poor Eliza's means, both torn from newspapers, are pinned up on the wall. A birdcage hangs in the window; but its tenant died long ago: it remains as a memorial only. These are the only visible luxuries: the rest is the irreducible minimum of poverty's needs: a wretched bed heaped with all sorts of coverings that have any warmth in them, a draped packing case with a basin and jug on it and a little looking glass over it, a chair and table, the refuse of some suburban kitchen, and an American alarm clock on the shelf above the unused fireplace: the whole lighted with a gas lamp with a penny in the slot meter. Rent: four shillings a week.*]

Here Eliza, chronically weary, but too excited to go to bed, sits, counting her new riches and dreaming and planning what to do with them, until the gas goes out, when she enjoys for the first time the sensation of being able to put in another penny without grudging it. This prodigal mood does not extinguish her gnawing sense of the need for economy sufficiently to prevent her from calculating that she can dream and plan in bed more cheaply and warmly than sitting up without a fire. So she takes off her shawl and skirt and adds them to the miscellaneous bedclothes. Then she kicks off her shoes and gets into bed without any further change.

ACT II

SCENE: *Next day at 11* A.M. HIGGINS'S *laboratory in Wimpole Street. It is a room on the first floor, looking on the street, and was meant for the drawing room. The double doors are in the middle of the back wall; and persons entering find in the corner to their right two tall file cabinets at right angles to one another against the walls. In this corner stands a flat writing table, on which are a phonograph, a laryngoscope, a row of tiny organ pipes with a bellows, a set of lamp chimneys for singing flames with burners attached to a gas plug in the wall by an indiarubber tube, several tuning forks of different sizes, a life-size image of half a human head, showing in section the vocal organs, and a box containing a supply of wax cylinders for the phonograph.*

Further down the room, on the same side, is a fireplace, with a comfortable leather-covered easy-chair at the side of the hearth nearest the door, and a coal scuttle. There is a clock on the mantlepiece. Between the fireplace and the phonograph table is a stand for newspapers.

On the other side of the central door, to the left of the visitor, is a cabinet of shallow drawers. On it is a telephone and the telephone directory. The corner beyond, and most of the side wall, is occupied by a grand piano, with the keyboard at the end furthest from the door, and a bench for the players extending the full length of the keyboard. On the piano is a dessert dish heaped with fruit and sweets, mostly chocolates.

The middle of the room is clear. Besides the easy-chair, the piano bench, and two chairs at the phonograph table, there is one stray chair. It stands near the fireplace. On the walls, engravings: mostly Piranesis and mezzotint portraits. No paintings.

PICKERING *is seated at the table, putting down some cards and a tuning fork which he has been using.* HIGGINS *is standing up near him, closing two or three file drawers which are hanging out. He appears in the morning light as a robust, vital, appetizing sort of man of forty or thereabouts, dressed in a professional looking black frock-coat with a white linen collar and black silk tie. He is of energetic, scientific type, heartily, even violently interested in everything that can be studied as a scientific subject, and careless about himself and other people, including their feelings. He is, in fact, but for his years and size, rather like a very impetuous baby "taking notice" eagerly and loudly, and requiring almost as much watching to keep him out of unintended mischief. His manner varies from genial bullying when he is in a good humor to stormy petulance when anything goes wrong; but he is so entirely frank and void of malice that he remains likeable even in his least reasonable moments.*

HIGGINS [*As he shuts the last drawer.*] Well, I think thats the whole show.

PICKERING It's really amazing. I havnt taken half of it in, you know.

HIGGINS Would you like to go over any of it again?

PICKERING [*Rising and coming to the fireplace, where he plants himself with his back to the fire.*] No, thank you: not now. I'm quite done up for this morning.

HIGGINS [*Following him, and standing beside him on his left.*] Tired of listening to sounds?

PICKERING Yes. It's a fearful strain. I rather fancied myself because I can pronounce twenty-four distinct vowel sounds; but your hundred and thirty beat me. I cant hear a bit of difference between most of them.

HIGGINS [*Chuckling, and going over to the piano to eat sweets.*] Oh, that comes with practice. You hear no difference at first; but you keep on listening, and presently you find theyre all as different as A from B. [MRS PEARCE *looks in: she is* HIGGINS's *housekeeper.*] Whats the matter?

MRS PEARCE [*Hesitating, evidently perplexed.*] A young woman asks to see you, sir.

HIGGINS A young woman! What does she want?

MRS PEARCE Well, sir, she says youll be glad to see her when you know what she's come about. She's quite a common girl, sir. Very common indeed. I should have sent her away, only I thought perhaps you wanted her to talk into your machines. I hope Ive not done wrong; but really you see such queer people sometimes—youll excuse me, I'm sure, sir . . .

HIGGINS Oh, thats all right, Mrs Pearce. Has she an interesting accent?

MRS PEARCE Oh, something dreadful, sir, really. I dont know how you can take an interest in it.

HIGGINS [*To* PICKERING.] Lets have her up. Show her up, Mrs Pearce. [*He rushes across to his working table and picks out a cylinder to use on the phonograph.*]

MRS PEARCE [*Only half resigned to it.*] Very well, sir. It's for you to say. [*She goes downstairs.*]

HIGGINS This is rather a bit of luck. I'll show you how I make records. We'll set her talking; and I'll take it down first in Bell's Visible Speech; then in broad Romic; and then we'll get her on the phonograph so that you can turn her on as often as you like with the written transcript before you.

MRS PEARCE [*Returning.*] This is the young woman, sir.

[*The flower girl enters in state. She has a hat with three ostrich feathers, orange, sky-blue, and red. She has a nearly clean apron, and the shoddy coat has been tidied a little. The pathos of this deplorable figure, with its innocent vanity and consequential air, touches* PICKERING, *who has already straightened himself in the presence of* MRS PEARCE. *But as to* HIGGINS, *the only distinction he makes between men and women is that when he is neither bullying nor exclaiming to the heavens against some featherweight cross, he coaxes women as a child coaxes its nurse when it wants to get anything out of her.*]

HIGGINS [*Brusquely, recognizing her with unconcealed disappointment, and at once, babylike, making an intolerable grievance of it.*] Why, this is the girl I jotted down last night. She's no use: Ive got all the records I want of the Lisson Grove lingo; and I'm not going to waste another cylinder on it. [*To the girl.*] Be off with you: I dont want you.

THE FLOWER GIRL Dont you be so saucy. You aint heard what I come for yet. [*To* MRS PEARCE, *who is waiting at the door for further instructions.*] Did you tell him I come in a taxi?

MRS PEARCE Nonsense, girl! what do you think a gentleman like Mr Higgins cares what you came in?

THE FLOWER GIRL Oh, we are proud! He aint above giving lessons, not him: I heard him say so. Well, I aint come here to ask for any compliment; and if my money's not good enough I can go elsewhere.

HIGGINS Good enough for what?

THE FLOWER GIRL Good enough for yə-oo. Now you know, don't you? I've come to have lessons, I am. And to pay for em tə-oo: make no mistake.

HIGGINS [*Stupent.*] Well!!! [*Recovering his breath with a gasp.*] What do you expect me to say to you?

THE FLOWER GIRL Well, if you was a gentleman, you might ask me to sit down, I think. Dont I tell you I'm bringing you business?

HIGGINS Pickering: shall we ask this baggage to sit down, or shall we throw her out of the window?

THE FLOWER GIRL [*Running away in terror to the piano, where she turns at bay.*] Ah-ah-oh-ow-ow-ow-oo! [*Wounded and whimpering.*] I wont be called a baggage when Ive offered to pay like any lady.

[*Motionless, the two men stare at her from the other side of the room, amazed.*]

PICKERING [*Gently.*] But what is it you want?

THE FLOWER GIRL I want to be a lady in a flower shop stead of sellin at the corner of Tottenham Court Road. But they wont take me unless I can talk more genteel. He said he could teach me. Well, here I am ready to pay him not asking any favor— and he treats me zif I was dirt.

MRS PEARCE How can you be such a foolish ignorant girl as to think you could afford to pay Mr Higgins?

THE FLOWER GIRL Why shouldnt I? I know what lessons cost as well as you do; and I'm ready to pay.

HIGGINS How much?

THE FLOWER GIRL [*Coming back to him, triumphant.*] Now youre talking! I thought youd come off it when you saw a chance of getting back a bit of what you chucked at me last night. [*Confidentially.*] Youd had a drop in, hadnt you?

HIGGINS [*Peremptorily.*] Sit down.

THE FLOWER GIRL Oh, if youre going to make a compliment of it . . .

HIGGINS [*Thundering at her.*] Sit down.

MRS PEARCE [*Severely.*] Sit down, girl. Do as youre told.

THE FLOWER GIRL Ah-ah-ah-ow-ow-oo! [*She stands, half rebellious, half bewildered.*]

PICKERING [*Very courteous.*] Wont you sit down? [*He places the stray chair near the hearthrug between himself and* HIGGINS.]

LIZA [*Coyly.*] Dont mind if I do. [*She sits down.* PICKERING *returns to the hearthrug.*]

HIGGINS Whats your name?

THE FLOWER GIRL Liza Doolittle.

HIGGINS [*Declaiming gravely.*]

Eliza, Elizabeth, Betsy and Bess,
They went to the woods to get a bird's nes':

PICKERING They found a nest with four eggs in it:

HIGGINS They took one apiece, and left three in it.

[*They laugh heartily at their own fun.*]

LIZA Oh, dont be silly.

MRS PEARCE [*Placing herself behind* ELIZA's *chair.*] You mustnt speak to the gentleman like that.

LIZA Well, why wont he speak sensible to me?

HIGGINS Come back to business. How much do you propose to pay me for the lessons?

LIZA Oh, I know whats right. A lady friend of mine gets French lessons for eighteenpence an hour from a real French gentleman. Well, you wouldnt have the face to ask me the same for teaching me my own language as you would for French; so I wont give more than a shilling. Take it or leave it.

HIGGINS [*Walking up and down the room, rattling his keys*

and his cash in his pockets.] You know, Pickering, if you consider a shilling, not as a simple shilling, but as a percentage of this girl's income, it works out as fully equivalent to sixty or seventy guineas from a millionaire.

PICKERING How so?

HIGGINS Figure it out. A millionaire has about £150 a day. She earns about half-a-crown.

LIZA [*Haughtily.*] Who told you I only . . .

HIGGINS [*Continuing.*] She offers me two-fifths of her day's income for a lesson. Two-fifths of a millionaire's income for a day would be somewhere about £60. It's handsome. By George, it's enormous! it's the biggest offer I ever had.

LIZA [*Rising, terrified.*] Sixty pounds! What are you talking about? I never offered you sixty pounds. Where would I get . . .

HIGGINS Hold your tongue.

LIZA [*Weeping.*] But I aint got sixty pounds. Oh . . .

MRS PEARCE Dont cry, you silly girl. Sit down. Nobody is going to touch your money.

HIGGINS Somebody is going to touch you, with a broomstick, if you dont stop snivelling. Sit down.

LIZA [*Obeying slowly.*] Ah-ah-ah-ow-oo-o! One would think you was my father.

HIGGINS If I decide to teach you, I'll be worse than two fathers to you. Here! [*He offers her his silk handkerchief.*]

LIZA Whats this for?

HIGGINS To wipe your eyes. To wipe any part of your face that feels moist. Remember: thats your handkerchief; and thats your sleeve. Dont mistake the one for the other if you wish to become a lady in a shop.

[LIZA, *utterly bewildered, stares helplessly at him.*]

MRS PEARCE It's no use talking to her like that, Mr Higgins: she doesnt understand you. Besides, youre quite wrong: she doesnt do it that way at all. [*She takes the handkerchief.*]

LIZA [*Snatching it.*] Here! You give me that handkerchief. He gev it to me, not to you.

PICKERING [*Laughing.*] He did. I think it must be regarded as her property, Mrs Pearce.

MRS PEARCE [*Resigning herself.*] Serve you right, Mr Higgins.

PICKERING Higgins: I'm interested. What about the ambassador's garden party? I'll say youre the greatest teacher alive if you make that good. I'll bet you all the expenses of the experiment you cant do it. And I'll pay for the lessons.

LIZA Oh, you are real good. Thank you, Captain.

HIGGINS [*Tempted, looking at her.*] It's almost irresistible. She's so deliciously low—so horribly dirty . . .

LIZA [*Protesting extremely.*] Ah-ah-ah-ah-ow-ow-oo-oo!!! I aint dirty: I washed my face and hands afore I come, I did.

PICKERING Youre certainly not going to turn her head with flattery, Higgins.

MRS PEARCE [*Uneasy.*] Oh, dont say that, sir: theres more ways than one of turning a girl's head; and nobody can do it better than Mr Higgins, though he may not always mean it. I do hope, sir, you wont encourage him to do anything foolish.

HIGGINS [*Becoming excited as the idea grows on him.*] What is life but a series of inspired follies? The difficulty is to find them to do. Never lose a chance: it doesnt come every day. I shall make a duchess of this draggletailed guttersnipe.

LIZA [*Strongly deprecating this view of her.*] Ah-ah-ah-ow-ow-oo!

HIGGINS [*Carried away.*] Yes: in six months—in three if she has a good ear and a quick tongue—I'll take her anywhere and pass her off as anything. We'll start today: now! this moment! Take her away and clean her, Mrs Pearce. Monkey Brand, if it wont come off any other way. Is there a good fire in the kitchen?

MRS PEARCE [*Protesting.*] Yes; but . . .

HIGGINS [*Storming on.*] Take all her clothes off and burn them. Ring up Whitely or somebody for new ones. Wrap her up in brown paper til they come.

LIZA Youre no gentleman, youre not, to talk of such things. I'm a good girl, I am; and I know what the like of you are, I do.

HIGGINS We want none of your Lisson Grove prudery here, young woman. Youve got to learn to behave like a duchess. Take her away, Mrs Pearce. If she gives you any trouble, wallop her.

LIZA [*Springing up and running between* PICKERING *and* MRS PEARCE *for protection.*] No! I'll call the police, I will.

MRS PEARCE But Ive no place to put her.

HIGGINS Put her in the dustbin.

LIZA Ah-ah-ah-ow-ow-oo!

PICKERING Oh come, Higgins! be reasonable.

MRS PEARCE [*Resolutely.*] You must be reasonable, Mr Higgins: really you must. You cant walk over everybody like this.

[HIGGINS, *thus scolded, subsides. The hurricane is succeeded by a zephyr of amiable surprise.*]

HIGGINS [*With professional exquisiteness of modulation.*] *I* walk over everybody! My dear Mrs Pearce, my dear Pickering, I never had the slightest intention of walking over anyone. All I propose is that we should be kind to this poor girl. We must help her to prepare and fit herself for her new station in life. If I did not express myself clearly it was because I did not wish to hurt her delicacy, or yours.

[LIZA, *reassured, steals back to her chair.*]

MRS PEARCE [*To* PICKERING.] Well, did you ever hear anything like that, sir?

PICKERING [*Laughing heartily.*] Never, Mrs Pearce: never.

HIGGINS [*Patiently.*] Whats the matter?

MRS PEARCE Well, the matter is, sir, that you cant take a girl up like that as if you were picking up a pebble on the beach.

HIGGINS Why not?

MRS PEARCE Why not! But you dont know anything about her. What about her parents? She may be married.

LIZA Garn!

HIGGINS There! As the girl very properly says, Garn! Married indeed! Dont you know that a woman of that class looks a worn out drudge of fifty a year after she's married?

LIZA Whood marry me?

HIGGINS [*Suddenly resorting to the most thrillingly beautiful low tones in his best elocutionary style.*] By George, Eliza, the streets will be strewn with the bodies of men shooting themselves for your sake before Ive done with you.

MRS PEARCE Nonsense, sir. You mustnt talk like that to her.

LIZA [*Rising and squaring herself determinedly.*] I'm going away. He's off his chump, he is. I dont want no balmies teaching me.

HIGGINS [*Wounded in his tenderest point by her insensibility to his elocution.*] Oh, indeed! I'm mad, am I? Very well, Mrs Pearce: you neednt order the new clothes for her. Throw her out.

LIZA [*Whimpering.*] Nah-ow. You got no right to touch me.

MRS PEARCE You see now what comes of being saucy. [*Indicating the door.*] This way, please.

LIZA [*Almost in tears.*] I didnt want no clothes. I wouldnt have taken them. [*She throws away the handkerchief.*] I can buy my own clothes.

HIGGINS [*Deftly retrieving the handkerchief and intercepting her on her reluctant way to the door.*] Youre an ungrateful wicked girl. This is my return for offering to take you out of the gutter and dress you beautifully and make a lady of you.

MRS PEARCE Stop, Mr Higgins. I wont allow it. It's you that are wicked. Go home to your parents, girl; and tell them to take better care of you.

LIZA I aint got no parents. They told me I was big enough to earn my own living and turned me out.

MRS PEARCE Wheres your mother?

LIZA I aint got no mother. Her that turned me out was my sixth stepmother. But I done without them. And I'm a good girl, I am.

HIGGINS Very well, then, what on earth is all this fuss about? The girl doesnt belong to anybody—is no use to anybody but me. [*He goes to* MRS PEARCE *and begins coaxing.*] You can adopt her, Mrs Pearce: I'm sure a daughter would be a great amusement to you. Now dont make any more fuss. Take her downstairs; and . . .

MRS PEARCE But whats to become of her? Is she to be paid anything? Do be sensible, sir.

HIGGINS Oh, pay her whatever is necessary: put it down in the housekeeping book. [*Impatiently.*] What on earth will she want with money? She'll have her food and her clothes. She'll only drink if you give her money.

LIZA [*Turning on him.*] Oh you are a brute. It's a lie: nobody ever saw the sign of liquor on me. [*To* PICKERING.] Oh, sir: youre a gentleman: dont let him speak to me like that.

PICKERING [*In good-humored remonstrance.*] Does it occur to you, Higgins, that the girl has some feelings?

HIGGINS [*Looking critically at her.*] Oh no, I dont think so. Not any feelings that we need bother about. [*Cheerily.*] Have you, Eliza?

LIZA I got my feelings same as anyone else.

HIGGINS [*To* PICKERING, *reflectively.*] You see the difficulty?

PICKERING Eh? What difficulty?

HIGGINS To get her to talk grammar. The mere pronunciation is easy enough.

LIZA I dont want to talk grammar. I want to talk like a lady in a flowershop.

MRS PEARCE Will you please keep to the point, Mr Higgins. I want to know on what terms the girl is to be here. Is she to have any wages? And what is to become of her when youve finished your teaching? You must look ahead a little.

HIGGINS [*Impatiently.*] Whats to become of her if I leave her in the gutter? Tell me that, Mrs Pearce.

MRS PEARCE Thats her own business, not yours, Mr Higgins.

HIGGINS Well, when Ive done with her, we can throw her back into the gutter; and then it will be her own business again; so thats all right.

LIZA Oh, youve no feeling heart in you: you dont care for nothing but yourself. [*She rises and takes the floor resolutely.*] Here! Ive had enough of this. I'm going. [*Making for the door.*] You ought to be ashamed of yourself, you ought.

HIGGINS [*Snatching a chocolate cream from the piano, his eyes suddenly beginning to twinkle with mischief.*] Have some chocolates, Eliza.

LIZA [*Halting, tempted.*] How do I know what might be in them? Ive heard of girls being drugged by the like of you.

[HIGGINS *whips out his penknife; cuts a chocolate in two; puts one half into his mouth and bolts it; and offers her the other half.*]

HIGGINS Pledge of good faith, Eliza. I eat one half: you eat the other. [LIZA *opens her mouth to retort: he pops the half chocolate into it.*] You shall have boxes of them, barrels of them, every day. You shall live on them. Eh?

LIZA [*Who has disposed of the chocolate after being nearly choked by it.*] I wouldnt have ate it, only I'm too ladylike to take it out of my mouth.

HIGGINS Listen, Eliza. I think you said you came in a taxi.

LIZA Well, what if I did? Ive as good a right to take a taxi as anyone else.

HIGGINS You have, Eliza; and in future you shall have as many taxis as you want. You shall go up and down and round the town in a taxi every day. Think of that, Eliza.

MRS PEARCE Mr Higgins: youre tempting the girl. It's not right. She should think of the future.

HIGGINS At her age! Nonsense! Time enough to think of the future when you havnt any future to think of. No, Eliza: do as this lady does: think of other people's futures; but never think of your own. Think of chocolates, and taxis, and gold, and diamonds.

LIZA No: I dont want no gold and no diamonds. I'm a good girl, I am. [*She sits down again, with an attempt at dignity.*]

HIGGINS You shall remain so, Eliza, under the care of Mrs Pearce. And you shall marry an officer in the Guards, with a beautiful mustache: the son of a marquis, who will disinherit him for marrying you, but will relent when he sees your beauty and goodness . . .

PICKERING Excuse me, Higgins; but I really must interfere. Mrs Pearce is quite right. If this girl is to put herself in your hands for six months for an experiment in teaching, she must understand thoroughly what she's doing.

HIGGINS How can she? She's incapable of understanding anything. Besides, do any of us understand what we are doing? If we did, would we ever do it?

PICKERING Very clever, Higgins; but not to the present point. [*To* ELIZA.] Miss Doolittle . . .

LIZA [*Overwhelmed.*] Ah-ah-ow-oo!

HIGGINS There! Thats all youll get out of Eliza. Ah-ah-ow-oo!

No use explaining. As a military man you ought to know that. Give her her orders: thats enough for her. Eliza: you are to live here for the next six months, learning how to speak beautifully, like a lady in a florist's shop. If youre good and do whatever youre told, you shall sleep in a proper bedroom, and have lots to eat, and money to buy chocolates and take rides in taxis. If youre naughty and idle you will sleep in the back kitchen among the black beetles, and be walloped by Mrs Pearce with a broomstick. At the end of six months you shall go to Buckingham Palace in a carriage, beautifully dressed. If the King finds out youre not a lady, you will be taken by the police to the Tower of London, where your head will be cut off as a warning to other presumptuous flower girls. If you are not found out, you shall have a present of seven-and-sixpence to start life with as a lady in a shop. If you refuse this offer you will be a most ungrateful wicked girl; and the angels will weep for you. [*To* PICKERING.] Now are you satisfied, Pickering? [*To* MRS PEARCE.] Can I put it more plainly and fairly, Mrs Pearce?

MRS PEARCE [*Patiently.*] I think youd better let me speak to the girl properly in private. I dont know that I can take charge of her or consent to the arrangement at all. Of course I know you dont mean her any harm; but when you get what you call interested in people's accents, you never think or care what may happen to them or you. Come with me, Eliza.

HIGGINS Thats all right. Thank you, Mrs Pearce. Bundle her off to the bathroom.

LIZA [*Rising reluctantly and suspiciously.*] Youre a great bully, you are. I wont stay here if I dont like. I wont let nobody wallop me. I never asked to go to Bucknam Palace, I didnt. I was never in trouble with the police, not me. I'm a good girl . . .

MRS PEARCE Dont answer back, girl. You dont understand the gentleman. Come with me. [*She leads the way to the door, and holds it open for* ELIZA.]

LIZA [*As she goes out.*] Well, what I say is right. I wont go near the King, not if I'm going to have my head cut off. If I'd known what I was letting myself in for, I wouldnt have come here. I always been a good girl; and I never offered to say a word to him; and I dont owe him nothing; and I dont care; and I wont be put upon; and I have my feelings the same as anyone else . . .

[MRS PEARCE *shuts the door; and* ELIZA'S *plaints are no longer audible.*]

* * * * * *

Eliza is taken upstairs to the third floor greatly to her surprise; for she expected to be taken down to the scullery. There Mrs Pearce opens a door and takes her into a spare bedroom.

MRS PEARCE I will have to put you here. This will be your bedroom.

LIZA O-h, I couldn't sleep here, missus. It's too good for the likes of me. I should be afraid to touch anything. I aint a duchess yet, you know.

MRS PEARCE You have got to make yourself as clean as the room: then you wont be afraid of it. And you must call me Mrs Pearce, not missus. [*She throws open the door of the dressing-room, now modernized as a bathroom.*]

LIZA Gawd! whats this? Is this where you wash clothes? Funny sort of copper I call it.

MRS PEARCE It is not a copper. This is where we wash ourselves, Eliza, and where I am going to wash you.

LIZA You expect me to get into that and wet myself all over! Not me. I should catch my death. I knew a woman did it every Saturday night; and she died of it.

MRS PEARCE Mr Higgins has the gentlemen's bathroom downstairs; and he has a bath every morning, in cold water.

LIZA Ugh! He's made of iron, that man.

MRS PEARCE If you are to sit with him and the Colonel and be taught you will have to do the same. They wont like the smell of you if you dont. But you can have the water as hot as you like. There are two taps: hot and cold.

LIZA [*Weeping.*] I couldnt. I dursnt. Its not natural: it would kill me. Ive never had a bath in my life: not what youd call a proper one.

MRS PEARCE Well, dont you want to be clean and sweet and

decent, like a lady? You know you cant be a nice girl inside if youre a dirty slut outside.

LIZA Boohoo!!!!

MRS PEARCE Now stop crying and go back into your room and take off all your clothes. Then wrap yourself in this [*taking down a gown from its peg and handing it to her*] and come back to me. I will get the bath ready.

LIZA [*All tears.*] I cant. I wont. I'm not used to it. Ive never took off all my clothes before. It's not right: it's not decent.

MRS PEARCE Nonsense, child. Dont you take off all your clothes every night when you go to bed?

LIZA [*Amazed.*] No. Why should I? I should catch my death. Of course I take off my skirt.

MRS PEARCE Do you mean that you sleep in the underclothes you wear in the daytime?

LIZA What else have I to sleep in?

MRS PEARCE You will never do that again as long as you live here. I will get you a proper nightdress.

LIZA Do you mean change into cold things and lie awake shivering half the night? You want to kill me, you do.

MRS PEARCE I want to change you from a frowzy slut to a clean respectable girl fit to sit with the gentlemen in the study. Are you going to trust me and do what I tell you or be thrown out and sent back to your flower basket?

LIZA But you dont know what the cold is to me. You dont know how I dread it.

MRS PEARCE Your bed won't be cold here: I will put a hot water bottle in it. [*Pushing her into the bedroom.*] Off with you and undress.

LIZA Oh, if only I'd known what a dreadful thing it is to be clean I'd never have come. I didnt know when I was well off. I . . . [MRS PEARCE *pushes her through the door, but leaves it partly open lest her prisoner should take to flight.*]

[MRS PEARCE *puts on a pair of white rubber sleeves, and fills the bath, mixing hot and cold, and testing the result with the bath thermometer. She perfumes it with a handful of bath salts and adds a palmful of mustard. She then takes a formidable looking long handled scrubbing brush and soaps it profusely with a ball of scented soap.*]

[ELIZA *comes back with nothing on but the bath gown huddled tightly round her, a piteous spectacle of abject terror.*]

MRS PEARCE Now come along. Take that thing off.

LIZA Oh I couldnt, Mrs Pearce: I reely couldnt. I never done such a thing.

MRS PEARCE Nonsense. Here: step in and tell me whether its hot enough for you.

LIZA Ah-oo! Ah-oo! It's too hot.

MRS PEARCE [*Deftly snatching the gown away and throwing* ELIZA *down on her back.*] It wont hurt you. [*She sets to work with the scrubbing brush.*]

[ELIZA's *screams are heartrending.*]

* * * * * *

Meanwhile the Colonel has been having it out with Higgins about Eliza. Pickering has come from the hearth to the chair and seated himself astride of it with his arms on the back to cross-examine him.

PICKERING Excuse the straight question, Higgins. Are you a man of good character where women are concerned?

HIGGINS [*Moodily.*] Have you ever met a man of good character where women are concerned?

PICKERING Yes: very frequently.

HIGGINS [*Dogmatically, lifting himself on his hands to the level of the piano, and sitting on it with a bounce.*] Well, I havnt. I find that the moment I let a woman make friends with me, she becomes jealous, exacting, suspicious, and a damned nuisance. I find that the moment I let myself make friends with a woman, I become selfish and tyrannical. Women upset everything. When you let them into your life, you find that the woman is driving at one thing and youre driving at another.

PICKERING At what, for example?

HIGGINS [*Coming off the piano restlessly.*] Oh, Lord knows!

I suppose the woman wants to live her own life; and the man wants to live his; and each tries to drag the other on to the wrong track. One wants to go north and the other south; and the result is that both have to go east, though they both hate the east wind. [*He sits down on the bench at the keyboard.*] So here I am, a confirmed old bachelor, and likely to remain so.

PICKERING [*Rising and standing over him gravely.*] Come, Higgins! You know what I mean. If I'm to be in this business I shall feel responsible for that girl. I hope it's understood that no advantage is to be taken of her position.

HIGGINS What! That thing! Sacred, I assure you. [*Rising to explain.*] You see, she'll be a pupil; and teaching would be impossible unless pupils were sacred. Ive taught scores of American millionairesses how to speak English: the best looking women in the world. I'm seasoned. They might as well be blocks of wood. *I* might as well be a block of wood. It's . . .

[MRS PEARCE *opens the door. She has* ELIZA's *hat in her hand.* PICKERING *retires to the easy-chair at the hearth and sits down.*]

HIGGINS [*Eagerly.*] Well, Mrs Pearce: is it all right?

MRS PEARCE [*At the door.*] I just wish to trouble you with a word, if I may, Mr Higgins.

HIGGINS Yes, certainly. Come in. [*She comes forward.*] Dont burn that, Mrs Pearce. I'll keep it as a curiosity. [*He takes the hat.*]

MRS PEARCE Handle it carefully, sir, please. I had to promise her not to burn it; but I had better put it in the oven for a while.

HIGGINS [*Putting it down hastily on the piano.*] Oh! thank you. Well, what have you to say to me?

PICKERING Am I in the way?

MRS PEARCE Not in the least, sir. Mr Higgins: will you please be very particular what you say before the girl?

HIGGINS [*Sternly.*] Of course. I'm always particular about what I say. Why do you say this to me?

MRS PEARCE [*Unmoved.*] No, sir: youre not at all particular when youve mislaid anything or when you get a little impatient. Now it doesnt matter before me: I'm used to it. But you really must not swear before the girl.

HIGGINS [*Indignantly.*] I swear! [*Most emphatically.*] I never swear. I detest the habit. What the devil do you mean?

MRS PEARCE [*Stolidly.*] Thats what I mean, sir. You swear a great deal too much. I dont mind your damning and blasting, and what the devil and where the devil and who the devil . . .

HIGGINS Mrs Pearce: this language from your lips! Really!

MRS PEARCE [*Not to be put off.*] . . . but there is a certain word I must ask you not to use. The girl used it herself when she began to enjoy the bath. It begins with the same letter as bath. She knows no better: she learnt it at her mother's knee. But she must not hear it from your lips.

HIGGINS [*Loftily.*] I cannot charge myself with having ever uttered it, Mrs Pearce. [*She looks at him steadfastly. He adds, hiding an uneasy conscience with a judicial air.*] Except perhaps in a moment of extreme and justifiable excitement.

MRS PEARCE Only this morning, sir, you applied it to your boots, to the butter, and to the brown bread.

HIGGINS Oh, that! Mere alliteration, Mrs Pearce, natural to a poet.

MRS PEARCE Well, sir, whatever you choose to call it, I beg you not to let the girl hear you repeat it.

HIGGINS Oh, very well, very well. Is that all?

MRS PEARCE No, sir. We shall have to be very particular with this girl as to personal cleanliness.

HIGGINS Certainly. Quite right. Most important.

MRS PEARCE I mean not to be slovenly about her dress or untidy in leaving things about.

HIGGINS [*Going to her solemnly.*] Just so, I intended to call your attention to that. [*He passes on to* PICKERING, *who is enjoying the conversation immensely.*] It is these little things that matter, Pickering. Take care of the pence and the pounds will take care of themselves is as true of personal habits as of money. [*He comes to anchor on the hearthrug, with the air of a man in an unassailable position.*]

MRS PEARCE Yes, sir. Then might I ask you not to come down to breakfast in your dressing gown, or at any rate not to use it as a napkin to the extent you do, sir. And if you would be so good as not to eat everything off the same plate, and to remember not to put the porridge saucepan out of your hand on the clean tablecloth, it would be a better example to the girl. You know you nearly choked yourself with a fishbone in a jam only last week.

HIGGINS [*Routed from the hearthrug and drifting back to the piano.*] I may do these things sometimes in absence of mind; but surely I dont do them habitually. [*Angrily.*] By the way: my dressing gown smells most damnably of benzine.

MRS PEARCE No doubt it does, Mr Higgins. But if you will wipe your fingers . . .

HIGGINS [*Yelling.*] Oh very well, very well: I'll wipe them in my hair in future.

MRS PEARCE I hope youre not offended, Mr Higgins.

HIGGINS [*Shocked at finding himself thought capable of an unamiable sentiment.*] Not at all, not at all. Youre quite right, Mrs Pearce: I shall be particularly careful before the girl. Is that all?

MRS PEARCE No, sir. Might she use some of those Japanese dresses you brought from abroad? I really cant put her back into her old things.

HIGGINS Certainly. Anything you like. Is that all?

MRS PEARCE Thank you, sir. Thats all. [*She goes out.*]

HIGGINS You know, Pickering, that woman has the most extraordinary ideas about me. Here I am, a shy, diffident sort of man. Ive never been able to feel really grown-up and tremendous, like other chaps. And yet she's firmly persuaded that I'm an arbitrary overbearing bossing kind of person. I cant account for it.

[MRS PEARCE *returns.*]

MRS PEARCE If you please, sir, the trouble's beginning already. Theres a dustman downstairs, Alfred Doolittle, wants to see you. He says you have his daughter here.

PICKERING [*Rising.*] Phew! I say!

HIGGINS [*Promptly.*] Send the blackguard up.

MRS PEARCE Oh, very well, sir. [*She goes out.*]

PICKERING He may not be a blackguard, Higgins.

HIGGINS Nonsense. Of course he's a blackguard.

PICKERING Whether he is or not, I'm afraid we shall have some trouble with him.

HIGGINS [*Confidently.*] Oh no: I think not. If theres any trouble he shall have it with me, not I with him. And we are sure to get something interesting out of him.

PICKERING About the girl?

HIGGINS No. I mean his dialect.

PICKERING Oh!

MRS PEARCE [*At the door.*] Doolittle, sir. [*She admits Doolittle and retires.*]

[ALFRED *is an elderly but vigorous dustman, clad in the costume of his profession, including a hat with a back brim covering his neck and shoulders. He has well-marked and rather interesting features, and seems equally free from fear and conscience. He has a remarkably expressive voice, the result of a habit of giving vent to his feelings without reserve. His present pose is that of wounded honor and stern resolution.*]

DOOLITTLE [*At the door, uncertain which of the two gentlemen is his man.*] Professor Iggins?

HIGGINS Here. Good morning. Sit down.

DOOLITTLE Morning, Governor. [*He sits down magisterially.*] I come about a very serious matter, Governor.

HIGGINS [*to* PICKERING.] Brought up in Hounslow. Mother Welsh, I should think. [DOOLITTLE *opens his mouth, amazed.* HIGGINS *continues.*] What do you want, Doolittle?

DOOLITTLE [*Menacingly.*] I want my daughter: thats what I want. See?

HIGGINS Of course you do. Youre her father, arnt you? You dont suppose anyone else wants her, do you? I'm glad to see you have some spark of family feeling left. She's upstairs. Take her away at once.

DOOLITTLE [*Rising, fearfully taken aback.*] What!

HIGGINS Take her away. Do you suppose I'm going to keep your daughter for you?

DOOLITTLE [*Remonstrating.*] Now, now, look here, Governor. Is this reasonable? Is it fairity to take advantage of a man like this? The girl belongs to me. You got her. Where do I come in? [*He sits down again.*]

HIGGINS Your daughter had the audacity to come to my house

and ask me to teach her how to speak properly so that she could get a place in a flowershop. This gentleman and my housekeeper have been here all the time. [*Bullying him.*] How dare you come here and attempt to blackmail me? You sent her here on purpose.

DOOLITTLE [*Protesting.*] No, Governor.

HIGGINS You must have. How else could you possibly know that she is here?

DOOLITTLE Dont take a man up like that, Governor.

HIGGINS The police shall take you up. This is a plant—a plot to extort money by threats. I shall telephone for the police. [*He goes resolutely to the telephone and opens the directory.*]

DOOLITTLE Have I asked you for a brass farthing? I leave it to the gentleman here: have I said a word about money?

HIGGINS [*Throwing the book aside and marching down on* DOOLITTLE *with a poser.*] What else did you come for?

DOOLITTLE [*Sweetly.*] Well, what would a man come for? Be human, Governor.

HIGGINS [*Disarmed.*] Alfred: did you put her up to it?

DOOLITTLE So help me, Governor, I never did. I take my Bible oath I aint seen the girl these two months past.

HIGGINS Then how did you know she was here?

DOOLITTLE [*"Most musical, most melancholy."*] I'll tell you, Governor, if youll only let me get a word in. I'm willing to tell you. I'm wanting to tell you. I'm waiting to tell you.

HIGGINS Pickering: this chap has a certain natural gift of rhetoric. Observe the rhythm of his native woodnotes wild. "I'm willing to tell you: I'm wanting to tell you: I'm waiting to tell you." Sentimental rhetoric! thats the Welsh strain in him. It also accounts for his mendacity and dishonesty.

PICKERING Oh, please, Higgins: I'm west country myself. [*To* DOOLITTLE.] How did you know the girl was here if you didnt send her?

DOOLITTLE It was like this, Governor. The girl took a boy in the taxi to give him a jaunt. Son of her landlady, he is. He hung about on the chance of her giving him another ride home. Well, she sent him back for her luggage when she heard you was willing for her to stop here. I met the boy at the corner of Long Acre and Endell Street.

HIGGINS Public house. Yes?

DOOLITTLE The poor man's club, Governor: why shouldnt I?

PICKERING Do let him tell his story, Higgins.

DOOLITTLE He told me what was up. And I ask you, what was my feelings and my duty as a father? I says to the boy, "You bring me the luggage," I says . . .

PICKERING Why didnt you go for it yourself?

DOOLITTLE Landlady wouldnt have trusted me with it, Governor. She's that kind of woman: you know. I had to give the boy a penny afore he trusted me with it, the little swine. I brought it to her just to oblige you like, and make myself agreeable. Thats all.

HIGGINS How much luggage?

DOOLITTLE Musical instrument, Governor. A few pictures, a trifle of jewelry, and a birdcage. She said she didnt want no clothes. What was I to think from that, Governor? I ask you as a parent what was I to think?

HIGGINS So you came to rescue her from worse than death, eh?

DOOLITTLE [*Appreciatively: relieved at being so well understood.*] Just so, Governor. Thats right.

PICKERING But why did you bring her luggage if you intended to take her away?

DOOLITTLE Have I said a word about taking her away? Have I now?

HIGGINS [*Determinedly.*] Youre going to take her away, double quick. [*He crosses to the hearth and rings the bell.*]

DOOLITTLE [*Rising.*] No, Governor. Dont say that. I'm not the man to stand in my girl's light. Heres a career opening for her, as you might say; and . . .

[MRS PEARCE *opens the door and awaits orders.*]

HIGGINS Mrs. Pearce: this is Eliza's father. He has come to take her away. Give her to him. [*He goes back to the piano, with an air of washing his hands of the whole affair.*]

DOOLITTLE No. This is a misunderstanding. Listen here . . .

MRS PEARCE He cant take her away, Mr Higgins: how can he? You told me to burn her clothes.

DOOLITTLE Thats right. I cant carry the girl through the streets like a blooming monkey, can I? I put it to you.

HIGGINS You have put it to me that you want your daughter. Take your daughter. If she has no clothes go out and buy her some.

DOOLITTLE [*Desperate.*] Wheres the clothes she come in? Did I burn them or did your missus here?

MRS PEARCE I am the housekeeper, if you please. I have sent for some clothes for your girl. When they come you can take her away. You can wait in the kitchen. This way, please.

[DOOLITTLE, *much troubled, accompanies her to the door; then hesitates; finally turns confidentially to* HIGGINS.]

DOOLITTLE Listen here, Governor. You and me is men of the world, aint we?

HIGGINS Oh! Men of the world, are we? Youd better go, Mrs Pearce.

MRS PEARCE I think so, indeed, sir. [*She goes, with dignity.*]

PICKERING The floor is yours, Mr Doolittle.

DOOLITTLE [*To* PICKERING.] I thank you, Governor. [*To* HIGGINS, *who takes refuge on the piano bench, a little overwhelmed by the proximity of his visitor; for* DOOLITTLE *has a professional flavor of dust about him.*] Well, the truth is, Ive taken a sort of fancy to you, Governor; and if you want the girl, I'm not so set on having her back home again but what I might be open to an arrangement. Regarded in the light of a young woman, she's a fine handsome girl. As a daughter she's not worth her keep; and so I tell you straight. All I ask is my rights as a father; and youre the last man alive to expect me to let her go for nothing; for I can see youre one of the straight sort, Governor. Well, whats a five-pound note to you? and whats Eliza to me? [*He turns to his chair and sits down judicially.*]

PICKERING I think you ought to know, Doolittle, that Mr Higgins's intentions are entirely honorable.

DOOLITTLE Course they are, Governor. If I thought they wasnt, I'd ask fifty.

HIGGINS [*Revolted.*] Do you mean to say that you would sell your daughter for £50?

DOOLITTLE Not in a general way I would; but to oblige a gentleman like you I'd do a good deal, I do assure you.

PICKERING Have you no morals, man?

DOOLITTLE [*Unabashed.*] Cant afford them, Governor. Neither could you if you was as poor as me. Not that I mean any harm, you know. But if Liza is going to have a bit out of this, why not me too?

HIGGINS [*Troubled.*] I dont know what to do, Pickering. There can be no question that as a matter of morals it's a positive crime to give this chap a farthing. And yet I feel a sort of rough justice in his claim.

DOOLITTLE Thats it, Governor. Thats all I say. A father's heart, as it were.

PICKERING Well, I know the feeling; but really it seems hardly right . . .

DOOLITTLE Dont say that, Governor. Dont look at it that way. What am I, Governors both? I ask you, what am I? I'm one of the undeserving poor: thats what I am. Think of what that means to a man. It means that he's up agen middle-class morality all the time. If theres anything going, and I put in for a bit of it, it's always the same story: "Youre undeserving; so you cant have it." But my needs is as great as the most deserving widow's that ever got money out of six different charities in one week for the death of the same husband. I dont need less than a deserving man: I need more. I dont eat less hearty than him; and I drink a lot more. I want a bit of amusement, cause I'm a thinking man. I want cheerfulness and a song and a band when I feel low. Well, they charge me just the same for everything as they charge the deserving. What is middle-class morality? Just an excuse for never giving me anything. Therefore, I ask you, as two gentlemen, not to play that game on me. I'm playing straight with you. I aint pretending to be deserving. I'm undeserving; and I mean to go on being undeserving. I like it; and thats the truth. Will you take advantage of a man's nature to do him out of the price of his own daughter what he's brought up and fed and clothed by the sweat of his brow until she's growed big enough to be interesting to you two gentlemen? Is five pounds unreasonable? I put it to you; and I leave it to you.

HIGGINS [*Rising, and going over to* PICKERING.] Pickering: if we were to take this man in hand for three months, he could choose between a seat in the Cabinet and a popular pulpit in Wales.

PICKERING What do you say to that, Doolittle?

DOOLITTLE Not me, Governor, thank you kindly. Ive heard all the preachers and all the prime ministers—for I'm a thinking man and game for politics or religion or social reform same as all the other amusements—and I tell you it's a dog's life any way you look at it. Undeserving poverty is my line. Taking one station in society with another, it's—it's—well, it's the only one that has any ginger in it, to my taste.

HIGGINS I suppose we must give him a fiver.

PICKERING He'll make a bad use of it, I'm afraid.

DOOLITTLE Not me, Governor, so help me I wont. Dont you be afraid that I'll save it and spare it and live idle on it. There wont be a penny of it left by Monday: I'll have to go to work same as if I'd never had it. It wont pauperize me, you bet. Just one good spree for myself and the missus, giving pleasure to ourselves and employment to others, and satisfaction to you to think it's not been throwed away. You couldnt spend it better.

HIGGINS [*Taking out his pocketbook and coming between* DOOLITTLE *and the piano.*] This is irresistible. Lets give him ten. [*He offers two notes to the dustman.*]

DOOLITTLE No, Governor. She wouldn't have the heart to spend ten; and perhaps I shouldnt neither. Ten pounds is a lot of money: it makes a man feel prudent like; and then goodbye to happiness. You give me what I ask you, Governor: not a penny more, and not a penny less.

PICKERING Why dont you marry that missus of yours? I rather draw the line at encouraging that sort of immorality.

DOOLITTLE Tell her so, Governor: tell her so. *I'm* willing. It's me that suffers by it. Ive no hold on her. I got to be agreeable to her. I got to give her presents. I got to buy her clothes something sinful. I'm a slave to that woman, Governor, just because I'm not her lawful husband. And she knows it too. Catch her marrying me! Take my advice, Governor: marry Eliza while she's young and dont know no better. If you dont you'll be sorry for it after. If you do, she'll be sorry for it after; but better her than you, because youre a man, and she's only a woman and dont know how to be happy anyhow.

HIGGINS Pickering: if we listen to this man another minute, we shall have no convictions left. [*To* DOOLITTLE.] Five pounds I think you said.

DOOLITTLE Thank you kindly, Governor.

HIGGINS Youre sure you wont take ten?

DOOLITTLE Not now. Another time, Governor.

HIGGINS [*Handing him a five-pound note.*] Here you are.

DOOLITTLE Thank you, Governor. Good morning. [*He hurries to the door, anxious to get away with his booty. When he opens it he is confronted with a dainty and exquisitely clean young Japanese lady in a simple blue cotton kimono printed cunningly with small white jasmine blossoms.* MRS PEARCE *is with her. He gets out of her way deferentially and apologizes.*] Beg pardon, miss.

THE JAPANESE LADY Garn! Dont you know your own daughter?

DOOLITTLE { *Exclaiming* } Bly me! it's Eliza!
HIGGINS { *simul-* } Whats that? This!
PICKERING { *taneously.* } By Jove!

LIZA Dont I look silly?

HIGGINS Silly?

MRS PEARCE [*At the door.*] Now, Mr Higgins, please dont say anything to make the girl conceited about herself.

HIGGINS [*Conscientiously.*] Oh! Quite right, Mrs Pearce. [*To* ELIZA.] Yes: damned silly.

MRS PEARCE Please, sir.

HIGGINS [*Correcting himself.*] I mean extremely silly.

LIZA I should look all right with my hat on. [*She takes up her hat; puts it on; and walks across the room to the fireplace with a fashionable air.*]

HIGGINS A new fashion, by George! And it ought to look horrible!

DOOLITTLE [*With fatherly pride.*] Well, I never thought she'd clean up as good looking as that, Governor. She's a credit to me, aint she?

LIZA I tell you, it's easy to clean up here. Hot and cold water on tap, just as much as you like, there is. Woolly towels, there is; and a towel horse so hot, it burns your fingers. Soft brushes to scrub yourself, and a wooden bowl of soap smelling like primroses. Now I know why ladies is so clean. Washing's a treat for them. Wish they could see what it is for the like of me!

HIGGINS I'm glad the bathroom met with your approval.

LIZA It didnt: not all of it; and I dont care who hears me say it. Mrs Pearce knows.

HIGGINS What was wrong, Mrs Pearce?

MRS PEARCE [*Blandly.*] Oh, nothing, sir. It doesnt matter.

LIZA I had a good mind to break it. I didnt know which way to look. But I hung a towel over it, I did.

HIGGINS Over what?

MRS PEARCE Over the looking glass, sir.

HIGGINS Doolittle: you have brought your daughter up too strictly.

DOOLITTLE Me! I never brought her up at all, except to give her a lick of a strap now and again. Dont put it on me, Governor. She aint accustomed to it, you see: thats all. But she'll soon pick up your free-and-easy ways.

LIZA I'm a good girl, I am; and I wont pick up no free-and-easy ways.

HIGGINS Eliza: if you say again that youre a good girl, your father shall take you home.

LIZA Not him. You dont know my father. All he come here for was to touch you for some money to get drunk on.

DOOLITTLE Well, what else would I want money for? To put into the plate in church, I suppose. [*She puts out her tongue at him. He is so incensed by this that* PICKERING *presently finds it necessary to step between them.*] Dont you give me none of your lip; and dont let me hear you giving this gentleman any of it neither, or youll hear from me about it. See?

HIGGINS Have you any further advice to give her before you go, Doolittle? Your blessing, for instance.

DOOLITTLE No, Governor: I aint such a mug as to put up my children to all I know myself. Hard enough to hold them in without that. If you want Eliza's mind improved, Governor, you do it yourself with a strap. So long, gentlemen. [*He turns to go.*]

HIGGINS [*Impressively.*] Stop. Youll come regularly to see your daughter. It's your duty, you know. My brother is a clergyman; and he could help you in your talks with her.

DOOLITTLE [*Evasively.*] Certainly, I'll come, Governor. Not just this week, because I have a job at a distance. But later on you may depend on me. Afternoon, gentlemen. Afternoon, maam. [*He touches his hat to* MRS PEARCE, *who disdains the salutation and goes out. He winks at* HIGGINS, *thinking him probably a fellow-sufferer from* MRS PEARCE'S *difficult disposition, and follows her.*]

LIZA Don't you believe the old liar. He'd as soon you set a bulldog on him as a clergyman. You wont see him again in a hurry.

HIGGINS I dont want to, Eliza. Do you?

LIZA Not me. I dont want never to see him again, I dont. He's a disgrace to me, he is, collecting dust, instead of working at his trade.

PICKERING What is his trade, Eliza?

LIZA Taking money out of other people's pockets into his own. His proper trade's a navvy; and he works at it sometimes too—for exercise—and earns good money at it. Aint you going to call me Miss Doolittle any more?

PICKERING I beg your pardon, Miss Doolittle. It was a slip of the tongue.

LIZA Oh, I dont mind; only it sounded so genteel. I should just like to take a taxi to the corner of Tottenham Court Road and get out there and tell it to wait for me, just to put the girls in their place a bit. I wouldnt speak to them, you know.

PICKERING Better wait til we get you something really fashionable.

HIGGINS Besides, you shouldnt cut your old friends now that you have risen in the world. Thats what we call snobbery.

LIZA You dont call the like of them my friends now, I should hope. Theyve took it out of me often enough with their ridicule when they had the chance; and now I mean to get a bit of my own back. But if I'm to have fashionable clothes, I'll wait. I should like to have some. Mrs Pearce says youre going to give me some to wear in bed at night different to what I wear in the daytime; but it do seem a waste of money when you could get something to show. Besides, I never could fancy changing into cold things on a winter night.

MRS PEARCE [*Coming back.*] Now, Eliza. The new things have come for you to try on.

LIZA Ah-ow-oo-ooh! [*She rushes out.*]

MRS PEARCE [*Following her.*] Oh, don't rush about like that, girl. [*She shuts the door behind her.*]

HIGGINS Pickering: we have taken on a stiff job.

PICKERING [*With conviction.*] Higgins: we have.

* * * * * *

There seems to be some curiosity as to what Higgins's lessons to Eliza were like. Well, here is a sample: the first one.

Picture Eliza, in her new clothes, and feeling her inside put out of step by a lunch, dinner, and breakfast of a kind to which it is unaccustomed, seated with Higgins and the Colonel in the study, feeling like a hospital out-patient at a first encounter with the doctors.

Higgins, constitutionally unable to sit still, discomposes her still more by striding restlessly about. But for the reassuring presence and quietude of her friend the Colonel she would run for her life, even back to Drury Lane.

HIGGINS Say your alphabet.

LIZA I know my alphabet. Do you think I know nothing? I dont need to be taught like a child.

HIGGINS [*Thundering.*] Say your alphabet.

PICKERING Say it, Miss Doolittle. You will understand presently. Do what he tells you; and let him teach you in his own way.

LIZA Oh well, if you put it like that—Ahyee, bəyee, cəyee, dəyee . . .

HIGGINS [*With the roar of a wounded lion.*] Stop. Listen to this, Pickering. This is what we pay for as elementary education. This unfortunate animal has been locked up for nine years in school at our expense to teach her to speak and read the language of Shakespear and Milton. And the result is Ahyee, Bə-yee, Cə-yee, Də-yee. [*To Eliza.*] Say A, B, C, D.

LIZA [*Almost in tears.*] But I'm sayin it. Ahyee, Bəyee, Cəyee . . .

HIGGINS Stop. Say a cup of tea.

LIZA A cappətə-ee.

HIGGINS Put your tongue forward until it squeezes against the top of your lower teeth. Now say cup.

LIZA C-c-c—I cant. C-Cup.

PICKERING Good. Splendid, Miss Doolittle.

HIGGINS By Jupiter, she's done it the first shot. Pickering: we shall make a duchess of her. [*To* ELIZA.] Now do you think you could possibly say tea? Not tə-yee, mind: if you ever say bə-yee cə-yee də-yee again you shall be dragged round the room three times by the hair of your head. [*Fortissimo.*] T, T, T, T.

LIZA [*Weeping.*] I cant hear no difference cep that it sounds more genteel-like when you say it.

HIGGINS Well, if you can hear that difference, what the devil are you crying for? Pickering: give her a chocolate.

PICKERING No, no. Never mind crying a little, Miss Doolittle: you are doing very well; and the lessons wont hurt. I promise you I wont let him drag you round the room by your hair.

HIGGINS Be off with you to Mrs Pearce and tell her about it. Think about it. Try to do it by yourself: and keep your tongue well forward in your mouth instead of trying to roll it up and swallow it. Another lesson at half-past four this afternoon. Away with you.

[ELIZA, *still sobbing, rushes from the room.*]

And that is the sort of ordeal poor Eliza has to go through for months before we meet her again on her first appearance in London society of the professional class.

ACT III

SCENE: *It is* MRS HIGGINS'S *at-home day. Nobody has yet arrived. Her drawing room, in a flat on Chelsea Embankment, has three windows looking on the river; and the ceiling is not so lofty as it would be in an older house of the same pretension. The windows are open, giving access to a balcony with flowers in pots. If you stand with your face to the windows, you have the fireplace on your left and the door in the right-hand wall close to the corner nearest the windows.*

MRS HIGGINS *was brought up on Morris and Burne Jones; and her room, which is very unlike her son's room in Wimpole Street, is not crowded with furniture and little tables and nicknacks. In the middle of the room there is a big ottoman; and this, with the carpet, the Morris wallpapers, and the Morris chintz window curtains and brocade covers of the ottoman and its cushions, supply all the ornament, and are much too handsome to be hidden by odds and ends of useless things. A few good oil paintings from the exhibitions in the Grosvenor Gallery thirty years ago (the Burne Jones, not the Whistler side of them) are on the walls. The only landscape is a Cecil Lawson on the scale of a Rubens. There is a portrait of* MRS HIGGINS *as she was when she defied the fashion in her youth in one of the beautiful Rossettian costumes which, when caricatured by people who did not understand, led to the absurdities of popular estheticism in the eighteen-seventies.*

In the corner diagonally opposite the door MRS HIGGINS, *now over sixty and long past taking the trouble to dress out of the fashion, sits writing at an elegantly simple writing table with a bell button within reach of her hand. There is a Chippendale chair further back in the room between her and the window nearest her side. At the other side of the room, further forward, is an Elizabethan chair roughly carved in the taste of Inigo Jones. On the same side a piano in a decorated case. The corner between the fireplace and the window is occupied by a divan cushioned in Morris chintz.*

It is between four and five in the afternoon.

The door is opened violently; and HIGGINS *enters with his hat on.*

MRS HIGGINS [*Dismayed.*] Henry! [*Scolding him.*] What are you doing here today? It is my at-home day: you promised not to come. [*As he bends to kiss her, she takes his hat off, and presents it to him.*]

HIGGINS Oh bother! [*He throws the hat down on the table.*]

MRS HIGGINS Go home at once.

HIGGINS [*Kissing her.*] I know, mother. I came on purpose.

MRS HIGGINS But you mustnt. I'm serious, Henry. You offend all my friends: they stop coming whenever they meet you.

HIGGINS Nonsense! I know I have no small talk; but people dont mind. [*He sits on the settee.*]

MRS HIGGINS Oh! dont they? Small talk indeed! What about your large talk? Really, dear, you mustnt stay.

HIGGINS I must. Ive a job for you. A phonetic job.

MRS HIGGINS No use, dear. I'm sorry; but I cant get round your vowels; and though I like to get pretty postcards in your patent shorthand, I always have to read the copies in ordinary writing you so thoughtfully send me.

HIGGINS Well, this isnt a phonetic job.

MRS HIGGINS You said it was.

HIGGINS Not your part of it. Ive picked up a girl.

MRS HIGGINS Does that mean that some girl has picked you up?

HIGGINS Not at all. I dont mean a love affair.

MRS HIGGINS What a pity!

HIGGINS Why?

MRS HIGGINS Well, you never fall in love with anyone under

forty-five. When will you discover that there are some rather nice-looking young women about?

HIGGINS Oh, I can't be bothered with young women. My idea of a lovable woman is somebody as like you as possible. I shall never get into the way of seriously liking young women: some habits lie too deep to be changed. [*Rising abruptly and walking about, jingling his money and his keys in his trouser pockets.*] Besides, theyre all idiots.

MRS HIGGINS Do you know what you would do if you really loved me, Henry?

HIGGINS Oh bother! What? Marry, I suppose.

MRS HIGGINS No. Stop fidgeting and take your hands out of your pockets. [*With a gesture of despair, he obeys and sits down again.*] Thats a good boy. Now tell me about the girl.

HIGGINS She's coming to see you.

MRS HIGGINS I dont remember asking her.

HIGGINS You didnt. *I* asked her. If youd known her you wouldnt have asked her.

MRS HIGGINS Indeed! Why?

HIGGINS Well, it's like this. She's a common flower girl. I picked her off the kerbstone.

MRS HIGGINS And invited her to my at-home!

HIGGINS [*Rising and coming to her to coax her.*] Oh, thatll be all right. Ive taught her to speak properly; and she has strict orders as to her behavior. She's to keep to two subjects: the weather and everybody's health—Fine day and How do you do, you know—and not to let herself go on things in general. That will be safe.

MRS HIGGINS Safe! To talk about our health! about our insides! perhaps about our outsides! How could you be so silly, Henry?

HIGGINS [*Impatiently.*] Well, she must talk about something. [*He controls himself and sits down again.*] Oh, she'll be all right: dont you fuss. Pickering is in it with me. Ive a sort of bet on that I'll pass her off as a duchess in six months. I started on her some months ago; and she's getting on like a house on fire. I shall win my bet. She has a quick ear; and she's easier to teach than my middle-class pupils because she's had to learn a complete new language. She talks English almost as you talk French.

MRS HIGGINS Thats satisfactory, at all events.

HIGGINS Well, it is and it isnt.

MRS HIGGINS What does that mean?

HIGGINS You see, Ive got her pronunciation all right; but you have to consider not only how a girl pronounces, but what she pronounces; and that's where . . .

[*They are interrupted by the parlormaid, announcing guests.*]

THE PARLORMAID Mrs and Miss Eynsford Hill. [*She withdraws.*]

HIGGINS Oh Lord! [*He rises; snatches his hat from the table; and makes for the door; but before he reaches it his mother introduces him.*]

[MRS *and* MISS EYNSFORD HILL *are the mother and daughter who sheltered from the rain in Covent Garden. The mother is well bred, quiet, and has the habitual anxiety of straitened means. The daughter has acquired a gay air of being very much at home in society: the bravado of genteel poverty.*]

MRS EYNSFORD HILL [*To* MRS HIGGINS.] How do you do? [*They shake hands.*]

MISS EYNSFORD HILL How d'you do? [*She shakes.*]

MRS HIGGINS [*Introducing.*] My son Henry.

MRS EYNSFORD HILL Your celebrated son! I have so longed to meet you, Professor Higgins.

HIGGINS [*Glumly, making no movement in her direction.*] Delighted. [*He backs against the piano and bows brusquely.*]

MISS EYNSFORD HILL [*Going to him with confident familiarity.*] How do you do?

HIGGINS [*Staring at her.*] Ive seen you before somewhere. I havnt the ghost of a notion where; but Ive heard your voice. [*Drearily.*] It doesnt matter. Youd better sit down.

MRS HIGGINS I'm sorry to say that my celebrated son has no manners. You mustnt mind him.

MISS EYNSFORD HILL [*Gaily.*] I don't. [*She sits in the Elizabethan chair.*]

MRS EYNSFORD HILL [*A little bewildered.*] Not at all. [*She sits on the ottoman between her daughter and* MRS HIGGINS, *who has turned her chair away from the writing table.*]

HIGGINS Oh, have I been rude? I didnt mean to be.

[*He goes to the central window, through which, with his back to the company, he contemplates the river and the flowers in Battersea Park on the opposite bank as if they were a frozen desert.*]

[*The parlormaid returns, ushering in* PICKERING.]

THE PARLORMAID Colonel Pickering. [*She withdraws.*]

PICKERING How do you do, Mrs Higgins?

MRS HIGGINS So glad youve come. Do you know Mrs Eynsford Hill—Miss Eynsford Hill? [*Exchange of bows. The* COLONEL *brings the Chippendale chair a little forward between* MRS HILL *and* MRS HIGGINS, *and sits down.*]

PICKERING Has Henry told you what weve come for?

HIGGINS [*Over his shoulder.*] We were interrupted: damn it!

MRS HIGGINS Oh Henry, Henry, really!

MRS EYNSFORD HILL [*Half rising.*] Are we in the way?

MRS HIGGINS [*Rising and making her sit down again.*] No, no. You couldnt have come more fortunately: we want you to meet a friend of ours.

HIGGINS [*Turning hopefully.*] Yes, by George! We want two or three people. Youll do as well as anybody else.

[*The parlormaid returns, ushering* FREDDY.]

THE PARLORMAID Mr Eynsford Hill.

HIGGINS [*Almost audibly, past endurance.*] God of Heaven! another of them.

FREDDY [*Shaking hands with* MRS HIGGINS.] Ahdedo?

MRS HIGGINS Very good of you to come. [*Introducing.*] Colonel Pickering.

FREDDY [*Bowing.*] Ahdedo?

MRS HIGGINS I dont think you know my son, Professor Higgins.

FREDDY [*Going to* HIGGINS.] Ahdedo?

HIGGINS [*Looking at him much as if he were a pickpocket.*] I'll take my oath Ive met you before somewhere. Where was it?

FREDDY I dont think so.

HIGGINS [*Resignedly.*] It doesnt matter, anyhow. Sit down.

[*He shakes* FREDDY'S *hand, and almost slings him on to the ottoman with his face to the window; then comes round to the other side of it.*]

HIGGINS Well, here we are, anyhow! [*He sits down on the ottoman next* MRS EYNSFORD HILL, *on her left.*] And now, what the devil are we going to talk about until Eliza comes?

MRS HIGGINS Henry: you are the life and soul of the Royal Society's soirées; but really youre rather trying on more commonplace occasions.

HIGGINS Am I? Very sorry. [*Beaming suddenly.*] I suppose I am, you know. [*Uproariously.*] Ha, ha!

MISS EYNSFORD HILL [*Who considers* HIGGINS *quite eligible matrimonially.*] I sympathize. *I* havnt any small talk. If people would only be frank and say what they really think!

HIGGINS [*Relapsing into gloom.*] Lord forbid!

MRS EYNSFORD HILL [*Taking up her daughter's cue.*] But why?

HIGGINS What they think they ought to think is bad enough, Lord knows; but what they really think would break up the whole show. Do you suppose it would be really agreeable if I were to come out now with what *I* really think?

MISS EYNSFORD HILL [*Gaily.*] Is it so very cynical?

HIGGINS Cynical! Who the dickens said it was cynical? I mean it wouldnt be decent.

MRS EYNSFORD HILL [*Seriously.*] Oh! I'm sure you dont mean that, Mr Higgins.

HIGGINS You see, we're all savages, more or less. We're supposed to be civilized and cultured—to know all about poetry and philosophy and art and science, and so on; but how many of us know even the meaning of these names? [*To* MISS HILL.] What do you know of poetry? [*To* MRS HILL.] What do you know of science? [*Indicating* FREDDY.] What does he know of art or science or anything else? What the devil do you imagine I know of philosophy?

MRS HIGGINS [*Warningly.*] Or of manners, Henry?

THE PARLORMAID [*Opening the door.*] Miss Doolittle. [*She withdraws.*]

HIGGINS [*Rising hastily and running to* MRS HIGGINS.] Here she is, mother. [*He stands on tiptoe and makes signs over his mother's head to* ELIZA *to indicate to her which lady is her hostess.*]

[ELIZA, *who is exquisitely dressed, produces an impression of such remarkable distinction and beauty as she enters that they all rise, quite fluttered. Guided by* HIGGINS'*s signals, she comes to* MRS HIGGINS *with studied grace.*]

LIZA [*Speaking with pedantic correctness of pronunciation and great beauty of tone.*] How do you do, Mrs Higgins? [*She gasps slightly in making sure of the H in Higgins, but is quite successful.*] Mr Higgins told me I might come.

MRS HIGGINS [*Cordially.*] Quite right: I'm very glad indeed to see you.

PICKERING How do you do, Miss Doolittle?

LIZA [*Shaking hands with him.*] Colonel Pickering, is it not?

MRS EYNSFORD HILL I feel sure we have met before, Miss Doolittle. I remember your eyes.

LIZA How do you do? [*She sits down on the ottoman gracefully in the place just left vacant by* HIGGINS.]

MRS EYNSFORD HILL [*Introducing.*] My daughter Clara.

LIZA How do you do?

CLARA [*Impulsively.*] How do you do? [*She sits down on the ottoman beside* ELIZA, *devouring her with her eyes.*]

FREDDY [*Coming to their side of the ottoman.*] Ive certainly had the pleasure.

MRS EYNSFORD HILL [*Introducing.*] My son Freddy.

LIZA How do you do?

[FREDDY *bows and sits down in the Elizabethan chair, infatuated.*]

HIGGINS [*Suddenly.*] By George, yes: it all comes back to me! [*They stare at him.*] Covent Garden! [*Lamentably.*] What a damned thing!

MRS HIGGINS Henry, please! [*He is about to sit on the edge of the table.*] Dont sit on my writing table: youll break it.

HIGGINS [*Sulkily.*] Sorry.

[*He goes to the divan, stumbling into the fender and over the fire-irons on his way; extricating himself with muttered imprecations; and finishing his disastrous journey by throwing himself so impatiently on the divan that he almost breaks it.* MRS HIGGINS *looks at him, but controls herself and says nothing.*]

[*A long and painful pause ensues.*]

MRS HIGGINS [*At last, conversationally.*] Will it rain, do you think?

LIZA The shallow depression in the west of these islands is likely to move slowly in an easterly direction. There are no indications of any great change in the barometrical situation.

FREDDY Ha! ha! how awfully funny!

LIZA What is wrong with that, young man? I bet I got it right.

FREDDY Killing!

MRS EYNSFORD HILL I'm sure I hope it wont turn cold. Theres so much influenza about. It runs right through our whole family regularly every spring.

LIZA [*Darkly.*] My aunt died of influenza: so they said.

MRS EYNSFORD HILL [*Clicks her tongue sympathetically.*]!!!

LIZA [*In the same tragic tone.*] But it's my belief they done the old woman in.

MRS HIGGINS [*Puzzled.*] Done her in?

LIZA Y-e-e-e-es, Lord love you! Why should she die of influenza? She come through diphtheria right enough the year before. I saw her with my own eyes. Fairly blue with it, she was. They all thought she was dead; but my father he kept ladling gin down her throat til she came to so sudden that she bit the bowl off the spoon.

MRS EYNSFORD HILL [*Startled.*] Dear me!

LIZA [*Piling up the indictment.*] What call would a woman with that strength in her have to die of influenza? What become of her new straw hat that should have come to me? Somebody pinched it; and what I say is, them as pinched it done her in.

MRS EYNSFORD HILL What does doing her in mean?

HIGGINS [*Hastily.*] Oh, thats the new small talk. To do a person in means to kill them.

MRS EYNSFORD HILL [*To* ELIZA, *horrified.*] You surely dont believe that your aunt was killed!

LIZA Do I not! Them she lived with would have killed her for a hat pin, let alone a hat.

MRS EYNSFORD HILL But it cant have been right for your

father to pour spirits down her throat like that. It might have killed her.

LIZA Not her. Gin was mother's milk to her. Besides, he'd poured so much down his own throat that he knew the good of it.

MRS EYNSFORD HILL Do you mean that he drank?

LIZA Drank! My word! Something chronic.

MRS EYNSFORD HILL How dreadful for you!

LIZA Not a bit. It never did him no harm what I could see. But then he did not keep it up regular. [*Cheerfully.*] On the burst, as you might say, from time to time. And always more agreeable when he had a drop in. When he was out of work, my mother used to give him fourpence and tell him to go out and not come back until he'd drunk himself cheerful and loving-like. Theres lots of women has to make their husbands drunk to make them fit to live with. [*Now quite at her ease.*] You see, it's like this. If a man has a bit of conscience, it always takes him when he's sober; and then it makes him low-spirited. A drop of booze just takes that off and makes him happy. [*To* FREDDY, *who is in convulsions of suppressed laughter.*] Here! what are you sniggering at?

FREDDY The new small talk. You do it so awfully well.

LIZA If I was doing it proper, what was you laughing at? [*To* HIGGINS.] Have I said anything I oughtnt?

MRS HIGGINS [*Interposing.*] Not at all, Miss Doolittle.

LIZA Well, thats a mercy, anyhow. [*Expansively.*] What I always say is . . .

HIGGINS [*Rising and looking at his watch.*] Ahem!

LIZA [*Looking round at him; taking the hint; and rising.*] Well: I must go. [*They all rise.* FREDDY *goes to the door.*] So pleased to have met you. Goodbye. [*She shakes hands with* MRS HIGGINS.]

MRS HIGGINS Goodbye.

LIZA Goodbye, Colonel Pickering.

PICKERING Goodbye, Miss Doolittle. [*They shake hands.*]

LIZA [*Nodding to the others.*] Goodbye, all.

FREDDY [*Opening the door for her.*] Are you walking across the Park, Miss Doolittle? If so . . .

LIZA [*With perfectly elegant diction.*] Walk! Not bloody likely. [*Sensation.*] I am going in a taxi. [*She goes out.*]

[PICKERING *gasps and sits down.* FREDDY *goes out on the balcony to catch another glimpse of* ELIZA.]

MRS EYNSFORD HILL [*Suffering from shock.*] Well, I really cant get used to the new ways.

CLARA [*Throwing herself discontentedly into the Elizabethan chair.*] Oh, it's all right, mamma, quite right. People will think we never go anywhere or see anybody if you are so old-fashioned.

MRS EYNSFORD HILL I daresay I am very old-fashioned; but I do hope you wont begin using that expression, Clara. I have got accustomed to hear you talking about men as rotters, and calling everything filthy and beastly; though I do think it horrible and unladylike. But this last is really too much. Dont you think so, Colonel Pickering?

PICKERING Dont ask me. Ive been away in India for several years; and manners have changed so much that I sometimes dont know whether I'm at a respectable dinnertable or in a ship's forecastle.

CLARA It's all a matter of habit. Theres no right or wrong in it. Nobody means anything by it. And it's so quaint, and gives such a smart emphasis to things that are not in themselves very witty. I find the new small talk delightful and quite innocent.

MRS EYNSFORD HILL [*Rising.*] Well, after that, I think it's time for us to go.

[PICKERING *and* HIGGINS *rise.*]

CLARA [*Rising.*] Oh yes: we have three at-homes to go to still. Goodbye, Mrs Higgins. Goodbye, Colonel Pickering. Goodbye, Professor Higgins.

HIGGINS [*Coming grimly at her from the divan, and accompanying her to the door.*] Goodbye. Be sure you try on that small talk at the three at-homes. Dont be nervous about it. Pitch it in strong.

CLARA [*All smiles.*] I will. Goodbye. Such nonsense, all this early Victorian prudery!

HIGGINS [*Tempting her.*] Such damned nonsense!

CLARA Such bloody nonsense!

MRS EYNSFORD HILL [*Convulsively.*] Clara!

CLARA Ha! ha! [*She goes out radiant, conscious of being thoroughly up to date, and is heard descending the stairs in a stream of silvery laughter.*]

FREDDY [*To the heavens at large.*] Well, I ask you . . . [*He gives it up, and comes to* MRS HIGGINS.] Goodbye.

MRS HIGGINS [*Shaking hands.*] Goodbye. Would you like to meet Miss Doolittle again?

FREDDY [*Eagerly.*] Yes, I should, most awfully.

MRS HIGGINS Well, you know my days.

FREDDY Yes. Thanks awfully. Goodbye. [*He goes out.*]

MRS EYNSFORD HILL Goodbye, Mr Higgins.

HIGGINS Goodbye. Goodbye.

MRS EYNSFORD HILL [*To* PICKERING.] It's no use. I shall never be able to bring myself to use that word.

PICKERING Dont. It's not compulsory, you know. Youll get on quite well without it.

MRS EYNSFORD HILL Only, Clara is so down on me if I am not positively reeking with the latest slang. Goodbye.

PICKERING Goodbye. [*They shake hands.*]

MRS EYNSFORD HILL [*To* MRS HIGGINS.] You mustnt mind Clara. [PICKERING, *catching from her lowered tone that this is not meant for him to hear, discreetly joins* HIGGINS *at the window.*] We're so poor! and she gets so few parties, poor child! She doesnt quite know. [MRS HIGGINS, *seeing that her eyes are moist, takes her hand sympathetically and goes with her to the door.*] But the boy is nice. Dont you think so?

MRS HIGGINS Oh, quite nice. I shall always be delighted to see him.

MRS EYNSFORD HILL Thank you, dear. Goodbye. [*She goes out.*]

HIGGINS [*Eagerly.*] Well? Is Eliza presentable? [*He swoops on his mother and drags her to the ottoman, where she sits down in* ELIZA'S *place with her son on her left.*]

[PICKERING *returns to his chair on her right.*]

MRS HIGGINS You silly boy, of course she's not presentable. She's a triumph of your art and of her dressmaker's; but if you suppose for a moment that she doesnt give herself away in every sentence she utters, you must be perfectly cracked about her.

PICKERING But dont you think something might be done? I mean something to eliminate the sanguinary element from her conversation.

MRS HIGGINS Not as long as she is in Henry's hands.

HIGGINS [*Aggrieved.*] Do you mean that my language is improper?

MRS HIGGINS No, dearest: it would be quite proper—say on a canal barge; but it would not be proper for her at a garden party.

HIGGINS [*Deeply injured.*] Well I must say . . .

PICKERING [*Interrupting him.*] Come, Higgins: you must learn to know yourself. I havnt heard such language as yours since we used to review the volunteers in Hyde Park twenty years ago.

HIGGINS [*Sulkily.*] Oh, well, if you say so, I suppose I dont always talk like a bishop.

MRS HIGGINS [*Quieting* HENRY *with a touch.*] Colonel Pickering: will you tell me what is the exact state of things in Wimpole Street?

PICKERING [*Cheerfully: as if this completely changed the subject.*] Well, I have come to live there with Henry. We work together at my Indian Dialects; and we think it more convenient . . .

MRS HIGGINS Quite so. I know all about that: it's an excellent arrangement. But where does this girl live?

HIGGINS With us, of course. Where should she live?

MRS HIGGINS But on what terms? Is she a servant? If not, what is she?

PICKERING [*Slowly.*] I think I know what you mean, Mrs Higgins.

HIGGINS Well, dash me if *I* do! Ive had to work at the girl every day for months to get her to her present pitch. Besides, she's useful. She knows where my things are, and remembers my appointments and so forth.

MRS HIGGINS How does your housekeeper get on with her?

HIGGINS Mrs Pearce? Oh, she's jolly glad to get so much taken off her hands; for before Eliza came, she used to have to find things and remind me of my appointments. But she's got some silly bee in her bonnet about Eliza. She keeps saying "You dont think, sir": doesnt she, Pick?

PICKERING Yes: thats the formula. "You dont think, sir." Thats the end of every conversation about Eliza.

HIGGINS As if I ever stop thinking about the girl and her confounded vowels and consonants. I'm worn out, thinking about her, and watching her lips and her teeth and her tongue, not to mention her soul, which is the quaintest of the lot.

MRS HIGGINS You certainly are a pretty pair of babies, playing with your live doll.

HIGGINS Playing! The hardest job I ever tackled: make no mistake about that, mother. But you have no idea how frightfully interesting it is to take a human being and change her into a quite different human being by creating a new speech for her. It's filling up the deepest gulf that separates class from class and soul from soul.

PICKERING [*Drawing his chair closer to* MRS HIGGINS *and bending over to her eagerly.*] Yes: it's enormously interesting. I assure you, Mrs Higgins, we take Eliza very seriously. Every week—every day almost—there is some new change. [*Closer again.*] We keep records of every stage—dozens of gramophone disks and photographs . . .

HIGGINS [*Assailing her at the other ear.*] Yes, by George: it's the most absorbing experiment I ever tackled. She regularly fills our lives up: doesnt she, Pick?

PICKERING We're always talking Eliza.

HIGGINS Teaching Eliza.

PICKERING Dressing Eliza.

MRS HIGGINS What!

HIGGINS Inventing new Elizas.

HIGGINS	[*Speaking together.*]	You know, she has the most extraordinary quickness of ear:
PICKERING		I assure you, my dear Mrs Higgins, that girl

HIGGINS } [*Speaking together.*] just like a parrot. Ive tried her with every
PICKERING } is a genius. She can play the piano quite beautifully.

HIGGINS possible sort of sound that a human being can make—
PICKERING We have taken her to classical concerts and to music

HIGGINS Continental dialects, African dialects, Hottentot
PICKERING halls; and it's all the same to her: she plays everything

HIGGINS clicks, things it took me years to get hold of; and
PICKERING she hears right off when she comes home, whether it's

HIGGINS she picks them up like a shot, right away, as if she had
PICKERING Beethoven and Brahms or Lehar and Lionel Monckton;

HIGGINS been at it all her life.
PICKERING though six months ago, she'd never as much as touched a piano . . .

MRS HIGGINS [*Putting her fingers in her ears, as they are by this time shouting one another down with an intolerable noise.*] Sh-sh-sh—sh! [*They stop.*]

PICKERING I beg your pardon. [*He draws his chair back apologetically.*]

HIGGINS Sorry. When Pickering starts shouting nobody can get a word in edgeways.

MRS HIGGINS Be quiet, Henry. Colonel Pickering: dont you realize that when Eliza walked in Wimpole Street, something walked in with her?

PICKERING Her father did. But Henry soon got rid of him.

MRS HIGGINS It would have been more to the point if her mother had. But as her mother didnt something else did.

PICKERING But what?

MRS HIGGINS [*Unconsciously dating herself by the word.*] A problem.

PICKERING Oh, I see. The problem of how to pass her off as a lady.

HIGGINS I'll solve that problem. Ive half solved it already.

MRS HIGGINS No, you two infinitely stupid male creatures: the problem of what is to be done with her afterwards.

HIGGINS I dont see anything in that. She can go her own way, with all the advantages I have given her.

MRS HIGGINS The advantages of that poor woman who was here just now! The manners and habits that disqualify a fine lady from earning her own living without giving her a fine lady's income! Is that what you mean?

PICKERING [*Indulgently, being rather bored.*] Oh, that will be all right, Mrs Higgins. [*He rises to go.*]

HIGGINS [*Rising also.*] We'll find her some light employment.

PICKERING She's happy enough. Dont you worry about her. Goodbye. [*He shakes hands as if he were consoling a frightened child, and makes for the door.*]

HIGGINS Anyhow, theres no good bothering now. The thing's done. Goodbye, mother. [*He kisses her, and follows* PICKERING.]

PICKERING [*Turning for a final consolation.*] There are plenty of openings. We'll do whats right. Goodbye.

HIGGINS [*To* PICKERING *as they go out together.*] Lets take her to the Shakespear exhibition at Earls Court.

PICKERING Yes: lets. Her remarks will be delicious.

HIGGINS She'll mimic all the people for us when we get home.

PICKERING Ripping. [*Both are heard laughing as they go downstairs.*]

MRS HIGGINS [*Rises with an impatient bounce, and returns to her work at the writing table. She sweeps a litter of disarranged papers out of the way; snatches a sheet of paper from her station-*

ery case; and tries resolutely to write. At the third time she gives it up; flings down her pen; grips the table angrily and exclaims.] Oh, men! men!! men!!!

* * * * * *

Clearly Eliza will not pass as a duchess yet; and Higgins's bet remains unwon. But the six months are not yet exhausted; and just in time Eliza does actually pass as a princess. For a glimpse of how she did it imagine an Embassy in London one summer evening after dark. The hall door has an awning and a carpet across the sidewalk to the kerb, because a grand reception is in progress. A small crowd is lined up to see the guests arrive.

A Rolls-Royce car drives up. Pickering in evening dress, with medals and orders, alights, and hands out Eliza, in opera cloak, evening dress, diamonds, fan, flowers and all accessories. Higgins follows. The car drives off; and the three go up the steps and into the house, the door opening for them as they approach.

Inside the house they find themselves in a spacious hall from which the grand staircase rises. On the left are the arrangements for the gentlemen's cloaks. The male guests are depositing their hats and wraps there.

On the right is a door leading to the ladies' cloakroom. Ladies are going in cloaked and coming out in splendor. Pickering whispers to Eliza and points out the ladies' room. She goes into it. Higgins and Pickering take off their overcoats and take tickets for them from the attendant.

One of the guests, occupied in the same way, has his back turned. Having taken his ticket, he turns round and reveals himself as an important looking young man with an astonishingly hairy face. He has an enormous mustache, flowing out into luxuriant whiskers. Waves of hair cluster on his brow. His hair is cropped closely at the back, and glows with oil. Otherwise he is very smart. He wears several worthless orders. He is evidently a foreigner, guessable as a whiskered Pandour from Hungary; but in spite of the ferocity of his mustache he is amiable and genially voluble.

Recognizing Higgins, he flings his arms wide apart and approaches him enthusiastically.

WHISKERS Maestro, maestro! [*He embraces* HIGGINS *and kisses him on both cheeks.*] You remember me?

HIGGINS No I dont. Who the devil are you?

WHISKERS I am your pupil: your first pupil, your best and greatest pupil. I am little Nepommuck, the marvelous boy. I have made your name famous throughout Europe. You teach me phonetic. You cannot forget ME.

HIGGINS Why dont you shave?

NEPOMMUCK I have not your imposing appearance, your chin, your brow. Nobody notice me when I shave. Now I am famous: they call me Hairy Faced Dick.

HIGGINS And what are you doing here among all these swells?

NEPOMMUCK I am interpreter. I speak 32 languages. I am indispensable at these international parties. You are great cockney specialist: you place a man anywhere in London the moment he open his mouth. I place any man in Europe.

[*A footman hurries down the grand staircase and comes to* NEPOMMUCK.]

FOOTMAN You are wanted upstairs. Her Excellency cannot understand the Greek gentleman.

NEPOMMUCK Thank you, yes, immediately.

[*The footman goes and is lost in the crowd.*]

NEPOMMUCK [*To* HIGGINS.] This Greek diplomatist pretends he cannot speak nor understand English. He cannot deceive me. He is the son of a Clerkenwell watchmaker. He speaks English so villainously that he dare not utter a word of it without betraying his origin. I help him to pretend; but I make him pay through the nose. I make them all pay. Ha ha! [*He hurries upstairs.*]

PICKERING Is this fellow really an expert? Can he find out Eliza and blackmail her?

HIGGINS We shall see. If he finds her out I lose my bet.

[ELIZA *comes from the cloakroom and joins them.*]

PICKERING Well, Eliza, now for it. Are you ready?

LIZA Are you nervous, Colonel?

PICKERING Frightfully. I feel exactly as I felt before my first battle. It's the first time that frightens.

LIZA It is not the first time for me, Colonel. I have done this fifty times—hundreds of times—in my little piggery in Angel Court in my daydreams. I am in a dream now. Promise me not to let Professor Higgins wake me; for if he does I shall forget everything and talk as I used to in Drury Lane.

PICKERING Not a word, Higgins. [*To* ELIZA.] Now, ready?

LIZA Ready.

PICKERING Go.

[*They mount the stairs,* HIGGINS *last.* PICKERING *whispers to the footman on the first landing.*]

FIRST LANDING FOOTMAN Miss Doolittle, Colonel Pickering, Professor Higgins.

SECOND LANDING FOOTMAN Miss Doolittle, Colonel Pickering, Professor Higgins.

[*At the top of the staircase the Ambassador and his wife, with* NEPOMMUCK *at her elbow, are receiving.*]

HOSTESS [*Taking* ELIZA'*s hand.*] How d'ye do?

HOST [*Same play.*] How d'ye do? How d'ye do, Pickering?

LIZA [*With a beautiful gravity that awes her hostess.*] How do you do? [*She passes on to the drawing room.*]

HOSTESS Is that your adopted daughter, Colonel Pickering? She will make a sensation.

PICKERING Most kind of you to invite her for me. [*He passes on.*]

HOSTESS [*To* NEPOMMUCK.] Find out all about her.

NEPOMMUCK [*Bowing.*] Excellency . . . [*He goes into the crowd.*]

HOST How d'ye do, Higgins? You have a rival here tonight. He introduced himself as your pupil. Is he any good?

HIGGINS He can learn a language in a fortnight—knows dozens of them. A sure mark of a fool. As a phonetician, no good whatever.

HOSTESS How d'ye do, Professor?

HIGGINS How do you do? Fearful bore for you this sort of thing. Forgive my part in it. [*He passes on.*]

In the drawing room and its suite of salons the reception is in full swing. Eliza passes through. She is so intent on her ordeal that she walks like a somnambulist in a desert instead of a débutante in a fashionable crowd. They stop talking to look at her, admiring her dress, her jewels, and her strangely attractive self. Some of the younger ones at the back stand on their chairs to see.

The Host and Hostess come in from the staircase and mingle with their guests. Higgins, gloomy and contemptuous of the whole business, comes into the group where they are chatting.

HOSTESS Ah, here is Professor Higgins: he will tell us. Tell us all about the wonderful young lady, Professor.

HIGGINS [*Almost morosely.*] What wonderful young lady?

HOSTESS You know very well. They tell me there has been nothing like her in London since people stood on their chairs to look at Mrs Langtry.

[NEPOMMUCK *joins the group, full of news.*]

HOSTESS Ah, here you are at last, Nepommuck. Have you found out all about the Doolittle lady?

NEPOMMUCK I have found out all about her. She is a fraud.

HOSTESS A fraud! Oh no.

NEPOMMUCK YES, yes. She cannot deceive me. Her name cannot be Doolittle.

HIGGINS Why?

NEPOMMUCK Because Doolittle is an English name. And she is not English.

HOSTESS Oh, nonsense! She speaks English perfectly.

NEPOMMUCK Too perfectly. Can you show me any English woman who speaks English as it should be spoken? Only foreigners who have been taught to speak it speak it well.

HOSTESS Certainly she terrified me by the way she said How d'ye do. I had a schoolmistress who talked like that; and I was mortally afraid of her. But if she is not English what is she?

NEPOMMUCK Hungarian.

ALL THE REST Hungarian!

NEPOMMUCK Hungarian. And of royal blood. I am Hungarian. My blood is royal.

HIGGINS Did you speak to her in Hungarian?

NEPOMMUCK I did. She was very clever. She said "Please speak to me in English: I do not understand French." French! She pretend not to know the difference between Hungarian and French. Impossible: she knows both.

HIGGINS And the blood royal? How did you find that out?

NEPOMMUCK Instinct, maestro, instinct. Only the Magyar races can produce that air of the divine right, those resolute eyes. She is a princess.

HOST What do you say, Professor?

HIGGINS I say an ordinary London girl out of the gutter and taught to speak by an expert. I place her in Drury Lane.

NEPOMMUCK Ha ha ha! Oh, maestro, maestro, you are mad on the subject of cockney dialects. The London gutter is the whole world for you.

HIGGINS [*To the* HOSTESS.] What does your Excellency say?

HOSTESS Oh, of course I agree with Nepommuck. She must be a princess at least.

HOST Not necessarily legitimate, of course. Morganatic perhaps. But that is undoubtedly her class.

HIGGINS I stick to my opinion.

HOSTESS Oh, you are incorrigible.

[*The group breaks up, leaving* HIGGINS *isolated.* PICKERING *joins him.*]

PICKERING Where is Eliza? We must keep an eye on her.

[ELIZA *joins them.*]

LIZA I dont think I can bear much more. The people all stare so at me. An old lady has just told me that I speak exactly like Queen Victoria. I am sorry if I have lost your bet. I have done my best; but nothing can make me the same as these people.

PICKERING You have not lost it, my dear. You have won it ten times over.

HIGGINS Let us get out of this. I have had enough of chattering to these fools.

PICKERING Eliza is tired; and I am hungry. Let us clear out and have supper somewhere.

ACT IV

SCENE: *The Wimpole Street laboratory. Midnight. Nobody in the room. The clock on the mantelpiece strikes twelve. The fire is not alight: it is a summer night.*

Presently HIGGINS *and* PICKERING *are heard on the stairs.*

HIGGINS [*Calling down to* PICKERING.] I say, Pick: lock up, will you? I shant be going out again.

PICKERING Right. Can Mrs Pearce go to bed? We dont want anything more, do we?

HIGGINS Lord, no!

[ELIZA *opens the door and is seen on the lighted landing in all the finery in which she has just won* HIGGINS'S *bet for him. She comes to the hearth, and switches on the electric lights there. She is tired: her pallor contrasts strongly with her dark eyes and hair; and her expression is almost tragic. She takes off her cloak; puts her fan and gloves on the piano; and sits down on the bench, brooding and silent.* HIGGINS, *in evening dress, with overcoat and hat, comes in, carrying a smoking jacket which he has picked up downstairs. He takes off the hat and overcoat; throws them carelessly on the newspaper stand; disposes of his coat in the same way; puts on the smoking jacket; and throws himself wearily into the easy-chair at the hearth.* PICKERING, *similarly attired, comes in. He also takes off his hat and overcoat, and is about to throw them on* HIGGINS'S *when he hesitates.*]

PICKERING I say: Mrs Pearce will row if we leave these things lying about in the drawing room.

HIGGINS Oh, chuck them over the bannisters into the hall. She'll find them there in the morning and put them away all right. She'll think we were drunk.

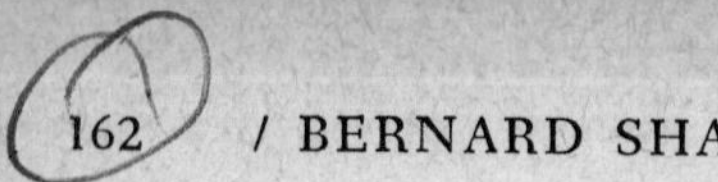

PICKERING We are, slightly. Are there any letters?

HIGGINS I didnt look. [PICKERING *takes the overcoats and hats and goes downstairs.* HIGGINS *begins half singing half yawning an air from La Fanciulla del Golden West. Suddenly he stops and exclaims.*] I wonder where the devil my slippers are!

[ELIZA *looks at him darkly; then rises suddenly and leaves the room.* HIGGINS *yawns again, and resumes his song.* PICKERING *returns, with the contents of the letter box in his hand.*]

PICKERING Only circulars, and this coroneted billet-doux for you. [*He throws the circulars into the fender, and posts himself on the hearthrug, with his back to the grate.*]

HIGGINS [*Glancing at the billet-doux.*] Moneylender. [*He throws the letter after the circulars.*]

[ELIZA *returns with a pair of large down-at-heel slippers. She places them on the carpet before* HIGGINS, *and sits as before without a word.*]

HIGGINS [*Yawning again.*] Oh Lord! What an evening! What a crew! What a silly tomfoolery! [*He raises his shoe to unlace it, and catches sight of the slippers. He stops unlacing and looks at them as if they had appeared there of their own accord.*] Oh! theyre there, are they?

PICKERING [*Stretching himself.*] Well, I feel a bit tired. It's been a long day. The garden party, a dinner party, and the reception! Rather too much of a good thing. But youve won your bet, Higgins. Eliza did the trick, and something to spare, eh?

HIGGINS [*Fervently.*] Thank God it's over!

[ELIZA *flinches violently; but they take no notice of her; and she recovers herself and sits stonily as before.*]

PICKERING Were you nervous at the garden party? *I* was. Eliza didnt seem a bit nervous.

HIGGINS Oh, she wasnt nervous. I knew she'd be all right. No: it's the strain of putting the job through all these months that has told on me. It was interesting enough at first, while we were at the phonetics; but after that I got deadly sick of it. If I hadnt backed myself to do it I should have chucked the whole thing up two months ago. It was a silly notion: the whole thing has been a bore.

PICKERING Oh come! the garden party was frightfully exciting. My heart began beating like anything.

HIGGINS Yes, for the first three minutes. But when I saw we were going to win hands down, I felt like a bear in a cage, hanging about doing nothing. The dinner was worse: sitting gorging there for over an hour, with nobody but a damned fool of a fashionable woman to talk to! I tell you, Pickering, never again for me. No more artificial duchesses. The whole thing has been simple purgatory.

PICKERING Youve never been broken in properly to the social routine. [*Strolling over to the piano.*] I rather enjoy dipping into it occasionally myself: it makes me feel young again. Anyhow, it was a great success: an immense success. I was quite frightened once or twice because Eliza was doing it so well. You see, lots of the real people cant do it at all: theyre such fools that they think style comes by nature to people in their position; and so they never learn. Theres always something professional about doing a thing superlatively well.

HIGGINS Yes: thats what drives me mad: the silly people dont know their own silly business. [*Rising.*] However, it's over and done with; and now I can go to bed at last without dreading tomorrow.

[ELIZA's *beauty becomes murderous.*]

PICKERING I think I shall turn in too. Still, it's been a great occasion: a triumph for you. Goodnight. [*He goes.*]

HIGGINS [*Following him.*] Goodnight. [*Over his shoulder, at the door.*] Put out the lights, Eliza; and tell Mrs Pearce not to make coffee for me in the morning: I'll take tea. [*He goes out.*]

[ELIZA *tries to control herself and feel indifferent as she rises and walks across to the hearth to switch off the lights. By the time she gets there she is on the point of screaming. She sits down in* HIGGINS's *chair and holds on hard to the arms. Finally she gives way and flings herself furiously on the floor, raging.*]

HIGGINS [*In despairing wrath outside.*] What the devil have I done with my slippers? [*He appears at the door.*]

LIZA [*Snatching up the slippers, and hurling them at him one after the other with all her force.*] There are your slippers. And there. Take your slippers; and may you never have a day's luck with them!

HIGGINS [*Astounded.*] What on earth . . . ! [*He comes to her.*] Whats the matter? Get up. [*He pulls her up.*] Anything wrong?

LIZA [*Breathless.*] Nothing wrong—with you. Ive won your bet for you, havnt I? Thats enough for you. *I* dont matter, I suppose.

HIGGINS You won my bet! You! Presumptuous insect! *I* won it. What did you throw those slippers at me for?

LIZA Because I wanted to smash your face. I'd like to kill you, you selfish brute. Why didnt you leave me where you picked me out of—in the gutter? You thank God it's all over, and that now you can throw me back again there, do you? [*She crisps her fingers frantically.*]

HIGGINS [*Looking at her in cool wonder.*] The creature is nervous, after all.

LIZA [*Gives a suffocated scream of fury, and instinctively darts her nails at his face.*]!!

HIGGINS [*Catching her wrists.*] Ah! would you? Claws in, you cat. How dare you show your temper to me? Sit down and be quiet. [*He throws her roughly into the easy-chair.*]

LIZA [*Crushed by superior strength and weight.*] Whats to become of me? Whats to become of me?

HIGGINS How the devil do I know whats to become of you? What does it matter what becomes of you?

LIZA You dont care. I know you dont care. You wouldnt care if I was dead. I'm nothing to you—not so much as them slippers.

HIGGINS [*Thundering.*] Those slippers.

LIZA [*With bitter submission.*] Those slippers. I didnt think it made any difference now.

[*A pause.* ELIZA *hopeless and crushed.* HIGGINS *a little uneasy.*]

HIGGINS [*In his loftiest manner.*] Why have you begun going on like this? May I ask whether you complain of your treatment here?

LIZA No.

HIGGINS Has anybody behaved badly to you? Colonel Pickering? Mrs Pearce? Any of the servants?

LIZA No.

HIGGINS I presume you dont pretend that *I* have treated you badly?

LIZA No.

HIGGINS I am glad to hear it. [*He moderates his tone.*] Perhaps youre tired after the strain of the day. Will you have a glass of champagne? [*He moves towards the door.*]

LIZA No. [*Recollecting her manners.*] Thank you.

HIGGINS [*Good-humored again.*] This has been coming on you for some days. I suppose it was natural for you to be anxious about the garden party. But thats all over now. [*He pats her kindly on the shoulder. She writhes.*] Theres nothing more to worry about.

LIZA No. Nothing more for you to worry about. [*She suddenly rises and gets away from him by going to the piano bench, where she sits and hides her face.*] Oh God! I wish I was dead.

HIGGINS [*Staring after her in sincere surprise.*] Why? In heaven's name, why? [*Reasonably, going to her.*] Listen to me, Eliza. All this irritation is purely subjective.

LIZA I dont understand. I'm too ignorant.

HIGGINS It's only imagination. Low spirits and nothing else. Nobody's hurting you. Nothing's wrong. You go to bed like a good girl and sleep it off. Have a little cry and say your prayers: that will make you comfortable.

LIZA I heard your prayers. "Thank God it's all over!"

HIGGINS [*Impatiently.*] Well, dont you thank God it's all over? Now you are free and can do what you like.

LIZA [*Pulling herself together in desperation.*] What am I fit for? What have you left me fit for? Where am I to go? What am I to do? Whats to become of me?

HIGGINS [*Enlightened, but not at all impressed.*] Oh, thats whats worrying you, is it? [*He thrusts his hands into his pockets, and walks about in his usual manner, rattling the contents of his pockets, as if condescending to a trivial subject out of pure kind-*

ness.] I shouldnt bother about it if I were you. I should imagine you wont have much difficulty in settling yourself somewhere or other, though I hadnt quite realized that you were going away. [*She looks quickly at him: he does not look at her, but examines the dessert stand on the piano and decides that he will eat an apple.*] You might marry, you know. [*He bites a large piece out of the apple and munches it noisily.*] You see, Eliza, all men are not confirmed old bachelors like me and the Colonel. Most men are the marrying sort (poor devils!); and youre not bad-looking: it's quite a pleasure to look at you sometimes—not now, of course, because youre crying and looking as ugly as the very devil; but when youre all right and quite yourself, youre what I should call attractive. That is, to the people in the marrying line, you understand. You go to bed and have a good nice rest; and then get up and look at yourself in the glass; and you wont feel so cheap.

[ELIZA *again looks at him, speechless, and does not stir. The look is quite lost on him: he eats his apple with a dreamy expression of happiness, as it is quite a good one.*]

HIGGINS [*A genial afterthought occurring to him.*] I daresay my mother could find some chap or other who would do very well.

LIZA We were above that at the corner of Tottenham Court Road.

HIGGINS [*Waking up.*] What do you mean?

LIZA I sold flowers. I didnt sell myself. Now youve made a lady of me I'm not fit to sell anything else. I wish youd left me where you found me.

HIGGINS [*Slinging the core of the apple decisively into the grate.*] Tosh, Eliza. Dont you insult human relations by dragging all this cant about buying and selling into it. You neednt marry the fellow if you dont like him.

LIZA What else am I to do?

HIGGINS Oh, lots of things. What about your old idea of a florist's shop? Pickering could set you up in one: he has lots of money. [*Chuckling.*] He'll have to pay for all those togs you have been wearing today; and that, with the hire of the jewelry, will make a big hole in two hundred pounds. Why, six months ago you would have thought it the millennium to have a flower shop of your own. Come! youll be all right. I must clear off to bed: I'm devilish sleepy. By the way, I came down for something: I forget what it was.

LIZA Your slippers.

HIGGINS Oh yes, of course. You shied them at me. [*He picks them up, and is going out when she rises and speaks to him.*]

LIZA Before you go, sir . . .

HIGGINS [*Dropping the slippers in his surprise at her calling him Sir.*] Eh?

LIZA Do my clothes belong to me or to Colonel Pickering?

HIGGINS [*Coming back into the room as if her question were the very climax of unreason.*] What the devil use would they be to Pickering?

LIZA He might want them for the next girl you pick up to experiment on.

HIGGINS [*Shocked and hurt.*] Is that the way you feel towards us?

LIZA I dont want to hear anything more about that. All I want to know is whether anything belongs to me. My own clothes were burnt.

HIGGINS But what does it matter? Why need you start bothering about that in the middle of the night?

LIZA I want to know what I may take away with me. I dont want to be accused of stealing.

HIGGINS [*Now deeply wounded.*] Stealing! You shouldnt have said that, Eliza. That shows a want of feeling.

LIZA I'm sorry. I'm only a common ignorant girl; and in my station I have to be careful. There cant be any feelings between the like of you and the like of me. Please will you tell me what belongs to me and what doesnt?

HIGGINS [*Very sulky.*] You may take the whole damned houseful if you like. Except the jewels. Theyre hired. Will that satisfy you? [*He turns on his heel and is about to go in extreme dudgeon.*]

LIZA [*Drinking in his emotion like nectar, and nagging him to provoke a further supply.*] Stop, please. [*She takes off her *jewels.*] Will you take these to your room and keep them safe? I dont want to run the risk of their being missing.

HIGGINS [*Furious.*] Hand them over. [*She puts them into his hands.*] If these belonged to me instead of to the jeweler, I'd ram them down your ungrateful throat. [*He perfunctorily thrusts them into his pockets, unconsciously decorating himself with the protruding ends of the chains.*]

LIZA [*Taking a ring off.*] This ring isnt the jeweler's: it's the one you bought me in Brighton. I dont want it now. [HIGGINS *dashes the ring violently into the fireplace, and turns on her so threateningly that she crouches over the piano with her hands over her face, and exclaims.*] Dont you hit me.

HIGGINS Hit you! You infamous creature, how dare you accuse me of such a thing? It is you who have hit me. You have wounded me to the heart.

LIZA [*Thrilling with hidden joy.*] I'm glad. Ive got a little of my own back, anyhow.

HIGGINS [*With dignity, in his finest professional style.*] You have caused me to lose my temper: a thing that has hardly ever happened to me before. I prefer to say nothing more tonight. I am going to bed.

LIZA [*Pertly.*] Youd better leave a note for Mrs Pearce about the coffee; for she wont be told by me.

HIGGINS [*Formally.*] Damn Mrs Pearce; and damn the coffee; and damn you; and [*wildly*] damn my own folly in having lavished my hard-earned knowledge and the treasure of my regard and intimacy on a heartless guttersnipe. [*He goes out with impressive decorum, and spoils it by slamming the door savagely.*]

[ELIZA *goes down on her knees on the hearthrug to look for the ring. When she finds it she considers for a moment what to do with it. Finally she flings it down on the dessert stand and goes upstairs in a tearing rage.*]

* * * * * *

The furniture of Eliza's room has been increased by a big wardrobe and a sumptuous dressing table. She comes in and switches on the electric light. She goes to the wardrobe; opens it; and pulls out a walking dress, a hat, and a pair of shoes, which she throws on the bed. She takes off her evening dress and shoes; then takes a padded hanger from the wardrobe; adjusts it carefully in the evening dress; and hangs it in the wardrobe, which she shuts with a slam. She puts on her walking shoes, her walking dress, and hat. She takes her wrist watch from the dressing table and fastens it on. She pulls on her gloves; takes her vanity bag; and looks into it to see that her purse is there before hanging it on her wrist. She makes for the door. Every movement expresses her furious resolution.

She takes a last look at herself in the glass.

She suddenly puts out her tongue at herself; then leaves the room, switching off the electric light at the door.

Meanwhile, in the street outside, Freddy Eynsford Hill, lovelorn, is gazing up at the second floor, in which one of the windows is still lighted.

The light goes out.

FREDDY Goodnight, darling, darling, darling.

[ELIZA *comes out, giving the door a considerable bang behind her.*]

LIZA Whatever are you doing here?

FREDDY Nothing. I spend most of my nights here. It's the only place where I'm happy. Dont laugh at me, Miss Doolittle.

LIZA Dont you call me Miss Doolittle, do you hear? Liza's good enough for me. [*She breaks down and grabs him by the shoulders.*] Freddy: you dont think I'm a heartless guttersnipe, do you?

FREDDY Oh no, no, darling: how can you imagine such a thing? You are the loveliest, dearest . . .

[*He loses all self control and smothers her with kisses. She, hungry for comfort, responds. They stand there in one another's arms. An elderly police constable arrives.*]

CONSTABLE [*Scandalized.*] Now then! Now then!! Now then!!!

[*They release one another hastily.*]

FREDDY Sorry, constable. Weve only just become engaged. [*They run away.*]

The constable shakes his head, reflecting on his own courtship and on the vanity of human hopes. He moves off in the opposite direction with slow professional steps.

The flight of the lovers takes them to Cavendish Square. There they halt to consider their next move.

LIZA [*Out of breath.*] He didnt half give me a fright, that copper. But you answered him proper.

FREDDY I hope I havent taken you out of your way. Where were you going?

LIZA To the river.

FREDDY What for?

LIZA To make a hole in it.

FREDDY [*Horrified.*] Eliza, darling. What do you mean? Whats the matter?

LIZA Never mind. It doesnt matter now. Theres nobody in the world now but you and me, is there?

FREDDY Not a soul.

[*They indulge in another embrace, and are again surprised by a much younger constable.*]

SECOND CONSTABLE Now then, you two! Whats this? Where do you think you are? Move along here, double quick. .

FREDDY As you say, sir, double quick.

They run away again, and are in Hanover Square before they stop for another conference.

FREDDY I had no idea the police were so devilishly prudish.

LIZA It's their business to hunt girls off the streets.

FREDDY We must go somewhere. We cant wander about the streets all night.

LIZA Cant we? I think it'd be lovely to wander about for ever.

FREDDY Oh, darling.

[*They embrace again, oblivious of the arrival of a crawling taxi. It stops.*]

TAXIMAN Can I drive you and the lady anywhere, sir?

[*They start asunder.*]

LIZA Oh, Freddy, a taxi. The very thing.

FREDDY But, damn it, Ive no money.

LIZA I have plenty. The Colonel thinks you should never go out without ten pounds in your pocket. Listen. We'll drive about all night; and in the morning I'll call on old Mrs Higgins and ask her what I ought to do. I'll tell you all about it in the cab. And the police wont touch us there.

FREDDY Righto! Ripping. [*To the* TAXIMAN.] Wimbledon Common. [*They drive off.*]

ACT V

SCENE: MRS HIGGINS'S *drawing room. She is at her writing table as before. The parlormaid comes in.*

THE PARLORMAID [*At the door.*] Mr Henry, maam, is downstairs with Colonel Pickering.

MRS HIGGINS Well, show them up.

THE PARLORMAID Theyre using the telephone, maam. Telephoning to the police, I think.

MRS HIGGINS What!

THE PARLORMAID [*Coming further in and lowering her voice.*] Mr Henry is in a state, maam. I thought I'd better tell you.

MRS HIGGINS If you had told me that Mr Henry was not in a state it would have been more surprising. Tell them to come up when theyve finished with the police. I suppose he's lost something.

THE PARLORMAID Yes, maam. [*Going.*]

MRS HIGGINS Go upstairs and tell Miss Doolittle that Mr Henry and the Colonel are here. Ask her not to come down til I send for her.

THE PARLORMAID Yes, maam.

[HIGGINS *bursts in. He is, as the parlormaid has said, in a state.*]

HIGGINS Look here, mother: heres a confounded thing!

MRS HIGGINS Yes, dear. Good morning. [*He checks his impatience and kisses her, whilst the parlormaid goes out.*] What is it?

HIGGINS Eliza's bolted.

MRS HIGGINS [*Calmly continuing her writing.*] You must have frightened her.

HIGGINS Frightened her! nonsense! She was left last night, as usual, to turn out the lights and all that; and instead of going to bed she changed her clothes and went right off: her bed wasnt slept in. She came in a cab for her things before seven this morning; and that fool Mrs Pearce let her have them without telling me a word about it. What am I to do?

MRS HIGGINS Do without, I'm afraid, Henry. The girl has a perfect right to leave if she chooses.

HIGGINS [*Wandering distractedly across the room.*] But I cant find anything. I dont know what appointments Ive got. I'm . . . [PICKERING *comes in.* MRS HIGGINS *puts down her pen and turns away from the writing table.*]

PICKERING [*Shaking hands.*] Good morning, Mrs Higgins. Has Henry told you? [*He sits down on the ottoman.*]

HIGGINS What does that ass of an inspector say? Have you offered a reward?

MRS HIGGINS [*Rising in indignant amazement.*] You dont mean to say you have set the police after Eliza?

HIGGINS Of course. What are the police for? What else could we do? [*He sits in the Elizabethan chair.*]

PICKERING The inspector made a lot of difficulties. I really think he suspected us of some improper purpose.

MRS HIGGINS Well, of course he did. What right have you to go to the police and give the girl's name as if she were a thief, or a lost umbrella, or something? Really! [*She sits down again, deeply vexed.*]

HIGGINS But we want to find her.

PICKERING We cant let her go like this, you know, Mrs Higgins. What were we to do?

MRS HIGGINS You have no more sense, either of you, than two children. Why . . .

[*The parlormaid comes in and breaks off the conversation.*]

THE PARLORMAID Mr. Henry: a gentleman wants to see you very particular. He's been sent on from Wimpole Street.

HIGGINS Oh, bother! I cant see anyone now. Who is it?

THE PARLORMAID A Mr Doolittle, sir.

PICKERING Doolittle! Do you mean the dustman?

THE PARLORMAID Dustman! Oh no, sir: a gentleman.

HIGGINS [*Springing up excitedly.*] By George, Pick, it's some relative of hers that she's gone to. Somebody we know nothing about. [*To the parlormaid.*] Send him up, quick.

THE PARLORMAID Yes, sir. [*She goes.*]

HIGGINS [*Eagerly, going to his mother.*] Genteel relatives! now we shall hear something. [*He sits down in the Chippendale chair.*]

MRS HIGGINS Do you know any of her people?

PICKERING Only her father: the fellow we told you about.

THE PARLORMAID [*Announcing.*] Mr Doolittle. [*She withdraws.*]

[DOOLITTLE *enters. He is resplendently dressed as for a fashionable wedding, and might, in fact, be the bridegroom. A flower in his buttonhole, a dazzling silk hat, and patent leather shoes complete the effect. He is too concerned with the business he has come on to notice* MRS HIGGINS. *He walks straight to* HIGGINS, *and accosts him with vehement reproach.*]

DOOLITTLE [*Indicating his own person.*] See here! Do you see this? You done this.

HIGGINS Done what, man?

DOOLITTLE This, I tell you. Look at it. Look at this hat. Look at this coat.

PICKERING Has Eliza been buying you clothes?

DOOLITTLE Eliza! not she. Why would she buy me clothes?

MRS HIGGINS Good morning, Mr Doolittle. Wont you sit down?

DOOLITTLE [*Taken aback as he becomes conscious that he has forgotten his hostess.*] Asking your pardon, maam. [*He approaches her and shakes her proffered hand.*] Thank you. [*He sits down on the ottoman, on* PICKERING'*s right.*] I am that full of what has happened to me that I cant think of anything else.

HIGGINS What the dickens has happened to you?

DOOLITTLE I shouldnt mind if it had only happened to me: anything might happen to anybody and nobody to blame but Providence, as you might say. But this is something that you done to me: yes, you, Enry Iggins.

HIGGINS Have you found Eliza?

DOOLITTLE Have you lost her?

HIGGINS Yes.

DOOLITTLE You have all the luck, you have. I aint found her; but she'll find me quick enough now after what you done to me.

MRS HIGGINS But what has my son done to you, Mr. Doolittle?

DOOLITTLE Done to me! Ruined me. Destroyed my happiness. Tied me up and delivered me into the hands of middle-class morality.

HIGGINS [*Rising intolerantly and standing over* DOOLITTLE.] Youre raving. Youre drunk. Youre mad. I gave you five pounds. After that I had two conversations with you, at half-a-crown an hour. Ive never seen you since.

DOOLITTLE Oh! Drunk am I? Mad am I? Tell me this. Did you or did you not write a letter to an old blighter in America that was giving five millions to found Moral Reform Societies all over the world, and that wanted you to invent a universal language for him?

HIGGINS What! Ezra D. Wannafeller! He's dead. [*He sits down again carelessly.*]

DOOLITTLE Yes: he's dead; and I'm done for. Now did you or did you not write a letter to him to say that the most original moralist at present in England, to the best of your knowledge, was Alfred Doolittle, a common dustman?

HIGGINS Oh, after your first visit I remember making some silly joke of the kind.

DOOLITTLE Ah! you may well call it a silly joke. It put the lid on me right enough. Just give him the chance he wanted to show that Americans is not like us: that they reckonize and respect merit in every class of life, however humble. Them words is in his blooming will, in which, Enry Iggins, thanks to your silly joking, he leaves me a share in his Pre-digested Cheese Trust worth four thousand a year on condition that I lecture for his Wannafeller Moral Reform World League as often as they ask me up to six times a year.

HIGGINS The devil he does! Whew! [*Brightening suddenly.*] What a lark!

PICKERING A safe thing for you, Doolittle. They wont ask you twice.

DOOLITTLE It aint the lecturing I mind. I'll lecture them blue in the face, I will, and not turn a hair. It's making a gentleman of me that I object to. Who asked him to make a gentleman of me? I was happy. I was free. I touched pretty nigh everybody for money when I wanted it, same as I touched you, Enry Iggins. Now I am worrited; tied neck and heels; and everybody touches me for money. It's a fine thing for you, says my solicitor. Is it? says I. You mean it's a good thing for you, I says. When I was a poor man and had a solicitor once when they found a pram in the dust cart, he got me off, and got shut of me and got me shut of him as quick as he could. Same with the doctors: used to shove me out of the hospital before I could hardly stand on my legs, and nothing to pay. Now they finds out that I'm not a healthy man and cant live unless they looks after me twice a day. In the house I'm not let do a hand's turn for myself: somebody else must do it and touch me for it. A year ago I hadnt a relative in the world except two or three that wouldnt speak to me. Now Ive fifty, and not a decent week's wages among the lot of them. I have to live for others and not for myself: that middle-class morality. You talk of losing Eliza. Dont you be anxious: I bet she's on my doorstep by this: she that could support herself easy by selling flowers if I wasnt respectable. And the next one to touch me will be you, Enry Iggins. I'll have to learn to speak middle-class language from you, instead of speaking proper English. Thats where youll come in; and I daresay thats what you done it for.

MRS HIGGINS But, my dear Mr Doolittle, you need not suffer all this if you are really in earnest. Nobody can force you to accept this bequest. You can repudiate it. Isnt that so, Colonel Pickering?

PICKERING I believe so.

DOOLITTLE [*Softening his manner in deference to her sex.*] Thats the tragedy of it, maam. It's easy to say chuck it; but I havnt the nerve. Which of us has? We're all intimidated. Intimidated, maam: thats what we are. What is there for me if I chuck it but the workhouse in my old age? I have to dye my hair already to keep my job as a dustman. If I was one of the deserving poor, and had put by a bit, I could chuck it; but then why should I, acause the deserving poor might as well be millionaires for all the happiness they ever has. They dont know what happiness is. But I, as one of the undeserving poor, have nothing between me and the pauper's uniform but this here blasted four thousand a year that shoves me into the middle class. (Excuse the expression, maam; youd use it yourself if you had my provocation.) Theyve got you every way you turn: it's a choice between the Skilly of the workhouse and the Char Bydis of the middle class; and I havnt the nerve for the workhouse. Intimidated: thats what I am. Broke. Bought up. Happier men than me will call for my dust, and touch me for their tip; and I'll look on helpless, and envy them. And thats what your son has brought me to. [*He is overcome by emotion.*]

MRS HIGGINS Well, I'm very glad youre not going to do anything foolish, Mr Doolittle. For this solves the problem of Eliza's future. You can provide for her now.

DOOLITTLE [*With melancholy resignation.*] Yes, maam: I'm expected to provide for everyone now, out of four thousand a year.

HIGGINS [*Jumping up.*] Nonsense! he cant provide for her. He shant provide for her. She doesnt belong to him. I paid him five pounds for her. Doolittle: either youre an honest man or a rogue.

DOOLITTLE [*Tolerantly.*] A little of both, Henry, like the rest of us: a little of both.

HIGGINS Well, you took that money for the girl; and you have no right to take her as well.

MRS HIGGINS Henry: dont be absurd. If you want to know where Eliza is, she is upstairs.

HIGGINS [*Amazed.*] Upstairs!!! Then I shall jolly soon fetch her downstairs. [*He makes resolutely for the door.*]

MRS HIGGINS [*Rising and following him.*] Be quiet, Henry. Sit down.

HIGGINS I . . .

MRS HIGGINS Sit down, dear; and listen to me.

HIGGINS Oh very well, very well, very well. [*He throws himself ungraciously on the ottoman, with his face towards the windows.*] But I think you might have told us this half an hour ago.

MRS HIGGINS Eliza came to me this morning. She told me of the brutal way you two treated her.

HIGGINS [*Bounding up again.*] What!

PICKERING [*Rising also.*] My dear Mrs Higgins, she's been telling you stories. We didnt treat her brutally. We hardly said a word to her; and we parted on particularly good terms. [*Turning on* HIGGINS.] Higgins: did you bully her after I went to bed?

HIGGINS Just the other way about. She threw my slippers in my face. She behaved in the most outrageous way. I never gave her the slightest provocation. The slippers came bang into my face the moment I entered the room—before I had uttered a word. And used perfectly awful language.

PICKERING [*Astonished.*] But why? What did we do to her?

MRS HIGGINS I think I know pretty well what you did. The girl is naturally rather affectionate, I think. Isnt she, Mr Doolittle?

DOOLITTLE Very tenderhearted, maam. Takes after me.

MRS HIGGINS Just so. She had become attached to you both. She worked very hard for you, Henry. I dont think you quite realize what anything in the nature of brain work means to a girl of her class. Well, it seems that when the great day of trial came, and she did this wonderful thing for you without making a single mistake, you two sat there and never said a word to her, but talked together of how glad you were that it was all over and how you had been bored with the whole thing. And then you were surprised because she threw your slippers at you! *I* should have thrown the fire-irons at you.

HIGGINS We said nothing except that we were tired and wanted to go to bed. Did we, Pick?

PICKERING [*Shrugging his shoulders.*] That was all.

MRS HIGGINS [*Ironically.*] Quite sure?

PICKERING Absolutely. Really, that was all.

MRS HIGGINS You didnt thank her, or pet her, or admire her, or tell her how splendid she'd been.

HIGGINS [*Impatiently.*] But she knew all about that. We didnt make speeches to her, if thats what you mean.

PICKERING [*Conscience stricken.*] Perhaps we were a little inconsiderate. Is she very angry?

MRS HIGGINS [*Returning to her place at the writing table.*] Well, I'm afraid she wont go back to Wimpole Street, especially now that Mr Doolittle is able to keep up the position you have thrust on her; but she says she is quite willing to meet you on friendly terms and to let bygones be bygones.

HIGGINS [*Furious.*] Is she, by George? Ho!

MRS HIGGINS If you promise to behave yourself, Henry, I'll ask her to come down. If not, go home; for you have taken up quite enough of my time.

HIGGINS Oh, all right. Very well. Pick: you behave yourself. Let us put on our best Sunday manners for this creature that we picked out of the mud. [*He flings himself sulkily into the Elizabethan chair.*]

DOOLITTLE [*Remonstrating.*] Now, now, Enry Iggins! Have some consideration for my feelings as a middle-class man.

MRS HIGGINS Remember your promise, Henry. [*She presses the bell button on the writing table.*] Mr Doolittle: will you be so good as to step out on the balcony for a moment. I dont want Eliza to have the shock of your news until she has made it up with these two gentlemen. Would you mind?

DOOLITTLE As you wish, lady. Anything to help Henry to keep her off my hands. [*He disappears through the window.*]

[*The parlormaid answers the bell.* PICKERING *sits down in* DOOLITTLE'S *place.*]

MRS HIGGINS Ask Miss Doolittle to come down, please.

THE PARLORMAID Yes, maam. [*She goes out.*]

MRS HIGGINS Now, Henry: be good.

HIGGINS I am behaving myself perfectly.

PICKERING He is doing his best, Mrs Higgins.

[*A pause.* HIGGINS *throws back his head; stretches out his legs; and begins to whistle.*]

MRS HIGGINS Henry, dearest, you dont look at all nice in that attitude.

HIGGINS [*Pulling himself together.*] I was not trying to look nice, mother.

MRS HIGGINS It doesnt matter, dear. I only wanted to make you speak.

HIGGINS Why?

MRS HIGGINS Because you cant speak and whistle at the same time.

[HIGGINS *groans. Another very trying pause.*]

HIGGINS [*Springing up, out of patience.*] Where the devil is that girl? Are we to wait here all day?

[ELIZA *enters, sunny, self-possessed, and giving a staggeringly convincing exhibition of ease of manner. She carries a little work-basket, and is very much at home.* PICKERING *is too much taken aback to rise.*]

LIZA How do you do, Professor Higgins? Are you quite well?

HIGGINS [*Choking.*] Am I . . . [*He can say no more.*]

LIZA But of course you are: you are never ill. So glad to see you again, Colonel Pickering. [*He rises hastily; and they shake hands.*] Quite chilly this morning, isn't it? [*She sits down on his left. He sits beside her.*]

HIGGINS Dont you dare try this game on me. I taught it to you; and it doesnt take me in. Get up and come home; and dont be a fool.

[ELIZA *takes a piece of needlework from her basket, and begins to stitch at it, without taking the least notice of this outburst.*]

MRS HIGGINS Very nicely put, indeed, Henry. No woman could resist such an invitation.

HIGGINS You let her alone, mother. Let her speak for herself. You will jolly soon see whether she has an idea that I havnt put into her head or a word that I havnt put into her mouth. I tell you I have created this thing out of the squashed cabbage leaves of Covent Garden; and now she pretends to play the fine lady with me.

MRS HIGGINS [*Placidly.*] Yes, dear; but youll sit down, wont you?

[HIGGINS *sits down again, savagely.*]

LIZA [*To* PICKERING, *taking no apparent notice of* HIGGINS, *and working away deftly.*] Will you drop me altogether now that the experiment is over, Colonel Pickering?

PICKERING Oh dont. You mustnt think of it as an experiment. It shocks me, somehow.

LIZA Oh, I'm only a squashed cabbage leaf . . .

PICKERING [*Impulsively.*] No.

LIZA [*Continuing quietly.*] . . . but I owe so much to you that I should be very unhappy if you forgot me.

PICKERING It's very kind of you to say so, Miss Doolittle.

LIZA It's not because you paid for my dresses. I know you are generous to everybody with money. But it was from you that I learnt really nice manners; and that is what makes one a lady, isnt it? You see it was so very difficult for me with the example of Professor Higgins always before me. I was brought up to be just like him, unable to control myself, and using bad language on the slightest provocation. And I should never have known that ladies and gentlemen didnt behave like that if you hadnt been there.

HIGGINS Well!!

PICKERING Oh, thats only his way, you know. He doesnt mean it.

LIZA Oh, *I* didnt mean it either, when I was a flower girl. It was only my way. But you see I did it; and thats what makes the difference after all.

PICKERING No doubt. Still, he taught you to speak; and I couldnt have done that, you know.

LIZA [*Trivially.*] Of course: that is his profession.

HIGGINS Damnation!

LIZA [*Continuing.*] It was just like learning to dance in the fashionable way: there was nothing more than that in it. But do you know what began my real education?

PICKERING What?

LIZA [*Stopping her work for a moment.*] Your calling me Miss Doolittle that day when I first came to Wimpole Street. That was the beginning of self-respect for me. [*She resumes her stitching.*] And there were a hundred little things you never noticed, because they came naturally to you. Things about standing up and taking off your hat and opening doors . . .

PICKERING Oh, that was nothing.

LIZA Yes: things that showed you thought and felt about me as if I were something better than a scullerymaid; though of course I know you would have been just the same to a scullerymaid if she had been let into the drawing room. You never took off your boots in the dining room when I was there.

PICKERING You mustnt mind that. Higgins takes off his boots all over the place.

LIZA I know. I am not blaming him. It is his way, isn't it? But it made such a difference to me that you didnt do it. You see, really and truly, apart from the things anyone can pick up (the dressing and the proper way of speaking, and so on), the difference between a lady and a flower girl is not how she behaves, but how she's treated. I shall always be a flower girl to Professor Higgins, because he always treats me as a flower girl, and always will; but I know I can be a lady to you, because you always treat me as a lady, and always will.

MRS HIGGINS Please dont grind your teeth, Henry.

PICKERING Well, this is really very nice of you, Miss Doolittle.

LIZA I should like you to call me Eliza, now, if you would.

PICKERING Thank you. Eliza, of course.

LIZA And I should like Professor Higgins to call me Miss Doolittle.

HIGGINS I'll see you damned first.

MRS HIGGINS Henry! Henry!

PICKERING [*Laughing.*] Why dont you slang back at him? Dont stand it. It would do him a lot of good.

LIZA I cant. I could have done it once; but now I cant go back to it. You told me, you know, that when a child is brought to a foreign country, it picks up the language in a few weeks, and forgets its own. Well, I am a child in your country. I have forgotten my own language, and can speak nothing but yours. Thats the real breakoff with the corner of Tottenham Court Road. Leaving Wimpole Street finishes it.

PICKERING [*Much alarmed.*] Oh! but youre coming back to Wimpole Street, arnt you? Youll forgive Higgins?

HIGGINS [*Rising.*] Forgive! Will she, by George! Let her go. Let her find out how she can get on without us. She will relapse into the gutter in three weeks without me at her elbow.

[DOOLITTLE *appears at the center window. With a look of dignified reproach at* HIGGINS, *he comes slowly and silently to his daughter, who, with her back to the window, is unconscious of his approach.*]

PICKERING He's incorrigible, Eliza. You wont relapse, will you?

LIZA No: not now. Never again. I have learnt my lesson. I dont believe I could utter one of the old sounds if I tried. [DOOLITTLE *touches her on the left shoulder. She drops her work, losing her self-possession utterly at the spectacle of her father's splendor.*] A-a-a-a-ah-ow-ooh!

HIGGINS [*With a crow of triumph.*] Aha! Just so. A-a-a-ahowooh! A-a-a-ahowooh! A-a-a-ahowooh! Victory! Victory! [*He throws himself on the divan, folding his arms, and spraddling arrogantly.*]

DOOLITTLE Can you blame the girl? Dont look at me like that, Eliza. It aint my fault. Ive come into some money.

LIZA You must have touched a millionaire this time, dad.

DOOLITTLE I have. But I'm dressed something special today. I'm going to St George's, Hanover Square. Your stepmother is going to marry me.

LIZA [*Angrily.*] Youre going to let yourself down to marry that low common woman!

PICKERING [*Quietly.*] He ought to, Eliza. [*To* DOOLITTLE.] Why has she changed her mind?

DOOLITTLE [*Sadly.*] Intimidated, Governor. Intimidated. Middle-class morality claims its victim. Wont you put on your hat, Liza, and come and see me turned off?

LIZA If the Colonel says I must, I—I'll [*almost sobbing*] I'll demean myself. And get insulted for my pains, like enough.

DOOLITTLE Dont be afraid: she never comes to words with anyone now, poor woman! respectability has broke all the spirit out of her.

PICKERING [*Squeezing* ELIZA's *elbow gently.*] Be kind to them, Eliza. Make the best of it.

LIZA [*Forcing a little smile for him through her vexation.*] Oh well, just to show theres no ill feeling. I'll be back in a moment. [*She goes out.*]

DOOLITTLE [*Sitting down beside* PICKERING.] I feel uncommon nervous about the ceremony, Colonel. I wish youd come and see me through it.

PICKERING But youve been through it before, man. You were married to Eliza's mother.

DOOLITTLE Who told you that, Colonel?

PICKERING Well, nobody told me. But I concluded—naturally . . .

DOOLITTLE No: that aint the natural way, Colonel: it's only the middle-class way. My way was always the undeserving way. But dont say nothing to Eliza. She dont know: I always had a delicacy about telling her.

PICKERING Quite right. We'll leave it so, if you dont mind.

DOOLITTLE And youll come to the church, Colonel, and put me through straight?

PICKERING With pleasure. As far as a bachelor can.

MRS HIGGINS May I come, Mr Doolittle? I should be very sorry to miss your wedding.

DOOLITTLE I should indeed be honored by your condescension,

maam; and my poor old woman would take it as a tremenjous compliment. She's been very low, thinking of the happy days that are no more.

MRS HIGGINS [*Rising.*] I'll order the carriage and get ready. [*The men rise, except* HIGGINS.] I shant be more than fifteen minutes. [*As she goes to the door* ELIZA *comes in, hatted and buttoning her gloves.*] I'm going to the church to see your father married, Eliza. You had better come in the brougham with me. Colonel Pickering can go on with the bridegroom.

[MRS HIGGINS *goes out.* ELIZA *comes to the middle of the room between the center window and the ottoman.* PICKERING *joins her.*]

DOOLITTLE Bridegroom. What a word! It makes a man realize his position, somehow. [*He takes up his hat and goes towards the door.*]

PICKERING Before I go, Eliza, do forgive Higgins and come back to us.

LIZA I dont think dad would allow me. Would you, dad?

DOOLITTLE [*Sad but magnanimous.*] They played you off very cunning, Eliza, them two sportsmen. If it had been only one of them, you could have nailed him. But you see, there was two; and one of them chaperoned the other, as you might say. [*To* PICKERING.] It was artful of you, Colonel; but I bear no malice: I should have done the same myself. I been the victim of one woman after another all my life, and I dont grudge you two getting the better of Liza. I shant interfere. It's time for us to go, Colonel. So long, Henry. See you in St George's, Eliza. [*He goes out.*]

PICKERING [*Coaxing.*] Do stay with us, Eliza. [*He follows* DOOLITTLE.]

[ELIZA *goes out on the balcony to avoid being alone with* HIGGINS. *He rises and joins her there. She immediately comes back into the room and makes for the door; but he goes along the balcony and gets his back to the door before she reaches it.*]

HIGGINS Well, Eliza, youve had a bit of your own back, as you call it. Have you had enough? and are you going to be reasonable? Or do you want any more?

LIZA You want me back only to pick up your slippers and put up with your tempers and fetch and carry for you.

HIGGINS I havnt said I wanted you back at all.

LIZA Oh, indeed. Then what are we talking about?

HIGGINS About you, not about me. If you come back I shall treat you just as I have always treated you. I cant change my nature; and I dont intend to change my manners. My manners are exactly the same as Colonel Pickering's.

LIZA Thats not true. He treats a flower girl as if she was a duchess.

HIGGINS And I treat a duchess as if she was a flower girl.

LIZA I see. [*She turns away composedly, and sits on the ottoman, facing the window.*] The same to everybody.

HIGGINS Just so.

LIZA Like father.

HIGGINS [*Grinning, a little taken down.*] Without accepting the comparison at all points, Eliza, it's quite true that your father is not a snob, and that he will be quite at home in any station of life to which his eccentric destiny may call him. [*Seriously.*] The great secret, Eliza, is not having bad manners or good manners or any other particular sort of manners, but having the same manner for all human souls: in short, behaving as if you were in Heaven, where there are no third-class carriages, and one soul is as good as another.

LIZA Amen. You are a born preacher.

HIGGINS [*Irritated.*] The question is not whether I treat you rudely, but whether you ever heard me treat anyone else better.

LIZA [*With sudden sincerity.*] I dont care how you treat me. I dont mind your swearing at me. I shouldnt mind a black eye: Ive had one before this. But [*standing up and facing him*] I wont be passed over.

HIGGINS Then get out of my way; for I wont stop for you. You talk about me as if I were a motor bus.

LIZA So you are a motor bus: all bounce and go, and no consideration for anyone. But I can do without you: dont think I cant.

HIGGINS I know you can. I told you you could.

LIZA [*Wounded, getting away from him to the other side of the ottoman with her face to the hearth.*] I know you did, you brute. You wanted to get rid of me.

HIGGINS Liar.

LIZA Thank you. [*She sits down with dignity.*]

HIGGINS You never asked yourself, I suppose, whether *I* could do without you.

LIZA [*Earnestly.*] Dont you try to get round me. Youll have to do without me.

HIGGINS [*Arrogant.*] I can do without anybody. I have my own soul: my own spark of divine fire. But [*with sudden humility*] I shall miss you, Eliza. [*He sits down near her on the ottoman.*] I have learnt something from your idiotic notions: I confess that humbly and gratefully. And I have grown accustomed to your voice and appearance. I like them, rather.

LIZA Well, you have both of them on your gramophone and in your book of photographs. When you feel lonely without me, you can turn the machine on. It's got no feelings to hurt.

HIGGINS I cant turn your soul on. Leave me those feelings; and you can take away the voice and the face. They are not you.

LIZA Oh, you are a devil. You can twist the heart in a girl as easy as some could twist her arms to hurt her. Mrs Pearce warned me. Time and again she has wanted to leave you; and you always got round her at the last minute. And you dont care a bit for her. And you dont care a bit for me.

HIGGINS I care for life, for humanity; and you are a part of it that has come my way and been built into my house. What more can you or anyone ask?

LIZA I wont care for anybody that doesnt care for me.

HIGGINS Commercial principles, Eliza. Like [*reproducing her Covent Garden pronunciation with professional exactness*] s'yollin voylets [*selling violets*], isnt it?

LIZA Dont sneer at me. It's mean to sneer at me.

HIGGINS I have never sneered in my life. Sneering doesnt become either the human face or the human soul. I am expressing my righteous contempt for Commercialism. I dont and wont trade in affection. You call me a brute because you couldnt buy a claim on me by fetching my slippers and finding my spectacles. You were a fool: I think a woman fetching a man's slippers is a disgusting sight: did I ever fetch your slippers? I think a good deal more of you for throwing them in my face. No use slaving for me and then saying you want to be cared for: who cares for a slave? If you come back, come back for the sake of good fellowship; for youll get nothing else. Youve had a thousand times as much out of me as I have out of you; and if you dare to set up your little dog's tricks of fetching and carrying slippers against my creation of a Duchess Eliza, I'll slam the door in your silly face.

LIZA What did you do it for if you didnt care for me?

HIGGINS [*Heartily.*] Why, because it was my job.

LIZA You never thought of the trouble it would make for me.

HIGGINS Would the world ever have been made if its maker had been afraid of making trouble? Making life means making trouble. Theres only one way of escaping trouble; and thats killing things. Cowards, you notice, are always shrieking to have troublesome people killed.

LIZA I'm no preacher: I dont notice things like that. I notice that you dont notice me.

HIGGINS [*Jumping up and walking about intolerantly.*] Eliza: youre an idiot. I waste the treasures of my Miltonic mind by spreading them before you. Once for all, understand that I go my way and do my work without caring twopence what happens to either of us. I am not intimidated, like your father and your stepmother. So you can come back or go to the devil: which you please.

LIZA What am I to come back for?

HIGGINS [*Bouncing up on his knees on the ottoman and leaning over it to her.*] For the fun of it. Thats why I took you on.

LIZA [*With averted face.*] And you may throw me out tomorrow if I dont do everything you want me to?

HIGGINS Yes; and you may walk out tomorrow if I dont do everything you want me to.

LIZA And live with my stepmother?

HIGGINS Yes, or sell flowers.

LIZA Oh! if I only could go back to my flower basket! I should be independent of both you and father and all the world! Why did you take my independence from me? Why did I give it up? I'm a slave now, for all my fine clothes.

HIGGINS Not a bit. I'll adopt you as my daughter and settle

money on you if you like. Or would you rather marry Pickering?

LIZA [*Looking fiercely round at him.*] I wouldnt marry you if you asked me; and youre nearer my age than what he is.

HIGGINS [*Gently.*] Than he is: not "than what he is."

LIZA [*Losing her temper and rising.*] I'll talk as I like. Youre not my teacher now.

HIGGINS [*Reflectively.*] I dont suppose Pickering would, though. He's as confirmed an old bachelor as I am.

LIZA Thats not what I want; and dont you think it. Ive always had chaps enough wanting me that way. Freddy Hill writes to me twice and three times a day, sheets and sheets.

HIGGINS [*Disagreeably surprised.*] Damn his impudence! [*He recoils and finds himself sitting on his heels.*]

LIZA He has a right to if he likes, poor lad. And he does love me.

HIGGINS [*Getting off the ottoman.*] You have no right to encourage him.

LIZA Every girl has a right to be loved.

HIGGINS What! By fools like that?

LIZA Freddy's not a fool. And if he's weak and poor and wants me, may be he'd make me happier than my betters that bully me and dont want me.

HIGGINS Can he make anything of you? Thats the point.

LIZA Perhaps I could make something of him. But I never thought of us making anything of one another; and you never think of anything else. I only want to be natural.

HIGGINS In short, you want me to be as infatuated about you as Freddy? Is that it?

LIZA No I dont. Thats not the sort of feeling I want from you. And dont you be too sure of yourself or of me. I could have been a bad girl if I'd liked. Ive seen more of some things than you, for all your learning. Girls like me can drag gentlemen down to make love to them easy enough. And they wish each other dead the next minute.

HIGGINS Of course they do. Then what in thunder are we quarrelling about?

LIZA [*Much troubled.*] I want a little kindness. I know I'm a common ignorant girl, and you a book-learned gentleman; but I'm not dirt under your feet. What I done [*correcting herself*] what I did was not for the dresses and the taxis: I did it because we were pleasant together and I come—came—to care for you; not to want you to make love to me, and not forgetting the difference between us, but more friendly like.

HIGGINS Well, of course. Thats just how I feel. And how Pickering feels. Eliza: youre a fool.

LIZA Thats not a proper answer to give me. [*She sinks on the chair at the writing table in tears.*]

HIGGINS It's all youll get until you stop being a common idiot. If youre going to be a lady, youll have to give up feeling neglected if the men you know dont spend half their time snivelling over you and the other half giving you black eyes. If you cant stand the coldness of my sort of life, and the strain of it, go back to the gutter. Work til youre more a brute than a human being; and then cuddle and squabble and drink til you fall asleep. Oh, it's a fine life, the life of the gutter. It's real: it's warm: it's violent: you can feel it through the thickest skin: you can taste it and smell it without any training or any work. Not like Science and Literature and Classical Music and Philosophy and Art. You find me cold, unfeeling, selfish, dont you? Very well: be off with you to the sort of people you like. Marry some sentimental hog or other with lots of money, and a thick pair of lips to kiss you with and a thick pair of boots to kick you with. If you cant appreciate what youve got, youd better get what you can appreciate.

LIZA [*Desperate.*] Oh, you are a cruel tyrant. I cant talk to you: you turn everything against me: I'm always in the wrong. But you know very well all the time that youre nothing but a bully. You know I cant go back to the gutter, as you call it, and that I have no real friends in the world but you and the Colonel. You know well I couldnt bear to live with a low common man after you two; and it's wicked and cruel of you to insult me by pretending I could. You think I must go back to Wimpole Street because I have nowhere else to go but father's. But dont you be too sure that you have me under your feet to be trampled on and talked down. I'll marry Freddy, I will, as soon as I'm able to support him.

HIGGINS [*Thunderstruck.*] Freddy!!! that young fool! That poor devil who couldnt get a job as an errand boy even if he had the guts to try for it! Woman: do you not understand that I have made you a consort for a king?

LIZA Freddy loves me: that makes him king enough for me. I dont want him to work: he wasnt brought up to it as I was. I'll go and be a teacher.

HIGGINS Whatll you teach, in heaven's name?

LIZA What you taught me. I'll teach phonetics.

HIGGINS Ha! ha! ha!

LIZA I'll offer myself as an assistant to that hairyfaced Hungarian.

HIGGINS [*Rising in a fury.*] What! That impostor! that humbug! that toadying ignoramus! Teach him my methods! my discoveries! You take one step in his direction and I'll wring your neck. [*He lays hands on her.*] Do you hear?

LIZA [*Defiantly nonresistant.*] Wring away. What do I care? I knew youd strike me some day. [*He lets her go, stamping with rage at having forgotten himself, and recoils so hastily that he stumbles back into his seat on the ottoman.*] Aha! Now I know how to deal with you. What a fool I was not to think of it before! You cant take away the knowledge you gave me. You said I had a finer ear than you. And I can be civil and kind to people, which is more than you can. Aha! [*Purposely dropping her aitches to annoy him.*] Thats done you, Enry Iggins, it az. Now I dont care that [*snapping her fingers*] for your bullying and your big talk. I'll advertise it in the papers that your duchess is only a flower girl that you taught, and that she'll teach anybody to be a duchess just the same in six months for a thousand guineas. Oh, when I think of myself crawling under your feet and being trampled on and called names, when all the time I had only to lift up my finger to be as good as you, I could just kick myself.

HIGGINS [*Wondering at her.*] You damned impudent slut, you! But it's better than snivelling; better than fetching slippers and finding spectacles, isnt it? [*Rising.*] By George, Eliza, I said I'd make a woman of you; and I have. I like you like this.

LIZA Yes: you turn round and make up to me now that I'm not afraid of you, and can do without you.

HIGGINS Of course I do, you little fool. Five minutes ago you were like a millstone round my neck. Now youre a tower of strength: a consort battleship. You and I and Pickering will be three old bachelors instead of only two men and a silly girl.

[MRS HIGGINS *returns, dressed for the wedding.* ELIZA *instantly becomes cool and elegant.*]

MRS HIGGINS The carriage is waiting, Eliza. Are you ready?

LIZA Quite. Is the Professor coming?

MRS HIGGINS Certainly not. He cant behave himself in church. He makes remarks out loud all the time on the clergyman's pronunciation.

LIZA Then I shall not see you again, Professor. Goodbye. [*She goes to the door.*]

MRS HIGGINS [*Coming to* HIGGINS.] Goodbye, dear.

HIGGINS Goodbye, mother. [*He is about to kiss her, when he recollects something.*] Oh, by the way, Eliza, order a ham and a Stilton cheese, will you? And buy me a pair of reindeer gloves, number eights, and a tie to match that new suit of mine. You can choose the color. [*His cheerful, careless, vigorous voic shows that he is incorrigible.*]

LIZA [*Disdainfully.*] Number eights are too small for you if you want them lined with lamb's wool. You have three new ties that you have forgotten in the drawer of your washstand. Colonel Pickering prefers double Gloucester to Stilton; and you dont notice the difference. I telephoned Mrs Pearce this morning not to forget the ham. What you are to do without me I cannot imagine. [*She sweeps out.*]

MRS HIGGINS I'm afraid youve spoilt that girl, Henry. I should be uneasy about you and her if she were less fond of Colonel Pickering.

HIGGINS Pickering! Nonsense: she's going to marry Freddy. Ha ha! Freddy! Freddy!! Ha ha ha ha ha!!!!! [*He roars with laughter as the play ends.*]

The rest of the story need not be shown in action, and indeed, would hardly need telling if our imaginations were not so enfeebled by their lazy dependence on the ready-mades and reach-me-downs of the ragshop in which Romance keeps its stock of "happy endings" to misfit all stories. Now, the history of Eliza Doolittle, though called a romance because the transfiguration it records seems exceedingly improbable, is common enough. Such transfigurations have been achieved by hundreds of resolutely ambitious young women since Nell Gwynne set them the example by playing queens and fascinating kings in the theatre in which she began by selling oranges. Nevertheless, people in all directions have assumed, for no other reason than that she became the heroine of a romance, that she must have married the hero of it. This is unbearable, not only because her little drama, if acted on such a thoughtless assumption, must be spoiled, but because the true sequel is patent to anyone with a sense of human nature in general, and of feminine instinct in particular.

Eliza, in telling Higgins she would not marry him if he asked her, was not coquetting: she was announcing a well-considered decision. When a bachelor interests, and dominates, and teaches, and becomes important to a spinster, as Higgins with Eliza, she always, if she has character enough to be capable of it, considers very seriously indeed whether she will play for becoming that bachelor's wife, especially if he is so little interested in marriage that a determined and devoted woman might capture him if she set herself resolutely to do it. Her decision will depend a good deal on whether she is really free to choose; and that, again, will depend on her age and income. If she is at the end of her youth, and has no security for her livelihood, she will marry him because she must marry anybody who will provide for her. But at Eliza's age a good-looking girl does not feel that pressure: she feels free to pick and choose. She is therefore guided by her instinct in the matter.

Eliza's instinct tells her not to marry Higgins. It does not tell her to give him up. It is not in the slightest doubt as to his remaining one of the strongest personal interests in her life. It would be very sorely strained if there was another woman likely to supplant her with him. But as she feels sure of him on that last point, she has no doubt at all as to her course, and would not have any, even if the difference of twenty years in age, which seems so great to youth, did not exist between them.

As our own instincts are not appealed to by her conclusion, let us see whether we cannot discover some reason in it. When Higgins excused his indifference to young women on the ground that they had an irresistible rival in his mother, he gave the clue to his inveterate old-bachelordom. The case is uncommon only to the extent that remarkable mothers are uncommon. If an imaginative boy has a sufficiently rich mother who has intelligence, personal grace, dignity of character without harshness, and a cultivated sense of the best art of her time to enable her to make her house beautiful, she sets a standard for him against which very few women can struggle, besides effecting for him a disengagement of his affections, his sense of beauty, and his idealism from his specifically sexual impulses. This makes him a standing puzzle to the huge number of uncultivated people who have been brought up in tasteless homes by commonplace or disagreeable parents, and to whom, consequently, literature, painting, sculpture, music, and affectionate personal relations come as modes of sex if they come at all. The word passion means nothing else to them; and that Higgins could have a passion for phonetics and idealize his mother instead of Eliza, would seem to them absurd and unnatural. Nevertheless, when we look round and see that hardly anyone is too ugly or disagreeable to find a wife or a husband if he or she wants one, whilst many old maids and bachelors are above the average in quality and culture, we cannot help suspecting that the disentanglement of sex from the associations with which it is so commonly confused, a disentanglement which persons of genius achieve by sheer intellectual analysis, is sometimes produced or aided by parental fascination.

Now, though Eliza was incapable of thus explaining to herself

Higgins's formidable powers of resistance to the charm that prostrated Freddy at the first glance, she was instinctively aware that she could never obtain a complete grip of him, or come between him and his mother (the first necessity of the married woman). To put it shortly, she knew that for some mysterious reason he had not the makings of a married man in him, according to her conception of a husband as one to whom she would be his nearest and fondest and warmest interest. Even had there been no mother-rival, she would still have refused to accept an interest in herself that was secondary to philosophic interests. Had Mrs Higgins died, there would still have been Milton and the Universal Alphabet. Landor's remark that to those who have the greatest power of loving, love is a secondary affair, would not have recommended Landor to Eliza. Put that along with her resentment of Higgins's domineering superiority, and her mistrust of his coaxing cleverness in getting round her and evading her wrath when he had gone too far with his impetuous bullying, and you will see that Eliza's instinct had good grounds for warning her not to marry her Pygmalion.

And now, whom did Eliza marry? For if Higgins was a predestinate old bachelor, she was most certainly not a predestinate old maid. Well, that can be told very shortly to those who have not guessed it from the indications she has herself given them.

Almost immediately after Eliza is stung into proclaiming her considered determination not to marry Higgins, she mentions the fact that young Mr Frederick Eynsford Hill is pouring out his love for her daily through the post. Now Freddy is young, practically twenty years younger than Higgins: he is a gentleman (or, as Eliza would qualify him, a toff), and speaks like one. He is nicely dressed, is treated by the Colonel as an equal, loves her unaffectedly, and is not her master, nor ever likely to dominate her in spite of his advantage of social standing. Eliza has no use for the foolish romantic tradition that all women love to be mastered, if not actually bullied and beaten. "When you go to women" says Nietzsche "take your whip with you." Sensible despots have never confined that precaution to women: they have taken their whips with them when they have dealt with men, and been slavishly idealized by the men over whom they have flourished the whip much more than by women. No doubt there are slavish women as well as slavish men; and women, like men, admire those that are stronger than themselves. But to admire a strong person and to live under that strong person's thumb are two different things. The weak may not be admired and heroworshiped; but they are by no means disliked or shunned; and they never seem to have the least difficulty in marrying people who are too good for them. They may fail in emergencies; but life is not one long emergency: it is mostly a string of situations for which no exceptional strength is needed, and with which even rather weak people can cope if they have a stronger partner to help them out. Accordingly, it is a truth everywhere in evidence that strong people, masculine or feminine, not only do not marry stronger people, but do not show any preference for them in selecting their friends. When a lion meets another with a louder roar "the first lion thinks the last a bore." The man or woman who feels strong enough for two, seeks for every other quality in a partner than strength.

The converse is also true. Weak people want to marry strong people who do not frighten them too much; and this often leads them to make the mistake we describe metaphorically as "biting off more than they can chew." They want too much for too little; and when the bargain is unreasonable beyond all bearing, the union becomes impossible: it ends in the weaker party being either discarded or borne as a cross, which is worse. People who are not only weak, but silly or obtuse as well, are often in these difficulties.

This being the state of human affairs, what is Eliza fairly sure to do when she is placed between Freddy and Higgins? Will she look forward to a lifetime of fetching Higgins's slippers or to a lifetime of Freddy fetching hers? There can be no doubt about the answer. Unless Freddy is biologically repulsive to her, and Higgins biologically attractive to a degree that overwhelms all her other instincts, she will, if she marries either of them, marry Freddy.

And that is just what Eliza did.

Complications ensued; but they were economic, not romantic. Freddy had no money and no occupation. His mother's jointure, a last relic of the opulence of Largelady Park, had enabled her to struggle along in Earlscourt with an air of gentility, but not to procure any serious secondary education for her children, much less give the boy a profession. A clerkship at thirty shillings a week was beneath Freddy's dignity, and extremely distasteful to him besides. His prospects consisted of a hope that if he kept up appearances somebody would do something for him. The something appeared vaguely to his imagination as a private secretaryship or a sinecure of some sort. To his mother it perhaps appeared as a marriage to some lady of means who could not resist her boy's niceness. Fancy her feelings when he married a flower girl who had become disclassed under extraordinary circumstances which were now notorious!

It is true that Eliza's situation did not seem wholly ineligible. Her father, though formerly a dustman, and now fantastically disclassed, had become extremely popular in the smartest society by a social talent which triumphed over every prejudice and every disadvantage. Rejected by the middle class, which he loathed, he had shot up at once into the highest circles by his wit, his dustmanship (which he carried like a banner), and his Nietzschean transcendence of good and evil. At intimate ducal dinners he sat on the right hand of the Duchess; and in country houses he smoked in the pantry and was made much of by the butler when he was not feeding in the dining room and being consulted by cabinet ministers. But he found it almost as hard to do all this on four thousand a year as Mrs Eynsford Hill to live in Earlscourt on an income so pitiably smaller that I have not the heart to disclose its exact figure. He absolutely refused to add the last straw to his burden by contributing to Eliza's support.

Thus Freddy and Eliza, now Mr and Mrs Eynsford Hill, would have spent a penniless honeymoon but for a wedding present of £500 from the Colonel to Eliza. It lasted a long time because Freddy did not know how to spend money, never having had any to spend, and Eliza, socially trained by a pair of old bachelors, wore her clothes as long as they held together and looked pretty, without the least regard to their being many months out of fashion. Still, £500 will not last two young people forever;

and they both knew, and Eliza felt as well, that they must shift for themselves in the end. She could quarter herself on Wimpole Street because it had come to be her home; but she was quite aware that she ought not to quarter Freddy there, and that it would not be good for his character if she did.

Not that the Wimpole Street bachelors objected. When she consulted them, Higgins declined to be bothered about her housing problem when that solution was so simple. Eliza's desire to have Freddy in the house with her seemed of no more importance than if she had wanted an extra piece of bedroom furniture. Pleas as to Freddy's character, and the moral obligation on him to earn his own living, were lost on Higgins. He denied that Freddy had any character, and declared that if he tried to do any useful work some competent person would have the trouble of undoing it: a procedure involving a net loss to the community, and great unhappiness to Freddy himself, who was obviously intended by Nature for such light work as amusing Eliza, which, Higgins declared, was a much more useful and honorable occupation than working in the city. When Eliza referred again to her project of teaching phonetics, Higgins abated not a jot of his violent opposition to it. He said she was not within ten years of being qualified to meddle with his pet subject; and as it was evident that the Colonel agreed with him, she felt she could not go against them in this grave matter, and that she had no right, without Higgins's consent, to exploit the knowledge he had given her; for his knowledge seemed to her as much his private property as his watch: Eliza was no communist. Besides, she was superstitiously devoted to them both, more entirely and frankly after her marriage than before it.

It was the Colonel who finally solved the problem, which had cost him much perplexed cogitation. He one day asked Eliza, rather shyly, whether she had quite given up her notion of keeping a flower shop. She replied that she had thought of it, but had put it out of her head, because the Colonel had said, that day at Mrs Higgins's, that it would never do. The Colonel confessed that when he said that, he had not quite recovered from the dazzling impression of the day before. They broke the matter to Higgins that evening. The sole comment vouchsafed by him very nearly led to a serious quarrel with Eliza. It was to the effect that she would have in Freddy an ideal errand boy.

Freddy himself was next sounded on the subject. He said he had been thinking of a shop himself; though it had presented itself to his pennilessness as a small place in which Eliza should sell tobacco at one counter whilst he sold newspapers at the opposite one. But he agreed that it would be extraordinarily jolly to go early every morning with Eliza to Covent Garden and buy flowers on the scene of their first meeting: a sentiment which earned him many kisses from his wife. He added that he had always been afraid to propose anything of the sort, because Clara would make an awful row about a step that must damage her matrimonial chances, and his mother could not be expected to like it after clinging for so many years to that step of the social ladder on which retail trade is impossible.

This difficulty was removed by an event highly unexpected by Freddy's mother. Clara, in the course of her incursions into those artistic circles which were the highest within her reach, discovered that her conversational qualifications were expected to include a grounding in the novels of Mr H. G. Wells. She borrowed them in various directions so energetically that she swallowed them all within two months. The result was a conversion of a kind quite common today. A modern Acts of the Apostles would fill fifty whole Bibles if anyone were capable of writing it.

Poor Clara, who appeared to Higgins and his mother as a disagreeable and ridiculous person, and to her own mother as in some inexplicable way a social failure, had never seen herself in either light; for, though to some extent ridiculed and mimicked in West Kensington like everybody else there, she was accepted as a rational and normal—or shall we say inevitable?—sort of human being. At worst they called her The Pusher; but to them no more than to herself had it ever occurred that she was pushing the air, and pushing it in a wrong direction. Still, she was not happy. She was growing desperate. Her one asset, the fact that her mother was what the Epsom greengrocer called a carriage lady, had no exchange value, apparently. It had prevented her from getting educated, because the only education she could have afforded was education with the Earlscourt greengrocer's daughter. It had led her to seek the society of her mother's class; and that class simply would not have her, because she was much poorer than the greengrocer, and, far from being able to afford a maid, could not afford even a housemaid, and had to scrape along at home with an illiberally treated general servant. Under such circumstances nothing could give her an air of being a genuine product of Largelady Park. And yet its tradition made her regard a marriage with anyone within her reach as an unbearable humiliation. Commercial people and professional people in a small way were odious to her. She ran after painters and novelists; but she did not charm them; and her bold attempts to pick up and practice artistic and literary talk irritated them. She was, in short, an utter failure, an ignorant, incompetent, pretentious, unwelcome, penniless, useless little snob; and though she did not admit these disqualifications (for nobody ever faces unpleasant truths of this kind until the possibility of a way out dawns on them) she felt their effects too keenly to be satisfied with her position.

Clara had a startling eyeopener when, on being suddenly wakened to enthusiasm by a girl of her own age who dazzled her and produced in her a gushing desire to take her for a model, and gain her friendship, she discovered that this exquisite apparition had graduated from the gutter in a few months time. It shook her so violently, that when Mr H. G. Wells lifted her on the point of his puissant pen, and placed her at the angle of view from which the life she was leading and the society to which she clung appeared in its true relation to real human needs and worthy social structure, he effected a conversion and a conviction of sin comparable to the most sensational feats of General Booth or Gypsy Smith. Clara's snobbery went bang. Life suddenly began to move with her. Without knowing how or why, she began to make friends and enemies. Some of the acquaintances to whom she had been a tedious or indifferent or ridiculous affliction, dropped her: others became cordial. To her amazement she found that some "quite nice" people were saturated with Wells, and that this accessibility to ideas was the secret of their niceness. People she had thought deeply religious, and had tried to conciliate on that tack with disastrous results, suddenly took an interest in her, and revealed a hostility to conventional religion which she had never conceived possible except among the most desperate characters. They made her read Galsworthy; and Galsworthy exposed the vanity of Largelady Park and finished her. It exasperated her to think that the dungeon in which she had languished for so many unhappy years had been unlocked all the time, and that the impulses she had so carefully struggled with and stifled for the sake of keeping well with society, were precisely those by which alone she could have come into any sort of sincere human contact. In the radiance of these discoveries, and the tumult of their reaction, she made a fool of herself as freely and conspicuously as when she so rashly adopted Eliza's expletive in Mrs Higgins's drawing room; for the new-born Wellsian had to find her bearings almost as ridiculously as a baby; but nobody hates a baby for its ineptitudes, or thinks the worse of it for trying to eat the matches; and Clara lost no friends by her follies. They laughed at her to her face this time; and she had to defend herself and fight it out as best she could.

When Freddy paid a visit to Earlscourt (which he never did when he could possibly help it) to make the desolating announcement that he and his Eliza were thinking of blackening the Largelady scutcheon by opening a shop, he found the little household already convulsed by a prior announcement from Clara that she also was going to work in an old furniture shop in Dover Street, which had been started by a fellow Wellsian. This appointment Clara owed, after all, to her old social accomplishment of Push. She had made up her mind that, cost what it might, she would see Mr Wells in the flesh; and she had achieved her end at a garden party. She had better luck than so rash an enterprise deserved. Mr Wells came up to her expectations. Age had not withered him, nor could custom stale his infinite variety in half an hour. His pleasant neatness and compactness, his small hands and feet, his teeming ready brain, his unaffected accessibility, and a certain fine apprehensiveness which stamped him as susceptible from his topmost hair to his tipmost toe, proved irresistible. Clara talked of nothing else for weeks and weeks afterwards. And as she happened to talk to the lady of the furniture shop, and that lady also desired above all things to know Mr Wells and sell pretty things to him, she offered Clara a job on the chance of achieving that end through her.

And so it came about that Eliza's luck held, and the expected opposition to the flower shop melted away. The shop is in the arcade of a railway station not very far from the Victoria and Albert Museum; and if you live in that neighborhood you may go there any day and buy a buttonhole from Eliza.

Now here is a last opportunity for romance. Would you not like to be assured that the shop was an immense success, thanks to Eliza's charms and her early business experience in Covent Garden? Alas! the truth is the truth: the shop did not pay for a long time, simply because Eliza and her Freddy did not know how to keep it. True, Eliza had not to begin at the very beginning: she knew the names and prices of the cheaper flowers; and her elation was unbounded when she found that Freddy, like all youths educated at cheap, pretentious, and thoroughly inefficient schools, knew a little Latin. It was very little, but enough to make him appear to her a Porson or Bentley, and to put him at his ease with botanical nomenclature. Unfortunately he knew nothing else; and Eliza, though she could count money up to eighteen shillings or so, and had acquired a certain familiarity with the language of Milton from her struggles to qualify herself for winning Higgins's bet, could not write out a bill without utterly disgracing the establishment. Freddy's power of stating in Latin that Balbus built a wall and that Gaul was divided into three parts did not carry with it the slightest knowledge of accounts or business: Colonel Pickering had to explain to him what a checkbook and a bank account meant. And the pair were by no means easily teachable. Freddy backed up Eliza in her obstinate refusal to believe that they could save money by engaging a bookkeeper with some knowledge of the business. How, they argued, could you possibly save money by going to extra expense when you already could not make both ends meet? But the Colonel, after making the ends meet over and over again, at last gently insisted; and Eliza, humbled to the dust by having to beg from him so often, and stung by the uproarious derision of Higgins, to whom the notion of Freddy succeeding at anything was a joke that never palled, grasped the fact that business, like phonetics, has to be learned.

On the piteous spectacle of the pair spending their evenings in shorthand schools and polytechnic classes, learning bookkeeping and typewriting with incipient junior clerks, male and female, from the elementary schools, let me not dwell. There were even classes at the London School of Economics, and a humble personal appeal to the director of that institution to recommend a course bearing on the flower business. He, being a humorist, explained to them the method of the celebrated Dickensian essay on Chinese Metaphysics by the gentleman who read an article on China and an article on Metaphysics and combined the information. He suggested that they should combine the London School with Kew Gardens. Eliza, to whom the procedure of the Dickensian gentleman seemed perfectly correct (as in fact it was) and not in the least funny (which was only her ignorance), took the advice with entire gravity. But the effort that cost her the deepest humiliation was a request to Higgins, whose pet artistic fancy, next to Milton's verse, was calligraphy, and who himself wrote a most beautiful Italian hand, that he would teach her to write. He declared that she was congenitally incapable of forming a single letter worthy of the least of Milton's words; but she persisted; and again he suddenly threw himself into the task of teaching her with a combination of stormy intensity, concentrated patience, and occasional bursts of interesting disquisition on the beauty and nobility, the august mission and destiny, of human handwriting. Eliza ended by acquiring an extremely uncommercial script which was a positive extension of her personal beauty, and spending three times as much on stationery as anyone else because certain qualities and shapes on paper became indispensable to her. She could not even address an envelope in the usual way because it made the margins all wrong.

Their commercial schooldays were a period of disgrace and despair for the young couple. They seemed to be learning nothing about flower shops. At last they gave it up as hopeless, and shook the dust of the shorthand schools, and the polytechnics, and the

London School of Economics from their feet forever. Besides, the business was in some mysterious way beginning to take care of itself. They had somehow forgotten their objections to employing other people. They came to the conclusion that their own way was the best, and that they had really a remarkable talent for business. The Colonel, who had been compelled for some years to keep a sufficient sum on current account at his bankers to make up their deficits, found that the provision was unnecessary: the young people were prospering. It is true that there was not quite fair play between them and their competitors in trade. Their week-ends in the country cost them nothing, and saved them the price of their Sunday dinners; for the motor car was the Colonel's; and he and Higgins paid the hotel bills. Mr F. Hill, florist and greengrocer (they soon discovered that there was money in asparagus; and asparagus led to other vegetables), had an air which stamped the business as classy; and in private life he was still Frederick Eynsford Hill, Esquire. Not that there was any swank about him: nobody but Eliza knew that he had been christened Frederick Challoner. Eliza herself swanked like anything.

That is all. That is how it has turned out. It is astonishing how much Eliza still manages to meddle in the housekeeping at Wimpole Street in spite of the shop and her own family. And it is notable that though she never nags her husband, and frankly loves the Colonel as if she were his favorite daughter, she has never got out of the habit of nagging Higgins that was established on the fatal night when she won his bet for him. She snaps his head off on the faintest provocation, or on none. He no longer dares to tease her by assuming an abysmal inferiority of Freddy's mind to his own. He storms and bullies and derides; but she stands up to him so ruthlessly that the Colonel has to ask her from time to time to be kinder to Higgins; and it is the only request of his that brings a mulish expression into her face. Nothing but some emergency or calamity great enough to break down all likes and dislikes, and throw them both back on their common humanity—and may they be spared any such trial!—will ever alter this. She knows that Higgins does not need her, just as her father did not need her.

The very scrupulousness with which he told her that day that he had become used to having her there, and dependent on her for all sorts of little services, and that he should miss her if she went away (it would never have occurred to Freddy or the Colonel to say anything of the sort) deepens her inner certainty that she is "no more to him than them slippers"; yet she has a sense, too, that his indifference is deeper than the infatuation of commoner souls. She is immensely interested in him. She has even secret mischievous moments in which she wishes she could get him alone, on a desert island, away from all ties and with nobody else in the world to consider, and just drag him off his pedestal and see him making love like any common man. We all have private imaginations of that sort. But when it comes to business, to the life that she really leads as distinguished from the life of dreams and fancies, she likes Freddy and she likes the Colonel; and she does not like Higgins and Mr Doolittle. Galatea never does quite like Pygmalion: his relation to her is too godlike to be altogether agreeable.

EUGENE O'NEILL

The Emperor Jones

CAST

BRUTUS JONES, *Emperor*

HENRY SMITHERS, *a Cockney Trader*

AN OLD NATIVE WOMAN

LEM, *a Native Chief*

SOLDIERS, *Adherents of Lem*

The Little Formless Fears

JEFF

The Negro Convicts

The Prison Guard

The Planters

The Auctioneer

The Slaves

The Congo Witch-Doctor

The Crocodile God

SCENE: *The action of the play takes place on an island in the West Indies as yet not self-determined by White Marines. The form of native government is, for the time being, an Empire.*

Expressionism + Drama:

the art of putting on the outside what the insides feel about something

N.B. Eugene O'Neills - The Hairy Ape -

In an expressionistic play:

1. usually short + compressed. 2. No sub-plots. 3. Nothing deviated from main idea. 4. Not too much dialogue.

Strindberg

5. Sometimes characters that are types - nameless.

6. Sucession of unrelated scenes.

7. Free use of symbol

8. Concentration on raw bold emotions: terror, agony. (intense)

9. sound + visual affects substituted for dialogue

Expressionism

Elmer Rice - The Adding Machine

Franz Werfel

Georg Kaiser

O'Neill - a real innovator

The Great God Brown

SCENE ONE

SCENE: *The audience chamber in the palace of the Emperor—a spacious, high-ceilinged room with bare, whitewashed walls. The floor is of white tiles. In the rear, to the left of center, a wide archway giving out on a portico with white pillars. The palace is evidently situated on high ground for beyond the portico nothing can be seen but a vista of distant hills, their summits crowned with thick groves of palm trees. In the right wall, center, a smaller arched doorway leading to the living quarters of the palace. The room is bare of furniture with the exception of one huge chair made of uncut wood which stands at center, its back to rear. This is very apparently the Emperor's throne. It is painted a dazzling, eye-smiting scarlet. There is a brilliant orange cushion on the seat and another smaller one is placed on the floor to serve as a foot-stool. Strips of matting, dyed scarlet, lead from the foot of the throne to the two entrances.*

It is late afternoon but the sunlight still blazes yellowly beyond the portico and there is an oppressive burden of exhausting heat in the air.

As the curtain rises, a native negro woman sneaks in cautiously from the entrance on the right. She is very old, dressed in cheap calico, barefooted, a red bandana handkerchief covering all but a few stray wisps of white hair. A bundle bound in colored cloth is carried over her shoulder on the end of a stick. She hesitates beside the doorway, peering back as if in extreme dread of being discovered. Then she begins to glide noiselessly, a step at a time, toward the doorway in the rear. At this moment, SMITHERS *appears beneath the portico.*

SMITHERS *is a tall, stoop-shouldered man about forty. His bald head, perched on a long neck with an enormous Adams apple, looks like an egg. The tropics have tanned his naturally pasty face with its small, sharp features to a sickly yellow, and native rum has painted his pointed nose to a startling red. His little, washy-blue eyes are red-rimmed and dart about him like a ferret's. His expression is one of unscrupulous meanness, cowardly and dangerous. He is dressed in a worn riding suit of dirty white drill, puttees, spurs, and wears a white cork helmet. A cartridge belt with an automatic revolver is around his waist. He carries a riding whip in his hand. He sees the woman and stops to watch her suspiciously. Then, making up his mind, he steps quickly on tiptoe into the room. The woman, looking back over her shoulder continually, does not see him until it is too late. When she does* SMITHERS *springs forward and grabs her firmly by the shoulder. She struggles to get away, fiercely but silently.*

SMITHERS [*Tightening his grasp—roughly.*] Easy! None o' that, me birdie. You can't wriggle out now. I got me 'ooks on yer.

WOMAN [*Seeing the uselessness of struggling, gives way to frantic terror, and sinks to the ground, embracing his knees supplicatingly.*] No tell him! No tell him, Mister!

SMITHERS [*With great curiosity.*] Tell 'im? [*Then scornfully.*] Oh, you mean 'is bloomin' Majesty. What's the gaime, any'ow? What are you sneakin' away for? Been stealin' a bit, I s'pose. [*He taps her bundle with his riding whip significantly.*]

WOMAN [*Shaking her head vehemently.*] No, me no steal.

SMITHERS Bloody liar! But tell me what's up. There's somethin' funny goin' on. I smelled it in the air first thing I got up this mornin'. You blacks are up to some devilment. This palace of 'is is like a bleedin' tomb. Where's all the 'ands? [*The woman keeps sullenly silent.* SMITHERS *raises his whip threateningly.*] Ow, yer won't, won't yer? I'll show yer what's what.

WOMAN [*Coweringly.*] I tell, Mister. You no hit. They go—all go. [*She makes a sweeping gesture toward the hills in the distance.*]

SMITHERS Run away—to the 'ills?

WOMAN Yes, Mister. Him Emperor—Great Father. [*She touches her forehead to the floor with a quick mechanical jerk.*] Him sleep after eat. Then they go—all go. Me old woman. Me left only. Now me go too.

SMITHERS [*His astonishment giving way to an immense, mean satisfaction.*] Ow! So that's the ticket! Well, I know bloody well wot's in the air—when they runs orf to the 'ills. The tom-tom 'll be thumping out there bloomin' soon. [*With extreme vindictiveness.*] And I'm bloody glad of it, for one! Serve 'im right! Puttin' on airs, the stinkin' nigger! 'Is Majesty! Gawd blimey! I only 'opes I'm there when they takes 'im out to shoot 'im. [*Suddenly.*] 'E's still 'ere all right, ain't 'e?

WOMAN Yes. Him sleep.

SMITHERS 'E's bound to find out soon as 'e wakes up. 'E's cunnin' enough to know when 'is time's come. [*He goes to the doorway on the right and whistles shrilly with his fingers in his mouth. The old woman springs to her feet and runs out of the doorway, rear.* SMITHERS *goes after her, reaching for his revolver.*] Stop or I'll shoot! [*Then stopping—indifferently.*] Pop orf then, if yer like, yer black cow. [*He stands in the doorway, looking after her.*]

[JONES *enters from the right. He is a tall, powerfully built, full-blooded Negro of middle age. His features are typically negroid, yet there is something decidedly distinctive about his face—an underlying strength of will, a hardy, self-reliant confidence in himself that inspires respect. His eyes are alive with a keen, cunning intelligence. In manner he is shrewd, suspicious, evasive. He wears a light blue uniform coat, sprayed with brass buttons, heavy gold chevrons on his shoulders, gold braid on the collar, cuffs, etc. His pants are bright red with a light blue stripe down the side. Patent leather laced boots with brass spurs, and a belt with a long-barreled, pearl-handled revolver in a holster complete his make-up. Yet there is something not altogether ridiculous about his grandeur. He has a way of carrying it off.*]

JONES [*Not seeing anyone—greatly irritated and blinking sleepily—shouts.*] Who dare whistle dat way in my palace? Who dare wake up de Emperor? I'll git de hide frayled off some o' you niggers sho'!

SMITHERS [*Showing himself—in a manner half-afraid and half-defiant.*] It was me whistled to yer. [*As* JONES *frowns angrily.*] I got news for yer.

JONES [*Putting on his suavest manner, which fails to cover up his contempt for the white man.*] Oh, it's you, Mister Smithers. [*He sits down on his throne with easy dignity.*] What news you got to tell me?

SMITHERS [*Coming close to enjoy his discomfiture.*] Don't yer notice nothin' funny today?

JONES [*Coldly.*] Funny? No. I ain't perceived nothin' of de kind.

SMITHERS Then yer ain't so foxy as I thought yer was. Where's all your court? [*Sarcastically.*] The Generals and the Cabinet Ministers and all?

JONES [*Imperturbably.*] Where dey mostly runs to minute I closes my eyes—drinkin' rum and talkin' big down in de town. [*Sarcastically.*] How come you don't know dat? Ain't you sousin' with 'em most every day?

SMITHERS [*Smug but pretending indifference—with a wink.*] That's part of the day's work. I got ter—ain't I—in my business?

JONES [*Contemptuously.*] Yo' business!

SMITHERS [*Imprudently enraged.*] Gawd blimey, you was glad enough for me ter take yer in on it when you landed here first. You didn't 'ave no 'igh and mighty airs in them days!

JONES [*His hand going to his revolver like a flash—menacingly.*] Talk polite, white man! Talk polite, you heah me! I'm boss heah now, is you fergettin'? [*The Cockney seems about to challenge this last statement with the facts but something in the other's eyes holds and cows him.*]

SMITHERS [*In a cowardly whine.*] No 'arm meant, old top.

JONES [*Condescendingly.*] I accepts yo' apology. [*Lets his hand fall from his revolver.*] No use'n you rakin' up ole times. What I was den is one thing. What I is now's another. You didn't let me in on yo' crooked work out o' no kind feelin's dat time. I done de dirty work fo' you—and most o' de brain work, too, fo' dat matter—and I was wu'th money to you, dat's de reason.

SMITHERS Well, blimey, I give yer a start, didn't I—when no one else would. I wasn't afraid to 'ire yer like the rest was—'count of the story about your breakin' jail back in the States.

JONES No, you didn't have no s'cuse to look down on me fo' dat. You been in jail you'self more'n once.

SMITHERS [*Furiously.*] It's a lie! [*Then trying to pass it off by an attempt at scorn.*] Garn! Who told yer that fairy tale?

JONES Dey's some tings I ain't got to be tole. I kin see 'em in folk's eyes. [*Then after a pause—meditatively.*] Yes, you sho' give me a start. And it didn't take long from dat time to git dese fool, woods' niggers right where I wanted dem. [*With pride.*] From stowaway to Emperor in two years! Dat's goin' some!

SMITHERS [*With curiosity.*] And I bet you got yer pile o' money 'id safe some place.

JONES [*With satisfaction.*] I sho' has! And it's in a foreign bank where no pusson don't get it out but me no matter what come. You didn't s'pose I was holdin' down dis Emperor job for de glory in it, did you? Sho'! De fuss and glory part of it, dat's only to turn de heads o' de low-flung, bush niggers dat's here. Dey wants de big circus show for deir money. I gives it to 'em an' I gits de money. [*With a grin.*] De long green, dat's me every time! [*Then rebukingly.*] But you ain't got no kick agin me, Smithers. I'se paid you back all you done for me many times. Ain't I pertected you and winked at all de crooked tradin' you been doin' right out in de broad day. Sho' I has—and me makin' laws to stop it at de same time! [*He chuckles.*]

SMITHERS [*Grinning.*] But, meanin' no 'arm, you been grabbin' right and left yourself, ain't yer? Look at the taxes you've put on 'em! Blimey! You've squeezed 'em dry!

JONES [*Chuckling.*] No, dey ain't *all* dry yet. I'se still heah, ain't I?

SMITHERS [*Smiling at his secret thought.*] They're dry right now, you'll find out. [*Changing the subject abruptly.*] And as for me breakin' laws, you've broke 'em all yerself just as fast as yer made 'em.

JONES Ain't I de Emperor? De laws don't go for him. [*Judicially.*] You heah what I tells you, Smithers. Dere's little stealin' like you does, and dere's big stealin' like I does. For de little stealin' dey gits you in jail soon or late. For de big stealin' dey makes you Emperor and puts you in de Hall o' Fame when you croaks. [*Reminiscently.*] If dey's one thing I learns in ten years on de Pullman ca's listenin' to de white quality talk, it's dat same fact. And when I gits a chance to use it I winds up Emperor in two years.

SMITHERS [*Unable to repress the genuine admiration of the small fry for the large.*] Yes, yer turned the bleedin' trick, all right. Blimey, I never seen a bloke 'as 'ad the bloomin' luck you 'as.

JONES [*Severely.*] Luck? What you mean—luck?

SMITHERS I suppose you'll say as that swank about the silver bullet ain't luck—and that was what first got the fool blacks on yer side the time of the revolution, wasn't it?

JONES [*With a laugh.*] Oh, dat silver bullet! Sho' was luck! But I makes dat luck, you heah? I loads de dice! Yessuh! When dat murderin' nigger ole Lem hired to kill me takes aim ten feet away and his gun misses fire and I shoots him dead, what you heah me say?

SMITHERS You said yer'd got a charm so's no lead bullet'd kill yer. You was so strong only a silver bullet could kill yer, you told 'em. Blimey, wasn't that swank for yer—and plain, fat-'eaded luck?

JONES [*Proudly.*] I got brains and I uses 'em quick. Dat ain't luck.

SMITHERS Yer know they wasn't 'ardly liable to get no silver bullets. And it was luck 'e didn't 'it you that time.

JONES [*Laughing.*] And dere all dem fool, bush niggers was kneelin' down and bumpin' deir heads on de ground like I was a miracle out o' de Bible. Oh Lawd, from dat time on I has dem all eatin' out of my hand. I cracks de whip and dey jumps through.

SMITHERS [*With a sniff.*] Yankee bluff done it.

JONES Ain't a man's talkin' big what makes him big—long as he makes folks believe it? Sho', I talks large when I ain't got nothin' to back it up, but I ain't talkin' wild just de same. I knows I kin fool 'em—I *knows* it—and dat's backin' enough fo' my game. And ain't I got to learn deir lingo and teach some of dem English befo' I kin talk to 'em? Ain't dat wuk? You ain't never learned ary word er it, Smithers, in de ten years you been heah, dough you knows it's money in yo' pocket tradin' wid' em if you does. But you'se too shiftless to take de trouble.

SMITHERS [*Flushing.*] Never mind about me. What's this I've 'eard about yer really 'avin' a silver bullet molded for yourself?

JONES It's playin' out my bluff. I has de silver bullet molded and I tells 'em when de time comes I kills myself wid it. I tells 'em dat's 'cause I'm de on'y man in de world big enuff to git me. No use'n deir tryin'. And dey falls down and bumps their heads. [*He laughs.*] I does dat so's I kin take a walk in peace widout no jealous nigger gunnin' at me from behind de trees.

SMITHERS [*Astonished.*] Then you 'ad it made—'onest?

JONES Sho' did. Heah she be. [*He takes out his revolver, breaks it, and takes the silver bullet out of one chamber.*] Five lead an' dis silver baby at de last. Don't she shine pretty? [*He holds it in his hand, looking at it admiringly, as if strangely fascinated.*]

SMITHERS Let me see. [*Reaches out his hand for it.*]

JONES [*Harshly.*] Keep yo' hands whar dey b'long, white man. [*He replaces it in the chamber and puts the revolver back on his hip.*]

SMITHERS [*Snarling.*] Gawd blimey! Think I'm a bleedin' thief, you would.

JONES No, 'tain't dat. I knows you'se scared to steal from me. On'y I ain't 'lowin' nary body to touch dis baby. She's my rabbit's foot.

SMITHERS [*Sneering.*] A bloomin' charm, wot? [*Venomously.*] Well, you'll need all the bloody charms you 'as before long, s' 'elp me!

JONES [*Judicially.*] Oh, I'se good for six months yit 'fore dey gits sick o' my game. Den, when I sees trouble comin', I makes my getaway.

SMITHERS Ho! You got it all planned, ain't yer?

JONES I ain't no fool. I knows dis Emperor's time is sho't. Dat why I make hay when de sun shine. Was you thinkin' I'se aimin' to hold down dis job for life? No, suh! What good is gittin' money if you stays back in dis raggedy country? I wants action when I spends. And when I sees dese niggers gettin' up deir nerve to tu'n me out, and I'se got all de money in sight, I resigns on de spot and beats it quick.

SMITHERS Where to?

JONES None o' yo' business.

SMITHERS Not back to the bloody States, I'll lay my oath.

JONES [*Suspiciously.*] Why don't I? [*Then with an easy laugh.*] You mean 'count of dat story 'bout me breakin' from jail back dere? Dat's all talk.

SMITHERS [*Skeptically.*] Ho, yes!

JONES [*Sharply.*] You ain't 'sinuatin' I'se a liar, is you?

SMITHERS [*Hastily.*] No, Gawd strike me! I was only thinkin' o' the bloody lies you told the blacks 'ere about killin' white men in the States.

JONES [*Angered*] How come dey're lies?

SMITHERS You'd 'ave been in jail if you 'ad, wouldn't yer then? [*With venom.*] And from what I've 'eard it ain't 'ealthy for a black to kill a white man in the States. They burns 'em in oil, don't they?

JONES [*With cool deadliness.*] You mean lynchin' 'd scare me? Well, I tells you, Smithers, maybe I does kill one white man back dere. Maybe I does. And maybe I kills another right heah 'fore long if he don't look out.

SMITHERS [*Trying to force a laugh.*] I was on'y spoofin' yer. Can't yer take a joke? And you was just sayin' you'd never been in jail.

JONES [*In the same tone—slightly boastful.*] Maybe I goes to jail dere for gettin' in an argument wid razors ovah a crap game. Maybe I gits twenty years when dat colored man die. Maybe I gits in 'nother argument wid de prison guard was overseer ovah us when we're wukin' de roads. Maybe he hits me wid a whip and I splits his head wid a shovel and runs away and files de chain off my leg and gits away safe. Maybe I does all dat an' maybe I don't. It's a story I tells you so's you knows I'se de kind of man dat if you evah repeats one word of it, I ends yo' stealin' on dis yearth mighty damn quick!

SMITHERS [*Terrified.*] Think I'd peach on yer? Not me! Ain't I always been yer friend?

JONES [*Suddenly relaxing.*] Sho' you has—and you better be.

SMITHERS [*Recovering his composure—and with it his malice.*] And just to show yer I'm yer friend, I'll tell yer that bit o' news I was goin' to.

JONES Go ahead! Shoot de piece. Must be bad news from de happy way you look.

SMITHERS [*Warningly.*] Maybe it's gettin' time for you to resign—with that bloomin' silver bullet, wot? [*He finishes with a mocking grin.*]

JONES [*Puzzled.*] What's dat you say? Talk plain.

SMITHERS Ain't noticed any of the guards or servants about the place today, I 'aven't.

JONES [*Carelessly.*] Dey're all out in de garden, sleepin' under de trees. When I sleeps, dey sneaks a sleep, too, and I pretends I never suspicions it. All I got to do is to ring de bell and dey come flyin', makin' a bluff dey was wukin' all de time.

SMITHERS [*In the same mocking tone.*] Ring the bell now an' you'll bloody well see what I means.

JONES [*Startled to alertness, but preserving the same careless tone.*] Sho' I rings. [*He reaches below the throne and pulls out a big, common dinner bell which is painted the same vivid scarlet as the throne. He rings this vigorously—then stops to listen. Then he goes to both doors, rings again, and looks out.*]

SMITHERS [*Watching him with malicious satisfaction, after a pause—mockingly.*] The bloody ship is sinkin' an' the bleedin' rats 'as slung their 'ooks.

JONES [*In a sudden fit of anger flings the bell clattering into a corner.*] Low-flung, woods' niggers! [*Then catching* SMITHERS' *eye on him, he controls himself and suddenly bursts into a low chuckling laugh.*] Reckon I overplays my hand dis once! A man can't take de pot on a bob-tailed flush all de time. Was I sayin' I'd sit in six months mo'? Well, I'se changed my mind den. I cashes in and resigns de job of Emperor right dis minute.

SMITHERS [*With real admiration.*] Blimey, but you're a cool bird, and no mistake.

JONES No use'n fussin'. When I knows de game's up I kisses it good-bye widout no long waits. Dey've all run off to de hills, ain't dey?

SMITHERS Yes—every bleedin' man jack of 'em.

JONES Den de revolution is at de post. And de Emperor better git his feet smokin' up de trail. [*He starts for the door in rear.*]

SMITHERS Goin' out to look for your 'orse? Yer won't find any. They steals the 'orses first thing. Mine was gone when I went for 'im this mornin'. That's wot first give me a suspicion of wot was up.

JONES [*Alarmed for a second, scratches his head, then philosophically.*] Well, den I hoofs it. Feet, do yo' duty! [*He pulls out a gold watch and looks at it.*] Three-thuty. Sundown's at six-thuty or dere-abouts. [*Puts his watch back—with cool confidence.*] I got plenty o'time to make it easy.

SMITHERS Don't be so bloomin' sure of it. They'll be after you 'ot and 'eavy. Ole Lem is at the bottom o' this business an' 'e 'ates you like 'ell. 'E'd rather do for you than eat 'is dinner, 'e would!

JONES [*Scornfully.*] Dat fool no-count nigger! Does you think I'se scared o' him? I stands him on his thick head more'n once befo' dis, and I does it again if he come in my way . . . [*Fiercely.*] And dis time I leave him a dead nigger fo' sho'!

SMITHERS You'll 'ave to cut through the big forest—an' these blacks 'ere can sniff and follow a trail in the dark like 'ounds. You'd 'ave to 'ustle to get through that forest in twelve hours even if you knew all the bloomin' trails like a native.

JONES [*With indignant scorn.*] Look-a-heah, white man! Does you think I'se a natural bo'n fool? Give me credit fo' havin' some sense, fo' Lawd's sake! Don't you s'pose I'se looked ahead and made sho' of all de chances? I'se gone out in dat big forest, pretendin' to hunt, so many times dat I knows it high an' low like a book. I could go through on dem trails wid my eyes shut. [*With great contempt.*] Think dese ign'rent bush niggers dat ain't got brains enuff to know deir own names even can catch Brutus Jones? Huh, I s'pects not! Not on yo' life! Why, man, de white men went after me wid bloodhounds where I came from an' I jes' laughs at 'em. It's a shame to fool dese black trash around heah, dey're sc easy. You watch me, man. I'll make dem look sick, I will. I'll be 'cross de plain to de edge of de forest by time dark comes. Once in de woods in de night, dey got a swell chance o' findin' dis baby! Dawn tomorrow I'll be out at de oder side and on de coast whar dat French gunboat is stayin'. She picks me up, take me to Martinique when she go dar, and dere I is safe wid a mighty big bankroll in my jeans. It's easy as rollin' off a log.

SMITHERS [*Maliciously.*] But s'posin' somethin' 'appens wrong an' they do nab yer?

JONES [*Decisively.*] Dey don't—dat's de answer.

SMITHERS But, just for argyment's sake—what'd you do?

JONES [*Frowning.*] I'se got five lead bullets in dis gun good enuff fo' common bush niggers—and after dat I got de silver bullet left to cheat 'em out o' gittin' me.

SMITHERS [*Jeeringly.*] Ho, I was fergettin' that silver bullet. You'll bump yourself orf in style, won't yer? Blimey!

JONES [*Gloomily.*] You kin bet yo' whole roll on one thing, white man. Dis baby plays out his string to de end and when he quits, he quits wid a bang de way he ought. Silver bullet ain't none too good for him when he go, dat's a fac'! [*Then shaking off his nervousness—with a confident laugh.*] Sho'! What is I talkin' about? Ain't come to dat yit and I never will—not wid trash niggers like dese yere. [*Boastfully.*] Silver bullet bring me luck anyway. I kin outguess, outrun, outfight, an' outplay de whole lot o' dem all ovah de board any time o' de day er night! You watch me! [*From the distant hills comes the faint, steady thump of a tom-tom, low and vibrating. It starts at a rate exactly corresponding to normal pulse beat—72 to the minute—and continues at a gradually accelerating rate from this point uninterruptedly to the very end of the play.*]

[JONES *starts at the sound. A strange look of apprehension creeps into his face for a moment as he listens. Then he asks, with an attempt to regain his most casual manner.*] What's dat drum beatin' fo'?

SMITHERS [*With a mean grin.*] For you. That means the bleedin' ceremony 'as started. I've 'eard it before and I knows.

JONES Cer'mony? What cer'mony?

SMITHERS The blacks is 'oldin' a bloody meetin', 'avin' a war dance, gettin' their courage worked up b'fore they starts after you.

JONES Let dem! Dey'll sho' need it!

SMITHERS And they're 'oldin' their 'eathen religious service— makin' no end of devil spells and charms to 'elp 'em against your silver bullets. [*He guffaws loudly.*] Blimey, but they're balmy as 'ell!

JONES [*A tiny bit awed and shaken in spite of himself.*] Huh! Takes more'n dat to scare dis chicken!

SMITHERS [*Scenting the other's feelings—maliciously.*] Ter-night when it's pitch black in the forest, they'll 'ave their pet devils and ghosts 'oundin' after you. You'll find yer bloody 'air 'll be standin' on end before termorrow mornin'. [*Seriously.*] It's a bleedin' queer place, that stinkin' forest, even in daylight. Yer don't know what might 'appen in there, it's that rotten still. Always sends the cold shivers down my back minute I gets in it.

JONES [*With a contemptuous sniff.*] I ain't no chicken-liver like you is. Trees an' me, we'se friends, and dar's a full moon comin' bring me light. And let dem po' niggers make all de fool spells dey'se a min' to. Does yo' s'pect I'se silly enuff to b'lieve in ghosts an' ha'nts an' all dat ole woman's talk? G'long, white man! You ain't talkin' to me. [*With a chuckle.*] Doesn't you know dey's got to do wid a man was member in good standin' o' de Baptist Church. Sho' I was dat when I was porter on de Pullmans, befo' I gits into my little trouble. Let dem try deir heathen tricks. De Baptist Church done pertect me and land dem all in hell. [*Then with more confident satisfaction.*] And I'se got little silver bullet o' my own, don't forgit.

SMITHERS Ho! You 'aven't give much 'eed to your Baptist Church since you been down 'ere. I've 'eard myself you 'ad turned yer coat an' was takin' up with their blarsted witch-doctors, or whatever the 'ell yer calls the swine.

JONES [*Vehemently.*] I pretends to! Sho' I pretends! Dat's part o' my game from de fust. If I finds out dem niggers believes dat black is white, den I yells it out louder 'n deir loudest. It don't git me nothin' to do missionary work for de Baptist Church. I'se after de coin, an' I lays my Jesus on de shelf for de time bein'. [*Stops abruptly to look at his watch—alertly.*] But I ain't got de time to waste no more fool talk wid you. I'se gwine away from heah dis secon'. [*He reaches in under the throne and pulls out an expensive Panama hat with a bright multicolored band and sets it jauntily on his head.*] So long, white man! [*With a grin.*] See you in jail sometime, maybe!

SMITHERS Not me, you won't. Well, I wouldn't be in yer bloody shoes for no bloomin' money, but 'ere's wishin' yer luck just the same.

JONES [*Contemptuously.*] You're de frightenedest man evah I see! I tells you I'se safe's 'f I was in New York City. It takes dem niggers from now to dark to git up de nerve to start somethin'. By dat time, I'se got a head start dey never kotch up wid.

SMITHERS [*Maliciously.*] Give my regards to any ghosts yer meets up with.

JONES [*Grinning.*] If dat ghost got money, I'll tell him never ha'nt you less'n he wants to lose it.

SMITHERS [*Flattered.*] Garn! [*Then curiously.*] Ain't yer takin' no baggage with yer?

JONES I travels light when I wants to move fast. And I got tinned grub buried on de edge o' de forest. [*Boastfully.*] Now say dat I don't look ahead an' use my brains! [*With a wide, liberal gesture.*] I will all dat's left in de palace to you—and you better grab all you kin sneak away wid befo' dey gits here.

SMITHERS [*Gratefully.*] Righto—and thanks ter yer. [*As* JONES *walks toward the door in rear—cautioningly.*] Say! Look 'ere, you ain't goin' out that way, are yer?

JONES Does you think I'd slink out de back door like a common nigger? I'se Emperor yit, ain't I? And de Emperor Jones leaves de way he comes, and dat black trash don't dare stop him —not yit, leastways. [*He stops for a moment in the doorway, listening to the far-off but insistent beat of the tom-tom.*] Listen to dat roll-call, will you? Must be mighty big drum carry dat far. [*Then with a laugh.*] Well, if dey ain't no whole brass band to see me off, I sho' got de drum part of it. So long, white man.

[*He puts his hand in his pockets and with studied carelessness, whistling a tune, he saunters out of the doorway and off to the left.*]

SMITHERS [*Looks after him with a puzzled admiration.*] 'E's got 'is bloomin' nerve with 'im, s'elp me. [*Then angrily.*] Ho—the bleedin' nigger—puttin' on 'is bloody airs! I 'opes they nabs 'im an' gives 'im what's what! [*Then putting business before the pleasure of this thought, looking around him with cupidity.*] A bloke ought to find a 'ole lot in this palace that'd go for a bit of cash. Let's take a look, 'Arry, me lad. [*He starts for the doorway on right as the curtain falls.*]

SCENE TWO

SCENE: *Nightfall. The end of the plain where the Great Forest begins. The foreground is sandy, level ground dotted by a few stones and clumps of stunted bushes cowering close against the earth to escape the buffeting of the trade wind. In the rear the forest is a wall of darkness dividing the world. Only when the eye becomes accustomed to the gloom can the outlines of separate trunks of the nearest trees be made out, enormous pillars of deeper blackness. A somber monotone of wind lost in the leaves moans in the air. Yet this sound serves but to intensify the impression of the forest's relentless immobility, to form a background throwing into relief its brooding, implacable silence.*

[JONES *enters from the left, walking rapidly. He stops as he nears the edge of the forest, looks around him quickly, peering into the dark as if searching for some familiar landmark. Then, apparently satisfied that he is where he ought to be, he throws himself on the ground, dog-tired.*]

Well, heah I is. In de nick o' time, too! Little mo' an' it'd be blacker'n de ace of spades heah-abouts. [*He pulls a bandana handkerchief from his hip pocket and mops off his perspiring face.*] Sho'! Gimme air! I'se tuckered out sho' 'nuff. Dat soft Emperor job ain't no trainin' fo' a long hike ovah dat plain in de brilin' sun. [*Then with a chuckle.*] Cheah up, nigger, de worst is yet to come. [*He lifts his head and stares at the forest. His chuckle peters out abruptly. In a tone of awe.*] My goodness, look at dem woods, will you? Dat no-count Smithers said dey'd be black an' he sho' called de turn. [*Turning away from them quickly and looking down at his feet, he snatches at a chance to change the subject—solicitously.*] Feet, you is holdin' up yo' end fine an' I sutinly hopes you ain't blisterin' none. It's time you git a rest. [*He takes off his shoes, his eyes studiously avoiding the forest. He feels of the soles of his feet gingerly.*] You is still in de pink—on'y a little mite feverish. Cool yo'selfs. Remember you done got a long journey yit befo' you. [*He sits in a weary attitude, listening to the rhythmic beating of the tom-tom. He grumbles in a loud tone to cover up a growing uneasiness.*] Bush niggers! Wonder dey wouldn' git sick o' beatin' dat drum. Sound louder, seem like. I wonder if dey's startin' after me? [*He scrambles to his feet, looking back across the plain.*] Couldn't see dem, nohow, if dey was hundred feet away. [*Then shaking himself like a wet dog to get rid of these depressing thoughts.*] Sho', dey's miles an' miles behind. What you gittin' fidgety about? [*But he sits down and begins to lace up his shoes in great haste, all the time muttering reassuringly.*] You know what? Yo' belly is empty, dat's what's de matter wid you. Come time to eat! Wid nothin' but wind on yo' stumach, o' course you feels jiggedy. Well, we eats right heah an' now soon's I git dese pesky shoes laced up! [*He finishes lacing up his shoes.*] Dere! Now let's see. [*Gets on his hands and knees and searches the ground around him with his eyes.*] White stone, white stone, where is you? [*He sees the first white stone and crawls to it—with satisfaction.*] Heah you is! I knowed dis was de right place. Box of grub, come to me. [*He turns over the stone and feels in under it—in a tone of dismay.*] Ain't heah! Gorry, is I in de right place or isn't I? Dere's 'nother stone. Guess dat's it. [*He scrambles to the next stone and turns it over.*] Ain't heah, neither! Grub, whar is you? Ain't heah. Gorry, has I got to go hungry into dem woods—all de night? [*While he is talking he scrambles from one stone to another, turning them over in frantic haste. Finally, he jumps to his feet excitedly.*] Is I lost de place? Must have! But how dat happen when I was followin' de trail across de plain in broad daylight? [*Almost plaintively.*] I'se hungry, I is! I gotta git my feed. Whar's my strength gonna come from if I doesn't? Gorry, I gotta find dat grub high an' low somehow! Why it come dark so quick like dat? Can't see nothin'. [*He scratches a match on his trousers and peers about him. The rate of the beat of the far-off tom-tom increases perceptibly as he does so. He mutters in a bewildered voice.*] How come all dese white stones come heah when I only remembers one? [*Suddenly, with a frightened gasp, he flings the match on the ground and stamps on it.*] Nigger, is you gone crazy mad? Is you lightin' matches to show dem whar you is? Fo' Lawd's sake use yo' haid. Gorry, I'se got to be careful! [*He stares at the plain behind him apprehensively, his hand on his revolver.*] But how come all dese white stones? And whar's dat tin box o' grub I hid all wrapped up in oil cloth?

[*While his back is turned, the* LITTLE FORMLESS FEARS *creep out from the deeper blackness of the forest. They are black, shapeless, only their glittering little eyes can be seen. If they have any describable form at all it is that of a grubworm about the size of a creeping child. They move noiselessly, but with deliberate, painful effort, striving to raise themselves on end, failing and sinking prone again.* JONES *turns about to face the forest. He stares up at the tops of the trees, seeking vainly to discover his whereabouts by their conformation.*]

Can't tell nothin' from dem trees! Gorry, nothin' 'round heah look like I evah seed it befo'. I'se done lost de place sho' 'nuff! [*With mournful foreboding.*] It's mighty queer! It's mighty queer! [*With sudden forced defiance—in an angry tone.*] Woods, is you tryin' to put somethin' ovah on me?

[*From the formless creatures on the ground in front of him comes a tiny gale of low mocking laughter like a rustling of leaves. They squirm upward toward him in twisted attitudes.* JONES *looks down, leaps backward with a yell of terror, yanking out his revolver as he does so—in a quavering voice.*] What's dat? Who's dar? What is you? Git away from me befo' I shoots you up! You don't? . . .

[*He fires. There is a flash, a loud report, then silence broken only by the far-off, quickened throb of the tom-tom. The formless creatures have scurried back into the forest.* JONES *remains fixed in his position, listening intently. The sound of the shot, the reassuring feel of the revolver in his hand, have somewhat restored his shaken nerve. He addresses himself with renewed confidence.*]

Dey're gone. Dat shot fix 'em. Dey was only little animals—little wild pigs, I reckon. Dey've maybe rooted out yo' grub an' eat it. Sho' you fool nigger, what you think dey is—ha'nts? [*Excitedly.*] Gorry, you give de game away when you fire dat shot. Dem niggers heah dat fo' su'tin! Time you beat it in de woods widout no long waits. [*He starts for the forest—hesitates before the plunge—then urging himself in with manful resolution.*] Git in, nigger! What you skeered at? Ain't nothin' dere but de trees! Git in! [*He plunges boldly into the forest.*]

SCENE THREE

SCENE: *Nine o'clock. In the forest. The moon has just risen. Its beams, drifting through the canopy of leaves, make a barely perceptible, suffused, eerie glow. A dense low wall of underbrush and creepers is in the nearer foreground, fencing in a small triangular clearing. Beyond this is the massed blackness of the forest like an encompassing barrier. A path is dimly discerned leading down to the clearing from left, rear, and winding away from it again toward the right. As the scene opens nothing can be distinctly made out. Except for the beating of the tom-tom, which is a trifle louder and quicker than in the previous scene, there is silence, broken every few seconds by a queer, clicking sound. Then gradually the figure of the negro,* JEFF, *can be discerned crouching on his haunches at the rear of the triangle. He is middle aged, thin, brown in color, is dressed in a Pullman porter's uniform, cap, etc. He is throwing a pair of dice on the ground before him, picking them up, shaking them, casting them out with the regular, rigid, mechanical movements of an automaton. The heavy, plodding footsteps of someone approaching along the trail from the left are heard and* JONES' *voice, pitched in a slightly higher key and strained in a cheering effort to overcome its own tremors.*

De moon's rizen. Does you heah that, nigger? You gits more light from dis out. No mo' buttin' yo' fool head again' de trunks an' scratchin' de hide off yo' legs in de bushes. Now you sees whar yo'se gwine. So cheer up! From now on you has a snap. [*He steps just to the rear of the triangular clearing and mops off his face on his sleeve. He has lost his Panama hat. His face is scratched, his brilliant uniform shows several large rents.*] What time's it gittin' to be, I wonder? I dassent light no match to find out. Phoo'. It's wa'm an' dat's a fac'! [*Wearily.*] How long I been makin' tracks in dese woods? Must be hours an' hours. Seems like fo'evah! Yit can't be, when de moon's jes riz. Dis am a long night fo' yo', yo' Majesty! [*With a mournful chuckle.*] Majesty! Der ain't much majesty 'bout dis baby now. [*With attempted cheerfulness.*] Never min'. It's all part o' de game. Dis night come to an end like everything else. And when you gits dar safe and has dat bankroll in yo' hands you laughs at all dis. [*He starts to whistle but checks himself abruptly.*] What yo' whistlin' for, you po' dope! Want all de worl' to heah you? [*He stops talking to listen.*] Heah dat ole drum! Sho' gits nearer from de sound. Dey're packin' it along wid'em. Time fo' me to move. [*He takes a step forward, then stops —worriedly.*] What's dat odder queer clickety sound I heah? Dere it is! Sound close! Sound like—sound like—Fo' God sake, sound like some nigger was shootin' crap! [*Frightenedly.*] I better beat it quick when I gits dem notions. [*He walks quickly into the clear space—then stands transfixed as he sees* JEFF*—in a terrified gasp.*] Who dar? Who dat? Is dat you, Jeff? [*Starting toward the other, forgetful for a moment of his surroundings and really believing it is a living man that he sees—in a tone of happy relief.*] Jeff! I'se sho' mighty glad to see you! Dey tol' me you done died from dat razor cut I gives you. [*Stopping suddenly, bewilderedly.*] But how you come to be heah, nigger? [*He stares fascinatedly at the other who continues his mechanical play with the dice.* JONES' *eyes begin to roll wildly. He stutters.*] Ain't you gwine—look up—can't you speak to me? Is you—is you—a ha'nt?

[*He jerks out his revolver in a frenzy of terrified rage.*] Nigger, I kills you dead once. Has I got to kill you again? You take it den. [*He fires. When the smoke clears away* JEFF *has disappeared.* JONES *stands trembling—then with a certain reassurance.*] He's gone, anyway. Ha'nt or no ha'nt, dat shot fix him. [*The beat of the far-off tom-tom is perceptibly louder and more rapid.* JONES *becomes conscious of it—with a start, looking back over his shoulder.*] Dey's gittin' near! Dey'se comin' fast! And heah I is shootin' shots to let 'em know jus' whar I is. Oh, Gorry, I'se got to run. [*Forgetting the path he plunges wildly into the underbrush in the rear and disappears in the shadow.*]

SCENE FOUR

SCENE: *Eleven o'clock. In the forest. A wide dirt road runs diagonally from right, front, to left, rear. Rising sheer on both sides the forest walls it in. The moon is now up. Under its light the road glimmers ghastly and unreal. It is as if the forest had stood aside momentarily to let the road pass through and accomplish its veiled purpose. This done, the forest will fold in upon itself again and the road will be no more.* JONES *stumbles in from the forest on the right. His uniform is ragged and torn. He looks about him with numbed surprise when he sees the road, his eyes blinking in the bright moonlight. He flops down exhaustedly and pants heavily for a while. Then with sudden anger.*

I'm meltin' wid heat! Runnin' an' runnin' an' runnin'! Damn dis heah coat! Like a strait jacket! [*He tears off his coat and flings it away from him, revealing himself stripped to the waist.*] Dere! Dat's better! Now I kin breathe! [*Looking down at his feet, the spurs catch his eye.*] And to hell wid dese high fangled spurs. Dey're what's been a-trippin' me up an' breakin' my neck. [*He unstraps them and flings them away disgustedly.*] Dere! I gits rid o' dem frippety Emperor trappin's an' I travels lighter. Lawd! I'se tired! [*After a pause, listening to the insistent beat of the tom-tom in the distance.*] I must'a put some distance between myself an' dem—runnin' like dat—and yit—dat damn drum sound jes' de same—nearer, even. Well, I guess I a'most holds my lead anyhow. Dey won't never catch up. [*With a sigh.*] If on'y my fool legs stands up. Oh, I'se sorry I evah went in for dis. Dat Emperor job is sho' hard to shake. [*He looks around him supiciously.*] How'd dis road evah git heah? Good level road, too. I never remembers seein' it befo'. [*Shaking his head apprehensively.*] Dese woods is sho' full o' de queerest things at night. [*With a sudden terror.*] Lawd God, don't let me see no more o' dem ha'nts! Dey gits my goat! [*Then trying to talk himself into confidence.*] Ha'nts! You fool nigger, dey ain't no such things! Don't de Baptist parson tell you dat many time? Is you civilized, or is you like dese ign'rent black niggers heah? Sho'! Dat was all in yo' own head. Wasn't nothin' dere. Wasn't no Jeff! Know what? You jus' get seein' dem things 'cause yo' belly's empty and you's sick wid hunger inside. Hunger 'fects yo' head and yo' eyes. Any fool knows dat. [*Then pleading fervently.*] But bless God, I don't come across no more o' dem, whatever dey is! [*Then cautiously.*] Rest! Don't talk! Rest! You needs it. Den you gits on yo' way again. [*Looking at the moon.*] Night's half gone a'most. You hits de coast in de mawning! Den you'se all safe.

[*From the right forward a small gang of Negroes enter. They are dressed in striped convict suits, their heads are shaven, one leg drags limpingly, shackled to a heavy ball and chain. Some carry picks, the others shovels. They are followed by a white man dressed in the uniform of a prison guard. A Winchester rifle is slung across his shoulders and he carries a heavy whip. At a signal from the* GUARD *they stop on the road opposite where* JONES *is sitting.* JONES, *who has been staring up at the sky, unmindful of their noiseless approach, suddenly looks down and sees them. His eyes pop out, he tries to get to his feet and fly, but sinks back, too numbed by fright to move. His voice catches in a choking prayer.*]

Lawd Jesus!

[*The* PRISON GUARD *cracks his whip—noiselessly—and at that signal all the convicts start to work on the road. They swing their picks, they shovel, but not a sound comes from their labor. Their movements, like those of* JEFF *in the preceding scene, are those of automatons—rigid, slow, and mechanical. The* PRISON GUARD *points sternly at* JONES *with his whip, motions him to take his place among the other shovelers.* JONES *gets to his feet in a hypnotized stupor. He mumbles subserviently.*]

Yes, suh! Yes, suh! I'se comin'.

[*As he shuffles, dragging one foot, over to his place, he curses under his breath with rage and hatred.*]

God damn yo' soul, I gits even wid you yit, sometime.

[*As if there were a shovel in his hands he goes through weary, mechanical gestures of digging up dirt, and throwing it to the roadside. Suddenly the* GUARD *approaches him angrily, threateningly. He raises his whip and lashes* JONES *viciously across the shoulders with it.* JONES *winces with pain and cowers abjectly. The* GUARD *turns his back on him and walks away contemptuously. With arms upraised as if his shovel were a club in his hands he springs murderously at the unsuspecting* GUARD. *In the act of crashing down his shovel on the white man's skull,* JONES *suddenly becomes aware that his hands are empty. He cries despairingly.*]

Whar's my shovel? Gimme my shovel 'till I splits his damn head! [*Appealing to his fellow convicts.*] Gimme a shovel, one o' you, fo' God's sake!

[*They stand fixed in motionless attitudes, their eyes on the ground. The* GUARD *seems to wait expectantly, his back turned to the attacker.* JONES *bellows with baffled, terrified rage, tugging frantically at his revolver.*]

I kills you, you white debil, if it's de last thing I evah does! Ghost or debil, I kill you agin!

[*He frees the revolver and fires point blank at the* GUARD'S *back. Instantly the walls of the forest close in from both sides, the road and the figures of the convict gang are blotted out in an enshrouding darkness. The only sounds are a crashing in the underbrush as* JONES *leaps away in mad flight and the throbbing of the tom-tom, still far distant, but increased in volume of sound and rapidity of beat.*]

SCENE FIVE

SCENE: *One o'clock. A large circular clearing, enclosed by the serried ranks of gigantic trunks of tall trees whose tops are lost to view. In the center is a big dead stump worn by time into a curious resemblance to an auction block. The moon floods the clearing with a clear light.* JONES *forces his way in through the forest on the left. He looks wildly about the clearing with hunted, fearful glances. His pants are in tatters, his shoes cut and misshapen, flapping about his feet. He slinks cautiously to the stump in the center and sits down in a tense position, ready for instant flight. Then he holds his head in his hands and rocks back and forth, moaning to himself miserably.*

Oh Lawd, Lawd! Oh Lawd, Lawd! [*Suddenly he throws himself on his knees and raises his clasped hands to the sky—in a voice of agonized pleading.*] Lawd Jesus, heah my prayer! I'se a po' sinner, a po' sinner! I knows I done wrong. I knows it! When I cotches Jeff cheatin' wid loaded dice my anger overcomes me and I kills him dead! Lawd, I done wrong! When dat guard hits me wid de whip, my anger overcomes me, and I kills him dead. Lawd, I done wrong! And down heah whar dese fool bush niggers raises me up to the seat o' de mighty, I steals all I could grab. Lawd, I done wrong! I knows it! I'se sorry! Forgive me, Lawd! Forgive dis po' sinner! [*Then beseeching terrifiedly.*] And keep dem away, Lawd! Keep dem away from me! And stop dat drum soundin' in my ears! Dat begin to sound ha'nted, too. [*He gets to his feet, evidently slightly reassured by his prayer—with attempted confidence.*] De Lawd'll preserve me from dem ha'nts after dis. [*Sits down on the stump again.*] I ain't skeered o' real men. Let dem come. But dem odders . . . [*He shudders—then looks down at his feet, working his toes inside the shoes—with a groan.*] Oh, my po' feet! Dem shoes ain't no use no more 'ceptin' to hurt. I'se better off widout dem. [*He unlaces them and pulls them off—holds the wrecks of the shoes in his hands and regards them mournfully.*] You was real, A-one patin' leather, too. Look at you now. Emperor, yu'se gettin' mighty low!

[*He sits dejectedly and remains with bowed shoulders, staring down at the shoes in his hands as if reluctant to throw them away. While his attention is thus occupied, a crowd of figures silently enter the clearing from all sides. All are dressed in Southern costumes of the period of the fifties of the last century. There are middle-aged men who are evidently well-to-do planters. There is one spruce, authoritative individual—the* AUCTIONEER. *There is a crowd of curious spectators, chiefly young belles and dandies who have come to the slave market for diversion. All exchange courtly greetings in dumb show and chat silently together. There is something stiff, rigid, unreal, marionettish about their movements. They group themselves about the stump. Finally a batch of slaves are led in from the left by an attendant—three men of different ages, two women, one with a baby in her arms, nursing. They are placed to the left of the stump, beside* JONES.

The white planters look them over appraisingly as if they were cattle, and exchange judgments on each. The dandies point with their fingers and make witty remarks. The belles titter bewitchingly. All this in silence save for the ominous throb of the tom-tom. The AUCTIONEER *holds up his hand, taking his place at the stump. The groups strain forward attentively. He touches* JONES *on the shoulder peremptorily, motioning for him to stand on the stump—the auction block.*

JONES *looks up, sees the figures on all sides, looks wildly for some opening to escape, sees none, screams and leaps madly to the top of the stump to get as far away from them as possible. He stands there, cowering, paralyzed with horror. The* AUCTIONEER *begins his silent spiel. He points to* JONES, *appeals to the planters to see for themselves. Here is a good field hand, sound in wind and limb as they can see. Very strong still in spite of his being middle-aged. Look at that back. Look at those shoulders. Look at the muscles in his arms and his sturdy legs. Capable of any amount of hard labor. Moreover, of a good disposition, intelligent and tractable. Will any gentleman start the bidding? The* PLANTERS *raise their fingers, make their bids. They are apparently all eager to possess* JONES.

The bidding is lively, the crowd interested. While this has been going on, JONES *has been seized by the courage of desperation. He dares to look down and around him. Over his face abject terror gives way to mystification, to gradual realization—stutteringly.*]

What you all doin', white folks? What's all dis? What you all lookin' at me fo'? What you doin' wid me, anyhow? [*Suddenly convulsed with raging hatred and fear.*] Is dis a auction? Is you sellin' me like dey uster befo' de war? [*Jerking out his revolver just as the* AUCTIONEER *knocks him down to one of the planters—glaring from him to the purchaser.*] And *you* sells me? And *you* buys me? I shows you I'se a free nigger, damn yo' souls! [*He fires at the* AUCTIONEER *and at the* PLANTER *with such rapidity that the two shots are almost simultaneous. As if this were a signal the walls of the forest fold in. Only blackness remains and silence broken by* JONES *as he rushes off, crying with fear—and by the quickened, ever louder beat of the tom-tom.*]

SCENE SIX

SCENE: *Three o'clock. A cleared space in the forest. The limbs of the trees meet over it forming a low ceiling about five feet from the ground. The interlocked ropes of creepers reaching upward to entwine the tree trunks give an arched appearance to the sides. The space thus enclosed is like the dark noisome hold of some ancient vessel. The moonlight is almost completely shut out and only a vague, wan light filters through. There is the noise of some-one approaching from the left, stumbling and crawling through the undergrowth.* JONES' *voice is heard between chattering moans.*

Oh, Lawd, what I gwine do now? Aint got no bullet left on'y de silver one. If mo' o' dem ha'nts come after me, how I gwine skeer dem away? Oh, Lawd, on'y de silver one left—an' I gotta save dat fo' luck. If I shoots dat one I'm a goner sho'! Lawd, it's black heah! Whar's de moon? Oh, Lawd, don't dis night evah come to an end? [*By the sounds, he is feeling his way cautiously forward.*] Dere! Dis feels like a clear space. I gotta lie down an' rest. I don't care if dem niggers does cotch me. I gotta rest. [*He is well forward now where his figure can be dimly made out. His pants have been so torn away that what is left of them is no better than a breech cloth. He flings himself full length, face downward on the ground, panting with exhaustion. Gradually it seems to grow lighter in the enclosed space and two rows of seated figures can be seen behind* JONES. *They are sitting in crumpled, despairing attitudes, hunched, facing one another with their backs touching the forest walls as if they were shackled to them. All Negroes, naked save for loin cloths. At first they are silent and motionless. Then they begin to sway slowly forward toward each other and back again in unison, as if they were laxly letting themselves follow the long roll of a ship at sea. At the same time, a low, melancholy murmur rises among them, increasing gradually by rhythmic degrees which seem to be directed and controlled by the throb of the tom-tom in the distance, to a long, tremulous wail of despair that reaches a certain pitch, unbearably acute, then falls by slow gradations of tone into silence and is taken up again.* JONES *starts, looks up, sees the figures, and throws himself down again to shut out the sight. A shudder of terror shakes his whole body as the wail rises up about him again. But the next time, his voice, as if under some uncanny compulsion, starts with the others. As their chorus lifts he rises to a sitting posture similar to the others, swaying back and forth. His voice reaches the highest pitch of sorrow, of desolation. The light fades out, the other voices cease, and only darkness is left.* JONES *can be heard scrambling to his feet and running off, his voice sinking down the scale and receding as he moves farther and farther away in the forest. The tom-tom beats louder, quicker, with a more insistent, triumphant pulsation.*]

SCENE SEVEN

SCENE: *Five o'clock. The foot of a gigantic tree by the edge of a great river. A rough structure of boulders, like an altar, is by the tree. The raised river bank is in the nearer background. Beyond this the surface of the river spreads out, brilliant and unruffled in the moonlight, blotted out and merged into a veil of bluish mist in the distance.* JONES' *voice is heard from the left rising and falling in the long, despairing wail of the chained slaves, to the rhythmic beat of the tom-tom. As his voice sinks into silence, he enters the open space. The expression of his face is fixed and stony, his eyes have an obsessed glare, he moves with a strange deliberation like a sleepwalker or one in a trance. He looks around at the tree, the rough stone altar, the moonlit surface of the river beyond, and passes his hand over his head with a vague gesture of puzzled bewilderment. Then, as if in obedience to some obscure impulse, he sinks into a kneeling, devotional posture before the altar. Then he seems to come to himself partly, to have an uncertain realization of what he is doing, for he straightens up and stares about him horrifiedly—in an incoherent mumble.*

What—what is I doin'? What is—dis place? Seems like—seems like I know dat tree—an' dem stones—an' de river. I remember—seems like I been heah befo'. [*Tremblingly.*] Oh, Gorry, I'se skeered in dis place! I'se skeered! Oh, Lawd, pertect dis sinner!

[*Crawling away from the altar, he cowers close to the ground, his face hidden, his shoulders heaving with sobs of hysterical fright. From behind the trunk of the tree, as if he had sprung out of it, the figure of the* CONGO WITCH-DOCTOR *appears. He is wizened and old, naked except for the fur of some small animal tied about his waist, its bushy tail hanging down in front. His body is stained all over a bright red. Antelope horns are on each side of his head, branching upward. In one hand he carries a bone rattle, in the other a charm stick with a bunch of white cockatoo feathers tied to the end. A great number of glass beads and bone ornaments are about his neck, ears, wrists, and ankles. He struts noiselessly with a queer prancing step to a position in the clear ground between* JONES *and the altar. Then with a preliminary, summoning stamp of his foot on the earth, he begins to dance and to chant. As if in response to his summons the beating of the tom-tom grows to a fierce, exultant boom whose throbs seem to fill the air with vibrating rhythm.* JONES *looks up, starts to spring to his feet, reaches a half-kneeling, half-squatting position and remains rigidly fixed there, paralyzed with awed fascination by this new apparition. The* WITCH-DOCTOR *sways, stamping with his foot, his bone rattle clicking the time. His voice rises and falls in a weird, monotonous croon, without articulate word divisions. Gradually his dance becomes clearly one of a narrative in pantomime, his croon is an incantation, a charm to allay the fierceness of some implacable deity demanding sacrifice. He flees, he is pursued by devils, he hides, he flees again. Ever wilder and wilder becomes his flight, nearer and nearer draws the pursuing evil, more and more the spirit of terror gains possession of him. His croon, rising to intensity, is punctuated by shrill cries.* JONES *has become completely hypnotized. His voice joins in the incantation, in the cries, he beats time with his hands and sways his body to and fro from the waist. The whole spirit and meaning of the dance has entered into him, has become his spirit. Finally the theme to the pantomime halts on a howl of despair, and is taken up again in a note of savage hope. There is a salvation. The forces of evil demand sacrifice. They must be appeased. The* WITCH-DOCTOR *points with his wand to the sacred tree, to the river beyond, to the altar, and finally to* JONES *with a ferocious command.* JONES *seems to sense the meaning of this. It is he who must offer himself for sacrifice. He beats his forehead abjectly to the ground, moaning hysterically.*]

Mercy, Oh Lawd! Mercy! Mercy on dis po' sinner.

[*The* WITCH-DOCTOR *springs to the river bank. He stretches out his arms and calls to some God within its depths. Then he starts backward slowly, his arms remaining out. A huge head of a crocodile appears over the bank and its eyes, glittering greenly, fasten upon* JONES. *He stares into them fascinatedly. The* WITCH-DOCTOR *prances up to him, touches him with his wand, motions him with his hideous command toward the waiting monster.* JONES *squirms on his belly nearer and nearer, moaning continually.*]

Mercy, Lawd! Mercy!

[*The crocodile heaves more of his enormous hulk onto the land.* JONES *squirms toward him. The* WITCH-DOCTOR'S *voice shrills out in furious exultation, the tom-tom beats madly.* JONES *cries out in fierce, exhausted spasm of anguished pleading.*]

Lawd, save me! Lawd Jesus, heah my prayer!

[*Immediately in answer to his prayer, comes the thought of the one bullet left him. He snatches at his hip, shouting defiantly.*]

De silver bullet! You don't git me yit!

[*He fires at the green eyes in front of him. The head of the crocodile sinks back behind the river bank, the* WITCH-DOCTOR *springs behind the sacred tree and disappears.* JONES *lies with his face to the ground, his arms outstretched, whimpering with fear as the throb of the tom-tom fills the silence about him with a somber pulsation, a baffled but revengeful power.*]

SCENE EIGHT

SCENE: *Dawn. Same as Scene Two, the dividing line of forest and plain. The nearest tree trunks are dimly revealed but the forest behind them is still a mass of glooming shadow. The tom-tom seems on the very spot, so loud and continuously vibrating are its beats.* LEM *enters from the left, followed by a small squad of his soldiers, and by the Cockney trader,* SMITHERS. LEM *is a heavy-set, ape-faced old savage of the extreme African type, dressed only in a loin cloth. A revolver and cartridge belt are about his waist. His soldiers are in different degrees of rag-concealed nakedness. All wear broad palm-leaf hats. Each one carries a rifle.* SMITHERS *is the same as in Scene One. One of the soldiers, evidently a tracker, is peering about keenly on the ground. He grunts and points to the spot where* JONES *entered the forest.* LEM *and* SMITHERS *come to look.*

SMITHERS [*After a glance, turns away in disgust.*] That's where 'e went in right enough. Much good it'll do yer. 'E's miles orf by this an' safe to the Coast, damn 'is 'ide! I tole yer yer'd lose 'im, didn't I?—wastin' the 'ole bloomin' night beatin' yer bloody drum and castin' yer silly spells! Gawd blimey, wot a pack!

LEM [*Gutturally.*] We cotch him. You see. [*He makes a motion to his soldiers who squat down on their haunches in a semicircle.*]

SMITHERS [*Exasperatedly.*] Well, ain't yer goin' in an' 'unt 'im in the woods? What the 'ell's the good of waitin'?

LEM [*Imperturbably—squatting down himself.*] We cotch him.

SMITHERS [*Turning away from him comtemptuously.*] Aw! Garn! 'E's a better man than the lot o' you put together. I 'ates the sight o' 'im but I'll say that for 'im. [*A sound of snapping twigs comes from the forest. The soldiers jump to their feet, cocking their rifles alertly.* LEM *remains sitting with an imperturbable expression, but listening intently. The sound from the woods is repeated.* LEM *makes a quick signal with his hand. His followers creep quietly but noiselessly into the forest, scattering so that each enters at a different spot.*]

SMITHERS [*In the silence that follows—in a contemptuous whisper.*] You ain't thinkin' that would be 'im, I 'ope?

LEM [*Calmly.*] We cotch him.

SMITHERS Blarsted fat 'eads! [*Then after a second's thought—wonderingly.*] Still an' all, it might 'appen. If 'e lost 'is bloody way in these stinkin' woods 'e'd likely turn in a circle without 'is knowin' it. They all does.

LEM [*Peremptorily.*] Sssh! [*The reports of several rifles sound from the forest, followed a second later by savage, exultant yells. The beating of the tom-tom abruptly ceases.* LEM *looks up at the white man with a grin of satisfaction.*] We cotch him. Him dead.

SMITHERS [*With a snarl.*] 'Ow d'yer know it's 'im an' 'ow d'yer know 'e's dead?

LEM My mens dey got'um silver bullets. Dey kill him shore.

SMITHERS [*Astonished.*] They got silver bullets?

LEM Lead bullet no kill him. He got um strong charm. I cook um money, make um silver bullet, make um strong charm, too.

SMITHERS [*Light breaking upon him.*] So that's wot you was up to all night, wot? You was scared to put after 'im till you'd molded silver bullets, eh?

LEM [*Simply stating a fact.*] Yes. Him got strong charm. Lead no good.

SMITHERS [*Slapping his thigh and guffawing.*] Haw-haw! If yer don't beat all 'ell![*Then recovering himself—scornfully.*] I'll bet yer it ain't 'im they shot at all, yer bleedin' looney!

LEM [*Calmly.*] Dey come bring him now. [*The soldiers come out of the forest, carrying* JONES' *limp body. There is a little reddish-purple hole under his left breast. He is dead. They carry him to* LEM, *who examines his body with great satisfaction.* SMITHERS *leans over his shoulder—in a tone of frightened awe.*] Well, they did for yer right enough, Jonesey, me lad! Dead as a 'erring! [*Mockingly.*] Where's yer 'igh an' mighty airs now, yer bloomin' Majesty? [*Then with a grin.*] Silver bullets! Gawd blimey, but yer died in the 'eighth o' style, any'ow! [LEM *makes a motion to the soldiers to carry the body out left.* SMITHERS *speaks to him sneeringly.*]

SMITHERS And I s'pose you think it's yer bleedin' charms and yer silly beatin' the drum that made 'im run in a circle when 'e'd lost 'imself, don't yer? [*But* LEM *makes no reply, does not seem to hear the question, walks out left after his men.* SMITHERS *looks after him with contemptuous scorn.*] Stupid as 'ogs, the lot of 'em! Blarsted niggers!

[*Curtain falls.*]

ANTON CHEKHOV

The Cherry Orchard

A COMEDY IN FOUR ACTS

CAST

LYUBOV ANDREYEVNA RANEVSKY,
owner of the cherry orchard
ANYA, *her daughter, age 17*
VARYA, *her adopted daughter, age 24*
LEONID ANDREYEVICH GAEV, *Lyubov's brother*
YERMOLAY ALEXEYEVICH LOPAHIN, *a business man*
PYOTR SERGEYEVICH TROFIMOV, *a student*
BORIS BORISOVICH SEMYONOV-PISHCHIK, *a landowner*
CHARLOTTA IVANOVNA, *a governess*
SEMYON PANTALEYEVICH EPIHODOV,
a clerk on the Ranevsky estate
DUNYASHA, *a maid*
FEERS, *an old servant, age 87*
YASHA, *a young servant*
A TRAMP
THE STATION MASTER
A POST-OFFICE CLERK
GUESTS *and* SERVANTS

The action takes place on the estate of Madame Ranevsky

ACT I

A room which used to be the children's room and is still called the nursery. Several doors, one leading into ANYA'S *room. It is early in the morning and the sun is rising. It is early in May, but there is a morning frost. The windows are closed but through them can be seen the blossoming cherry trees. Enter* DUNYASHA, *carrying a candle, and* LOPAHIN *with a book in his hand.*

LOPAHIN The train's arrived, thank God. What time is it?

DUNYASHA It's nearly two. [*Blows out the candle.*] It's daylight already.

LOPAHIN The train must have been at least two hours late. [*Yawns and stretches.*] And what a fool I am! I make a special trip out here to meet them at the station, and then I fall asleep. . . . Just sat down in the chair and dropped off. What a nuisance. Why didn't you wake me up?

DUNYASHA I thought you'd gone. [*Listens.*] I think they're coming.

LOPAHIN [*Also listens.*] No . . . I should've been there to help them with their luggage and other things . . . [*Pause.*] Lyubov Andreyevna has been abroad for five years. I wonder what she's like now. She used to be such a kind and good person. So easy to get along with and always considerate. Why, I remember when I was fifteen, my father—he had a store in town then—hit me in the face and it made my nose bleed. . . . We'd come out here for something or other, and he was drunk. Oh, I remember it as if it happened yesterday. . . . She was so young and beautiful . . . Lyubov Andreyevna brought me into this very room—the nursery, and she fixed my nose and she said to me, "Don't cry, little peasant, it'll be better by the time you get married.". . . [*Pause.*] "Little peasant". . . She was right, my father was a peasant. And look at me now—going about in a white waistcoat and brown shoes, like a crown in peacock's feathers. Oh, I am rich all right, I've got lots of money, but when you think about it, I'm still just a peasant. [*Turning over pages of the book.*] Here, I've been reading this book, and couldn't understand a word of it. Fell asleep reading it. [*Pause.*]

DUNYASHA The dogs have been awake all night: they know their mistress is coming.

LOPAHIN Why, what's the matter with you, Dunyasha?

DUNYASHA My hands are shaking. I think I'm going to faint.

LOPAHIN You've become too delicate and refined, Dunyasha. You get yourself all dressed up like a lady, and you fix your hair like one, too. You shouldn't do that, you know. You must remember your place.

[*Enter* EPIHODOV *with a bouquet of flowers; he wears a jacket and brightly polished high boots which squeak loudly. As he enters he drops the flowers.*]

EPIHODOV [*Picks up the flowers.*] The gardener sent these. He says they're to go in the dining room. [*Hands the flowers to* DUNYASHA.]

LOPAHIN And bring me some kvass.

DUNYASHA All right.

EPIHODOV It's chilly outside this morning, three degrees of frost, and here the cherry trees are all in bloom. I can't say much for this climate of ours, you know. [*Sighs.*] No, I really can't. It doesn't contribute to—well, you know, things . . . And what do you think, Yermolay Alexeyevich, the day before yesterday I bought myself a pair of boots and they squeak so much . . . well, I mean to say, they're impossible. . . . What can I use to fix them?

LOPAHIN Oh, be quiet! And don't bother me!

EPIHODOV Every day something unpleasant happens to me. But I don't complain; I'm used to it, why I even laugh. [*Enter* DUNYASHA: *she serves* LOPAHIN *with kvass.*] Well, I have to be going. [*Bumps into a chair which falls over.*] There, you see! [*Triumphantly.*] You can see for yourself what I mean, you see . . . so to speak . . . It's absolutely amazing! [*Goes out.*]

DUNYASHA I must tell you a secret, Yermolay Alexeyevich. Epihodov proposed to me.

LOPAHIN Really!

DUNYASHA I don't know what to do. . . . He's a quiet man, but then sometimes he starts talking, and then you can't understand a word he says. It sounds nice, and he says it with so much feeling, but it doesn't make any sense. I think I like him a little, and he's madly in love with me. But the poor man, he's sort of unlucky! Do you know, something unpleasant seems to happen to him every day. That's why they tease him and call him "two-and-twenty misfortunes."

LOPAHIN [*Listens.*] I think I hear them coming. . . .

DUNYASHA Coming! . . . Oh, what's the matter with me. . . . I feel cold all over.

LOPAHIN Yes, they're really coming! Let's go and meet them at the door. I wonder if she'll recognize me? We haven't seen each other for five years.

DUNYASHA [*Agitated.*] I'm going to faint . . . Oh, I'm going to faint! . . .

[*The sound of two carriages driving up to the house can be heard.* LOPAHIN *and* DUNYASHA *hurry out. The stage is empty. Then there are sounds of people arriving in the next room.* FEERS, *who has gone to meet the train, enters the room leaning on a cane. He crosses the stage as rapidly as he can. He is dressed in an old-fashioned livery coat and a top hat and is muttering to himself, though it is impossible to make out what he is saying. The noises off-stage become louder.*]

VOICE [*Off-stage.*] Let's go through here.

[*Enter* LYUBOV ANDREYEVNA, ANYA, *and* CHARLOTTA IVANOVNA, *leading a small dog, all in traveling clothes,* VARYA, *wearing an overcoat and a kerchief over her head,* GAEV, SEMYONOV-PISHCHIK, LOPAHIN, DUNYASHA, *carrying a bundle and parasol, and other servants with luggage.*]

ANYA Let's go through here. Do you remember what room this is, Mamma?

LYUBOV [*Joyfully, through her tears.*] The nursery!

VARYA How cold it is! My hands are numb. [*To* LYUBOV.] Your rooms are the same as always, Mamma dear, the white one, and the lavender one.

LYUBOV The nursery, my dear, beautiful room! . . . I used to sleep here when I was little. [*Cries.*] And here I am again, like a little child . . . [*She kisses her brother, then* VARYA, *then her brother again.*] And Varya hasn't changed a bit, looking like a nun. And I recognized Dunyasha, *too.* [*Kisses* DUNYASHA.]

GAEV The train was two hours late. Just think of it! Such efficiency!

CHARLOTTA [*To* PISHCHIK.] And my dog eats nuts, too.

PISHCHIK [*Astonished.*] Think of that!

[*They all go out except* ANYA *and* DUNYASHA.]

DUNYASHA We've waited and waited for you . . . [*Helps* ANYA *to take off her hat and coat.*]

ANYA I haven't slept for four nights . . . I'm freezing.

DUNYASHA It was Lent when you left, and it was snowing and freezing; but it's spring now. Darling! [*She laughs and kisses her.*] Oh, how I've missed you! I could hardly stand it. My pet, my precious . . . But I must tell you . . . I can't wait another minute . . .

ANYA [*Without enthusiasm.*] What time is it? . . .

DUNYASHA Epihodov, the clerk, proposed to me right after Easter.

ANYA You never talk about anything else . . . [*Tidies her hair.*] I've lost all my hairpins. . . . [*She's so tired she can hardly keep on her feet.*]

DUNYASHA I really don't know what to think. He loves me . . . he loves me very much!

ANYA [*Looking through the door into her room, tenderly.*] My own room, my own windows, just as if I'd never left them! I'm home again! Tomorrow I'm going to get up and run right to the garden! Oh, if only I could fall asleep! I couldn't sleep all the way back, I've been so worried.

DUNYASHA Pyotr Sergeyevich came the day before yesterday.

ANYA [*Joyfully.*] Pyeta!

DUNYASHA We put him in the bathhouse, he's probably asleep now. He said he didn't want to inconvenience you. [*Looks at her watch.*] I should have gotten him up, but Varya told me not to. "Don't you dare get him up," she said

[*Enter* VARYA *with a bunch of keys at her waist.*]

VARYA Dunyasha, get some coffee, and hurry! Mamma wants some.

DUNYASHA I'll get it right away. [*Goes out.*]

VARYA Thank God, you're back! You're home again. [*Embracing her.*] My little darling's come home! How are you, my precious?

ANYA If you only knew what I've had to put up with!

VARYA I can just imagine . . .

ANYA You remember, I left just before Easter and it was cold then. And Charlotta never stopped talking the whole time, talking and those silly tricks of hers. Why did you make me take Charlotta?

VARYA But you couldn't go all alone, darling. At seventeen!

ANYA When we got to Paris it was cold and snowing. My French was terrible. Mamma was living on the fifth floor, and the place was filled with people—some French ladies, and an old priest with a little book, and the room was full of cigarette smoke. It was so unpleasant. All of a sudden I felt so sorry for Mamma that I put my arms around her neck and hugged her and wouldn't let go I was so upset. Later Mamma cried and was very kind.

VARYA [*Tearfully.*] I can't stand to hear it! . . .

ANYA She had already sold her villa at Mentone, and she had nothing left, not a thing. And I didn't have any money left either, not a penny. In fact, I barely had enough to get to Paris. And Mamma didn't understand it at all. On the way, we'd eat at the best restaurants and she'd order the most expensive dishes and tip the waiters a rouble each. Charlotta's the same way. And Yasha expected a full-course dinner for himself; it was horrible. You know, Yasha is Mamma's valet, now, we brought him with us.

VARYA Yes, I've seen the scoundrel.

ANYA Well, how's everything here? Have you paid the interest on the mortgage?

VARYA With what?

ANYA Oh dear! Oh dear!

VARYA The time runs out in August, and then it will be up for sale.

ANYA Oh dear!

LOPAHIN [*Puts his head through the door and moos like a cow.*] Moo-o. . . . [*Disappears.*]

VARYA [*Tearfully.*] I'd like to hit him . . . [*Clenches her fist.*]

ANYA [*Her arms round* VARYA, *dropping her voice.*] Varya, has he proposed to you? [VARYA *shakes her head.*] But he loves you. . . . Why don't you talk to him, what are you waiting for?

VARYA Nothing will come of it. He's too busy to have time to think of me . . . He doesn't notice me at all. It's easier when he isn't around, it makes me miserable just to see him. Everybody talks of our wedding and congratulates me, but in fact there's nothing to it, it's all a dream. [*In a different tone.*] You've got a new pin, it looks like a bee.

ANYA [*Sadly.*] Mamma bought it for me. [*She goes into her room and then with childlike gaiety.*] Did you know that in Paris I went up in a balloon?

VARYA My darling's home again! My precious one's home. [DUNYASHA *returns with a coffeepot and prepares coffee. Standing by* ANYA'*s door.*] You know, all day long, as I go about the house doing my work, I'm always dreaming. If only we could marry you to some rich man, I'd be more at peace. Then they could go away; first I'd go to the cloisters, and then I'd go on a pilgrimage to Kiev, and then Moscow . . . I'd spend my life just walking from one holy place to another. On and on. Oh, what a wonderful life that would be!

ANYA The birds are singing in the garden. What time is it?

VARYA It must be nearly three. Time you went to bed, darling. [*Goes into* ANYA'*s room.*] Oh, what a wonderful life!

[*Enter* YASHA, *with a blanket and a small bag.*]

YASHA [*Crossing the stage, in an affectedly genteel voice.*] May I go through here?

DUNYASHA My, how you've changed since you've been abroad, Yasha. I hardly recognized you.

YASHA Hm! And who are you?

DUNYASHA When you went away, I was no bigger than this . . . [*Shows her height from the floor.*] I'm Dunyasha, Fyodor's daughter. You don't remember me!

YASHA Hm! You're quite a little peach! [*Looks around and em-*

braces her; she screams and drops a saucer. YASHA *goes out quickly.*]

VARYA [*In the doorway, crossly.*] What's happening in here?

DUNYASHA [*Tearfully.*] I've broken a saucer.

VARYA That's good luck.

ANYA [*Coming out of her room.*] We ought to warn Mamma that Petya's here.

VARYA I gave strict orders not to wake him up.

ANYA [*Pensively.*] Six years ago father died, and then a month later Grisha was drowned in the river. He was such a beautiful little boy—and only seven! Mamma couldn't stand it so she went away . . . and never looked back. [*Shivers.*] How well I understand her! If she only knew! [*Pause.*] And, Petya was Grisha's tutor, he might remind her . . .

[*Enter* FEERS, *wearing a jacket and a white waistcoat.*]

FEERS [*Goes over and is busy with the samovar.*] The mistress will have her coffee in here. [*Puts on white gloves.*] Is it ready? [*To* DUNYASHA, *severely.*] Where's the cream?

DUNYASHA Oh, I forgot! [*Goes out quickly.*]

FEERS [*Fussing around the coffeepot.*] That girl's hopeless. . . . [*Mutters.*] They've come from Paris . . . Years ago the master used to go to Paris . . . Used to go by carriage . . . [*Laughs.*]

VARYA Feers, what are you laughing at?

FEERS What would you like? [*Happily.*] The mistress has come home! Home at last! I don't mind if I die now . . . [*Weeps with joy.*]

[*Enter* LYUBOV, LOPAHIN, GAEV *and* SEMYONOV-PISHCHIK, *the latter in a long peasant coat of fine cloth and full trousers tucked inside high boots.* GAEV, *as he comes in, moves his arms and body as if he were playing billiards.*]

LYUBOV How does it go now? Let me think . . . The red off the side and into the middle pocket!

GAEV That's right! Then I put the white into the corner pocket! . . . Years ago we used to sleep in this room, and now I'm fifty-one, strange as it may seem.

LOPAHIN Yes, time flies.

GAEV What?

LOPAHIN Time flies, I say.

GAEV This place smells of patchouli . . .

ANYA I'm going to bed. Goodnight, Mamma. [*Kisses her.*]

LYUBOV My precious child! [*Kisses her hands.*] Are you glad you're home? I still can't get used to it.

ANYA Goodnight, Uncle.

GAEV [*Kisses her face and hands.*] God bless you. You're so much like your mother! [*To his sister.*] You looked exactly like her at her age, Lyuba.

ANYA [*Shakes hands with* LOPAHIN *and* PISHCHIK, *goes out and shuts the door after her.*]

LYUBOV She's very tired.

PISHCHIK It's been a long trip for her.

VARYA [*To* LOPAHIN *and* PISHCHIK.] Well, gentlemen? It's nearly three o'clock, time to say good-bye.

LYUBOV [*Laughs.*] You haven't changed a bit, Varya. [*Draws* VARYA *to her and kisses her.*] Let me have some coffee, then we'll all turn in. [FEERS *places a cushion under her feet.*] Thank you, my dear. I've got into the habit of drinking coffee. I drink it day and night. Thank you, my dear old friend. [*Kisses* FEERS.]

VARYA I'd better see if they brought all the luggage in. [*Goes out.*]

LYUBOV Is it really me sitting here? [*Laughing.*] I'd like to dance and wave my arms about. [*Covering her face with her hands.*] But am I just dreaming? God, how I love it here—my own country! Oh, I love it so much, I could hardly see anything from the train, I was crying so hard. [*Through tears.*] Here, but I must drink my coffee. Thank you, Feers, thank you, my dear old friend. I'm so glad you're still alive.

FEERS The day before yesterday.

GAEV He doesn't hear very well.

LOPAHIN I've got to leave for Kharkov a little after four. What a nuisance! It's so good just to see you, and I want to talk with you . . . You look as lovely as ever.

PISHCHIK [*Breathing heavily.*] Prettier. In her fancy Parisian clothes . . . She's simply ravishing!

LOPAHIN Your brother here—Leonid Andreyevich—says that I'm nothing but a hick from the country, a tight-fisted peasant, but it doesn't bother me. Let him say what he likes. All I want is that you trust me as you always have. Merciful God! My father was your father's serf, and your grandfather's, too, but you've done so much for me that I've forgotten all that. I love you as if you were my own sister . . . more than that even.

LYUBOV I just can't sit still, I can't for the life of me! [*She jumps up and walks about in great excitement.*] I'm so happy, it's too much for me. It's all right, you can laugh at me. I know I'm being silly . . . My wonderful old bookcase! [*Kisses bookcase.*] And my little table!

GAEV You know, the old Nurse died while you were away.

LYUBOV [*Sits down and drinks coffee.*] Yes, you wrote to me about it. May she rest in peace.

GAEV Anastasy died, too. And Petrushka quit and is working in town for the chief of police. [*Takes a box of gumdrops out of his pocket and puts one in his mouth.*]

PISHCHIK My daughter, Dashenka, sends you her greetings.

LOPAHIN I feel like telling you some good news, something to cheer you up. [*Looks at his watch.*] I'll have to leave in a minute, so there's not much time to talk. But briefly it's this. As you know, the cherry orchard is going to be sold to pay your debts. They've set August 22nd as the date for the auction, but you can sleep in peace and not worry about it; there's a way out. Here's my plan, so please pay close attention. Your estate is only twenty miles from town, and the railroad is close by. Now, if the cherry orchard and the land along the river were subdivided and leased for the building of summer cottages, you'd have a yearly income of at least twenty-five thousand roubles.

GAEV Such nonsense!

LYUBOV I'm afraid I don't quite understand, Yermolay Alexeyevich.

LOPAHIN You'd divide the land into one acre lots and rent them for at least twenty-five roubles a year. I'll bet you, that if you advertise it now there won't be a lot left by the fall; they'll be snapped up almost at once. You see, you're saved! And really, I must congratulate you; it's a perfect setup. The location is marvelous and the river's deep enough for swimming. Of course, the land will have to be cleared and cleaned up a bit. For instance, all those old buildings will have to be torn down . . . And this house, too . . . but then it's not really good for anything any more. . . . And then, the old cherry orchard will have to be cut down . . .

LYUBOV Cut down? My good man, forgive me, but you don't seem to understand. If there's one thing that's interesting and really valuable in this whole part of the country, it's our cherry orchard.

LOPAHIN The only valuable thing about it is that it's very large. It only produces a crop every other year and then who wants to buy it?

GAEV Why, this orchard is even mentioned in the Encyclopedia.

LOPAHIN [*Looking at his watch.*] If you don't decide now, and do something about it before August, the cherry orchard as well as the estate will be auctioned off. So make up your minds! There's no other way out, I promise you. There's no other way.

FEERS In the old days, forty or fifty years ago, the cherries were dried, preserved, pickled, made into jam, and sometimes. . . .

GAEV Be quiet, Feers.

FEERS And sometimes, whole wagon-loads of dried cherries were shipped to Moscow and Kharkov. We used to make a lot of money on them then! And the dried cherries used to be soft, juicy, sweet, and very good . . . They knew how to do it then . . . they had a way of cooking them . . .

LYUBOV And where is that recipe now?

FEERS They've forgotten it. Nobody can remember it.

PISHCHIK [*To* LYUBOV.] What's it like in Paris? Did you eat frogs?

LYUBOV I ate crocodiles.

PISHCHIK Well, will you imagine that!

LOPAHIN Until recently only rich people and peasants lived in the country, but now lots of people come out for the summer. Almost every town, even the small ones, is surrounded with summer places. And probably within the next twenty years there'll be more and more of these people. Right now, all they do is sit on the porch and drink tea, but later on they might begin to grow a few things, and then your cherry orchard would be full of life again . . . rich and prosperous.

GAEV [*Indignantly.*] Such a lot of nonsense!

[*Enter* VARYA *and* YASHA.]

VARYA There were two telegrams for you, Mamma dear. [*Takes out the keys and opens the old bookcase, making a great deal of noise.*] Here they are.

LYUBOV They're from Paris. [*Tears them up without reading them.*] I'm through with Paris.

GAEV Do you know, Lyuba, how old this bookcase is? Last week I pulled out the bottom drawer, and I found the date it was made burned in the wood. Just think, it's exactly a hundred years old. What do you think of that, eh? We ought to celebrate its anniversary. I know it's an inanimate object, but still—it's a bookcase!

PISHCHIK [*Astonished.*] A hundred years! Can you imagine that!

GAEV Yes . . . That's quite something. [*Feeling round the bookcase with his hands.*] Dear, most honored bookcase! I salute you! For one hundred years you have served the highest ideals of goodness and justice. For one hundred years you have made us aware of the need for creative work; several generations of our family have had their courage sustained and their faith in a brighter future fortified by your silent call; you have fostered in us the ideals of public service and social consciousness. [*Pause.*]

LOPAHIN Yes . . .

LYUBOV You haven't changed a bit, Leonia.

GAEV [*Slightly embarrassed.*] I shoot it off the corner into the middle pocket! . . .

LOPAHIN [*Looks at his watch.*] Well, I've got to go.

YASHA [*Brings medicine to* LYUBOV.] Would you like to take your pills now; it's time.

PISHCHIK You shouldn't take medicine, my dear . . . they don't do you any good . . . or harm either. Let me have them. [*Takes the box from her, pours the pills into the palm of his hand, blows on them, puts them all into his mouth and drinks them down with kvass.*] There!

LYUBOV [*Alarmed.*] You're out of your mind!

PISHCHIK I took all the pills.

LOPAHIN What a stomach! [*All laugh.*]

FEERS His honor was here during Holy Week, and he ate half a bucket of pickles. [*Mutters.*]

LYUBOV What's he saying?

VARYA He's been muttering like that for three years now. We're used to it.

YASHA It's his age. . . .

[CHARLOTTA IVANOVNA, *very thin, and tightly laced in a white dress, with a lorgnette at her waist, passes across the stage.*]

LOPAHIN Excuse me, Charlotta Ivanovna, for not greeting you. I didn't have a chance. [*Tries to kiss her hand.*]

CHARLOTTA [*Withdrawing her hand.*] If I let you kiss my hand, then you'd want to kiss my elbow next, and then my shoulder.

LOPAHIN This just isn't my lucky day. [*All laugh.*] Charlotta Ivanovna, do a trick for us.

CHARLOTTA Not now. I want to go to bed. [*Goes out.*]

LOPAHIN I'll be back in three weeks. [*Kisses* LYUBOV'*s hand.*] It's time I'm going so I'll say good-bye. [*To* GAEV.] Au revoir. [*Embraces* PISHCHIK.] Au revoir. [*Shakes hands with* VARYA, *then with* FEERS *and* YASHA.] I don't want to go, really. [*To* LYUBOV.] Think over the idea of the summer cottages and if you decide anything, let me know, and I'll get you a loan of at least fifty thousand. So think it over seriously.

VARYA [*Crossly.*] Won't you ever go?

LOPAHIN I'm going, I'm going. [*Goes out.*]

GAEV What a boor! I beg your pardon . . . Varya's going to marry him, he's Varya's fiancé.

VARYA Please don't talk like that, Uncle.

LYUBOV Well, Varya, I'd be delighted. He's a good man.

PISHCHIK He's a man . . . you have to say that . . . a most worthy fellow . . . My Dashenka says so too . . . she says all sorts of things. . . . [*He drops asleep and snores, but wakes up again at once.*] By the way, my dear, will you lend me two hundred and forty roubles? I've got to pay the interest on the mortgage tomorrow . . .

VARYA [*In alarm.*] We haven't got it, really we haven't!

LYUBOV It's true, I haven't got a thing.

PISHCHIK It'll turn up. [*Laughs.*] I never lose hope. There are times when I think everything's lost, I'm ruined, and then—suddenly!—a railroad is built across my land, and they pay me for it! Something's bound to happen, if not today, then tomorrow, or the next day. Perhaps Dashenka will win two hundred thousand—she's got a lottery ticket.

LYUBOV Well, we've finished our coffee; now we can go to bed.

FEERS [*Brushing* GAEV, *admonishing him.*] You've got on the trousers again! What am I going to do with you?

VARYA [*In a low voice.*] Anya's asleep. [*Quietly opens a window.*] The sun's rising and see how wonderful the trees are! And the air smells so fragrant! The birds are beginning to sing.

GAEV [*Coming to the window.*] The orchard is all white. You haven't forgotten, Lyuba? How straight that lane is . . . just like a ribbon. And how it shines on moonlight nights. Do you remember? You haven't forgotten, have you?

LYUBOV [*Looks through the window at the orchard.*] Oh, my childhood, my innocent childhood! I used to sleep here, and I'd look out at the orchard and every morning when I woke up I was so happy. The orchard was exactly the same, nothing's changed. [*Laughs happily.*] All, all white! Oh, my orchard! After the dark, gloomy autumn and the cold winter, you are young again and full of joy; the angels have not deserted you! If only this burden could be taken from me, if only I could forget my past!

GAEV Yes, and now the orchard's going to be sold to pay our debts, how strange it all is.

LYUBOV Look, there's Mother walking through the orchard . . . dressed all in white! [*Laughs happily.*] It is Mother!

GAEV Where?

VARYA Oh, please, Mamma dear!

LYUBOV You're right, it's no one, I only imagined it. Over there, you see, on the right, by the path that goes to the arbor, there's a small white tree that's bending so it looks just like a woman.

[*Enter* TROFIMOV. *He is dressed in a shabby student's uniform, and wears glasses.*]

What a wonderful orchard! Masses of white blossoms, the blue sky . . .

TROFIMOV Lyubov Andreyevna! [*She turns to him.*] I'll just say hello and leave at once. [*Kisses her hand warmly.*] They told me to wait until morning, but I couldn't wait any longer. [LYUBOV *looks at him, puzzled.*]

VARYA [*Through tears.*] This is Petya Trofimov.

TROFIMOV Petya Trofimov, I was Grisha's tutor. Have I changed that much?

[LYUBOV *puts her arms round him and weeps quietly.*]

GAEV [*Embarrassed.*] Now, now, Lyuba . . .

VARYA [*Weeps.*] Didn't I tell you to wait until tomorrow, Petya?

LYUBOV My Grisha . . . my little boy . . . Oh, Grisha . . . my son . . .

VARYA Don't cry, Mamma darling. There's nothing we can do, it was God's will.

TROFIMOV [*Gently, with emotion.*] Don't, don't . . . please.

LYUBOV [*Weeping quietly.*] My little boy was lost . . . drowned . . . Why? Why, my friend? [*More quietly.*] Anya's asleep in there, and here I'm crying and making a scene. But tell me, Petya, what's happened to your good looks? You've aged so.

TROFIMOV A peasant woman on the train called me "that moth-eaten man."

LYUBOV You used to be such an attractive boy, a typical young student. But now your hair is thin and you wear glasses. Are you still a student? [*She walks to the door.*]

TROFIMOV I expect I'll be a student as long as I live.

LYUBOV [*Kisses her brother, then* VARYA.] Well, go to bed now. You have aged, too, Leonid.

PISHCHIK [*Following her.*] Yes, I suppose it's time to get to bed. Oh, my gout! I'd better spend the night here, and in the morning, Lyubov Andreyevna, my dear, I'd like to borrow the two hundred and forty roubles.

GAEV Don't you ever stop?

PISHCHIK Just two hundred and forty roubles . . . To pay the interest on my mortgage.

LYUBOV I haven't any money, my friend.

PISHCHIK Oh, I'll pay you back, my dear. It's not much, after all.

LYUBOV Oh, all right. Leonid will give it to you. You give him the money, Leonid.

GAEV Why, of course; glad to. As much as he wants!

LYUBOV What else can we do? He needs it. He'll pay it back.

[LYUBOV, TROFIMOV, PISHCHIK *and* FEERS *go out.* GAEV, VARYA *and* YASHA *remain.*]

GAEV My sister hasn't lost her habit of throwing money away. [*To* YASHA.] Get out of the way, you smell like a barnyard.

YASHA [*With a sneer.*] And you haven't changed either, have you Leonid Andreyevich?

GAEV What's that? [*To* VARYA.] What did he say?

VARYA [*To* YASHA.] Your mother came out from town yesterday to see you, and she's been waiting out in the servant's quarters ever since.

YASHA I wish she wouldn't bother me.

VARYA Oh, you ought to be ashamed of yourself.

YASHA What's she in such a hurry for? She could have come tomorrow. [YASHA *goes out.*]

VARYA Mamma hasn't changed a bit. She'd give away everything we had, if she could.

GAEV Yes . . . You know, when many things are prescribed to cure a disease, that means it's incurable. I've been wracking my brains to find an answer, and I've come up with several solutions, plenty of them—which means there aren't any. It would be wonderful if we could inherit some money, or if our Anya were to marry some very rich man, or if one of us went to Yaroslavl and tried our luck with our old aunt, the Countess. You know she's very rich.

VARYA [*Weeping.*] If only God would help us.

GAEV Oh, stop blubbering! The Countess is very rich, but she doesn't like us . . . To begin with, my sister married a lawyer, and not a nobleman . . . [ANYA *appears in the doorway.*] She married a commoner . . . and since then no one can say she's behaved in the most virtuous way possible. She's good, kind, and lovable, and I love her very much, but no matter how much you may allow for extenuating circumstances, you've got to admit that her morals have not been beyond reproach. You can sense it in everything she does . . .

VARYA [*In a whisper.*] Anya's standing in the doorway.

GAEV What? [*A pause.*] Isn't that strange, something's gotten into my right eye . . . I'm having a terrible time seeing. And last Thursday, when I was in the District Court . . . [ANYA *comes in.*]

VARYA Anya, why aren't you asleep?

ANYA I don't feel like sleeping. I just can't.

GAEV My dear little girl! [*Kisses* ANYA*'s face and hands.*] My child! [*Tearfully.*] You're not just my niece, you're an angel, my whole world. Please believe me, believe . . .

ANYA I believe you, Uncle. Everyone loves you, respects you . . . but, dear Uncle, you shouldn't talk so much, just try to keep quiet. What were you saying just now about mother, about your own sister? What made you say that?

GAEV Yes, yes! [*He takes her hand and puts it over his face.*] You're quite right, it was a horrible thing to say! My God! My God! And that speech I made to the bookcase . . . so stupid! As soon as I finished it, I realized how stupid it was.

VARYA It's true, Uncle dear, you oughtn't to talk so much. Just keep quiet, that's all.

ANYA If you keep quiet, you'll find life is more peaceful.

GAEV I'll be quiet. [*Kisses* ANYA*'s and* VARYA*'s hands.*] I'll be quiet. But I must tell you something about all this business, it's important. Last Thursday I went to the District Court, and I got talking with some friends, and from what they said it looks as if it might be possible to get a second mortgage so we can pay the interest to the bank.

VARYA If only God would help us!

GAEV I'm going again on Tuesday to talk with them some more. [*To* VARYA.] Oh, stop crying. [*To* ANYA.] Your mother's going to talk with Lopahin, and he certainly won't refuse her. And after you've had a little rest, you can go to Yaroslavl to see your grandmother, the Countess. You see, we'll attack the problem from three sides, and—it's as good as solved! We'll pay the interest, I'm sure of it. [*He eats a gumdrop.*] On my honor, on anything you like, I swear the estate'll not be sold! [*Excited.*] I'll bet my happiness on it! Here's my hand, you can call me a worthless liar if I allow the auction to take place. I swear it with all my soul!

ANYA [*Calmer, with an air of happiness.*] How good you are, Uncle, and how sensible! [*Embracing him.*] I'm not afraid anymore. I feel so happy and at peace.

[*Enter* FEERS.]

FEERS [*Reproachfully.*] Leonid Andreyevich, aren't you ashamed of yourself? When are you going to bed?

GAEV In a minute. Now you go away, Feers. I can get ready for bed myself. Come along, children, time for bed. We'll talk about it some more tomorrow, you must go to bed now. [*Kisses* ANYA *and* VARYA.] You know, I'm a man of the 'eighties. People don't think much of that period these days, but still I can say that I've suffered a great deal in my lifetime because of my convictions. There's a reason why the peasants love me. You have to know the peasants! You have to know . . .

ANYA You're beginning again, Uncle!

VARYA Yes, you'd better keep quiet, Uncle dear.

FEERS [*Sternly.*] Leonid Andreyevich!

GAEV I'm coming, I'm coming! Go to bed now! Bank the white into the side pocket. There's a shot for you . . . [*Goes out;* FEERS *hobbles after him.*]

ANYA I feel better now, although I don't want to go to Yaroslavl, I don't like the Countess at all, but then, thanks to Uncle, we really don't have to worry at all. [*She sits down.*]

VARYA I've got to get some sleep. I'm going. Oh, by the way, we had a terrible scene while you were gone. You know, there are only a few old servants left out in the servants' quarters: just Yefmushka, Polya, Yevstignay, and Karp. Well, they let some tramp sleep out there, and at first I didn't say anything about it. But then later, I heard people saying that I had given orders to feed them nothing but beans. Because I was stingy, you see . . . Yevstignay was the cause of it all. "Well," I think to myself, "if that's how things are, just you wait!" So I called Yevstignay in. [*Yawns.*] So he came. "What's all this, Yevstignay," I said to him, "you're such a fool." [*She walks up to* ANYA.] Anichka! [*A pause.*] She's asleep! . . . [*Takes her arm.*] Let's go to bed! Come! [*Leads her away.*] My darling's fallen asleep! Come . . . [*They go towards the door. The sound of a shepherd's pipe is heard from far away, beyond the orchard.* TROFIMOV *crosses the stage, but, seeing* VARYA *and* ANYA, *stops.*] Sh-sh! She's asleep . . . asleep . . . Come along, come along.

ANYA [*Softly, half-asleep.*] I'm so tired. . . . I can hear the bells ringing all the time . . . Uncle . . . dear . . . Mamma and Uncle. . . .

VARYA Come, darling, come. . . . [*They go into* ANYA*'s room.*]

TROFIMOV [*Deeply moved.*] Oh, Anya . . . my sunshine! My spring!

[*Curtain.*]

ACT II

An old abandoned chapel in a field. Beside it are a well, an old bench, and some tombstones. A road leads to the Ranevsky estate. On one side a row of poplars casts a shadow; at that point the cherry orchard begins. In the distance, a line of telegraph poles can be seen, and beyond them, on the horizon, is the outline of a large town, visible only in very clear weather. It's nearly sunset. CHARLOTTA, YASHA *and* DUNYASHA *are sitting on the bench;* EPIHODOV *is standing near by, playing a guitar; everyone is lost in thought.* CHARLOTTA *is wearing an old hunting cap; she has taken a shotgun off her shoulder and is adjusting the buckle on the strap.*

CHARLOTTA [*Thoughtfully.*] I don't know how old I am. For you see, I haven't got a passport . . . but I keep pretending that I'm still very young. When I was a little girl, my father and mother traveled from fair to fair giving performances—oh, very good ones. And I used to do the "*salto-mortale*" and all sorts of other tricks, too. When Papa and Mamma died, a German lady took me to live with her and sent me to school. So when I grew up I became a governess. But where I come from and who I am, I don't know. Who my parents were—perhaps they weren't even married—I don't know. [*Taking a cucumber from her pocket and beginning to eat it.*] I don't know anything. [*Pause.*] I'm longing to talk to someone, but there isn't anybody. I haven't anybody . . .

EPIHODOV [*Plays the guitar and sings.*] "What care I for the noisy world? . . . What care I for friends and foes?" How pleasant it is to play the mandolin!

DUNYASHA That's a guitar, not a mandolin. [*She looks at herself in a little mirror and powders her face.*]

EPIHODOV To a man who's madly in love this is a mandolin. [*Sings quietly.*] "If only my heart were warmed by the fire of love requited.". . . [YASHA *joins in.*]

CHARLOTTA How dreadfully these people sing! . . . Ach! Like a bunch of jackals.

DUNYASHA [*To* YASHA.] You're so lucky to have been abroad!

YASHA Of course I am. Naturally. [*Yawns, then lights a cigar.*]

EPIHODOV Stands to reason. Abroad everything's reached its maturity . . . I mean to say, everything's been going on for such a long time.

YASHA Obviously.

EPIHODOV Now, I'm a cultured man, I read all kinds of extraordinary books, you know, but somehow I can't seem to figure out where I'm going, what it is I really want, I mean to say—whether to live or to shoot myself. Nevertheless, I always carry a revolver on me. Here it is. [*Shows the revolver.*]

CHARLOTTA That's finished, so now I'm going. [*Slips the strap of the gun over her shoulder.*] Yes, Epihodov, you are a very clever man, and frightening, too; the women must be wild about you! Brrr! [*Walks off.*] All these clever people are so stupid, I haven't anyone to talk to. I'm so lonely, always alone, I have nobody and . . . and who I am and what I'm here for, nobody knows . . . [*Wanders out.*]

EPIHODOV Frankly, and I want to keep to the point, I have to admit that Fate, so to speak, treats me absolutely without mercy, like a small ship is buffeted by the storm, as it were. I mean to say, suppose I'm mistaken, then why for instance should I wake up this morning and suddenly see a gigantic spider sitting on my chest? Like this . . . [*Showing the size with both hands.*] Or if I pick up a jug to have a drink of kvass, there's sure to be something horrible, like a cockroach, inside it. [*Pause.*] Have you read Buckle? [*Pause.*] May I trouble you for a moment, Dunyasha? I'd like to speak with you.

DUNYASHA Well, go ahead.

EPIHODOV I'd very much like to speak with you alone. [*Sighs.*]

DUNYASHA [*Embarrassed.*] Oh, all right . . . But first bring me my little cape . . . It's hanging by the cupboard. It's getting terribly chilly . . .

EPIHODOV Very well, I'll get it. . . . Now I know what to do with my revolver. [*Takes his guitar and goes off playing it.*]

YASHA Two-and-twenty misfortunes! Just between you and me, he's a stupid fool. [*Yawns.*]

DUNYASHA I hope to God he doesn't shoot himself. [*Pause.*] He makes me so nervous and I'm always worrying about him. I came to live here when I was still a little girl. Now I no longer know how to live a simple life, and my hands are as white . . . as white as a lady's. I've become such a delicate and sensitive creature. I'm afraid of everything . . . so frightened. If you deceive me, Yasha, I don't know what will happen to my nerves.

YASHA [*Kisses her.*] You sweet little peach! Just remember, a girl must always control herself. Personally I think nothing is worse than a girl who doesn't behave herself.

DUNYASHA I love you so much, so passionately! You're so intelligent, you can talk about anything. [*Pause.*]

YASHA [*Yawns.*] Yes, I suppose so . . . In my opinion, it's like this: if a girl loves someone it means she's immoral. [*Pause.*] I enjoy smoking a cigar in the fresh air . . . [*Listens.*] Someone's coming. It's the ladies and gentlemen. . . . [DUNYASHA *impulsively embraces him.*] Go to the house now, as though you'd been swimming down at the river. No, this way or they'll see you. I wouldn't want them to think I was interested in you.

DUNYASHA [*Coughing softly.*] That cigar has given me such a headache . . . [*Goes out.*]

[YASHA *remains sitting by the shrine. Enter* LYUBOV, GAEV *and* LOPAHIN.]

LOPAHIN You've got to make up your minds once and for all; there's no time to lose. After all, it's a simple matter. Will you lease your land for the cottages, or won't you? You can answer in one word: yes or no? Just one word!

LYUBOV Who's been smoking such wretched cigars? [*Sits down.*]

GAEV How very convenient everything is with the railroad nearby. [*Sits down.*] Well, here we are—we've been to town, had lunch and we're home already. I put the red into the middle pocket! I'd like to go in . . . just for one game. . . .

LYUBOV You've got lots of time.

LOPAHIN Just one word! [*Beseechingly.*] Please give me an answer!

GAEV [*Yawns.*] What did you say?

LYUBOV [*Looking into her purse.*] Yesterday I had lots of money, but today there's practically none left. My poor Varya feeds us all milk soups to economize; the old servants in the kitchen have nothing but dried peas, and here I am wasting money senselessly, I just don't understand it. . . . [*She drops her purse, scattering gold coins.*] Now I've dropped it again. . . . [*Annoyed.*]

YASHA Allow me, madam, I'll pick them right up. [*Picks up the money.*]

LYUBOV Thank you, Yasha . . . And why did we go out for lunch today? And that restaurant of yours . . . the food was vile, the music ghastly, and the tablecloths smelled of soap. And Leonia, why do you drink so much? And eat so much? And talk so much? Today at the restaurant you were at it again, and it was all so pointless. About the seventies, and the decadents. And to whom? Really, talking to the waiters about the decadents!

LOPAHIN Yes, that's too much.

GAEV [*Waving his hand.*] I know I'm hopeless. [*To* YASHA, *irritably.*] Why are you always bustling about in front of me?

YASHA [*Laughs.*] The minute you open your mouth I start laughing.

GAEV [*To his sister.*] Either he goes, or I do. . . .

LYUBOV Get along, Yasha, you'd better leave us now.

YASHA [*Hands the purse to* LYUBOV.] I'm going. [*He can hardly restrain his laughter.*] Right this minute. . . . [*Goes out.*]

LOPAHIN You know, that rich merchant Deriganov is thinking of buying your estate. They say he's coming to the auction himself.

LYUBOV Where did you hear that?

LOPAHIN That's what they say in town.

GAEV Our Aunt in Yaroslavl has promised to send us some money, but when and how much we don't know.

LOPAHIN How much will she send? A hundred thousand? Two hundred?

LYUBOV Well, hardly . . . Ten or fifteen thousand, perhaps. And we should be thankful for that.

LOPAHIN Forgive me for saying it, but really, in my whole life I've never met such unrealistic, unbusinesslike, queer people as you. You're told in plain language that your estate's going to be sold, and you don't seem to understand it at all.

LYUBOV But what are we to do? Please, tell us.

LOPAHIN I keep on telling you. Every day I tell you the same thing. You must lease the cherry orchard and the rest of the land for summer cottages, and you must do it now, as quickly as possible. It's almost time for the auction. Please, try to understand! Once you definitely decide to lease it for the cottages, you'll be able to borrow as much money as you like, and you'll be saved.

LYUBOV Summer cottages and vacationers! Forgive me, but it's so vulgar.

GAEV I agree with you entirely.

LOPAHIN Honestly, I'm going to burst into tears, or scream, or faint. I can't stand it any more! It's more than I can take! [*To* GAEV.] And you're an old woman!

GAEV What did you say?

LOPAHIN I said, you're an old woman!

LYUBOV [*Alarmed.*] No, don't go, please stay. I beg you! Perhaps we can think of something.

LOPAHIN What's there to think of?

LYUBOV Please don't go! I feel so much more cheerful when you're here. [*Pause.*] I keep expecting something horrible to happen . . . as though the house were going to collapse on top of us.

GAEV [*In deep thought.*] I bank it off the cushions, and then into the middle pocket. . . .

LYUBOV We've sinned too much. . . .

LOPAHIN Sinned! What sins have you . . .

GAEV [*Putting a gumdrop into his mouth.*] They say I've eaten up my fortune in gumdrops. [*Laughs.*]

LYUBOV Oh, my sins! Look at the way I've always wasted money. It's madness. And then I married a man who had nothing but debts. And he was a terrible drinker . . . Champagne killed him! And then, as if I hadn't enough misery, I fell in love with someone else. We went off together, and just at that time—it was my first punishment, a blow that broke my heart—my little boy was drowned right here in this river . . . so I went abroad. I went away for good, never to return, never to see this river again . . . I just shut my eyes and ran away in a frenzy of grief, but *he* . . . he followed me. It was so cruel and brutal of him! I bought a villa near Mentone because he fell ill there, and for three years, day and night, I never had any rest. He was very sick, and he completely exhausted me; my soul dried up completely. Then, last year when the villa had to be sold to pay the debts, I went to Paris, and there he robbed me of everything I had and left me for another woman. . . . I tried to poison myself. . . . It was all so stupid, so shameful! And then suddenly I felt an urge to come back to Russia, to my own country, to my little girl . . . [*Dries her tears.*] Oh, Lord, Lord, be merciful, forgive my sins! Don't punish me any more! [*Takes a telegram out of her pocket.*] This came from Paris today. He's asking my forgiveness, he's begging me to return. [*Tears up the telegram.*] Sounds like music somewhere. [*Listens.*]

GAEV That's our famous Jewish orchestra. Don't you remember, four violins, a flute, and a bass?

LYUBOV Are they still playing? Sometime we should have a dance and they could play for us.

LOPAHIN [*Listens.*] I can't hear anything . . . [*Sings quietly.*] "And the Germans, if you pay, will turn Russians into Frenchmen, so they say". . . [*Laughs.*] I saw a wonderful play last night. It was so funny.

LYUBOV It probably wasn't funny at all. Instead of going to plays, you should take a good look at yourself. Just think how dull your life is, and how much nonsense you talk!

LOPAHIN That's true, I admit it! Our lives are stupid . . . [*Pause.*] My father was a peasant, an idiot. He knew nothing and he taught me nothing. He only beat me when he was drunk, and always with a stick. And as a matter of fact, I'm just as much an idiot myself. I don't know anything and my handwriting's awful. I'm ashamed for people to see it—it's like a pig's.

LYUBOV You ought to get married, my friend.

LOPAHIN Yes . . . That's true.

LYUBOV You ought to marry our Varya. She's a fine girl.

LOPAHIN Yes.

LYUBOV She comes from simple people, and she works hard all day long without stopping. But the main thing is she loves you, and you've liked her for a long time yourself.

LOPAHIN Well. . . . I think it's a fine idea . . . She's a nice girl. [*Pause.*]

GAEV I've been offered a job at the bank. Six thousand a year. Did I tell you?

LYUBOV Yes, you did. You'd better stay where you are.

[FEERS *enters, bringing an overcoat.*]

FEERS [*To* GAEV.] Please put it on, sir, you might catch cold.

GAEV [*Puts on the overcoat.*] Oh, you *are* a nuisance.

FEERS You must stop this! You went off this morning without letting me know. [*Looks him over.*]

LYUBOV How you've aged, Feers!

FEERS What can I do for you, Madam?

LOPAHIN She says you've aged a lot.

FEERS I've lived for a long time. They were planning to marry me before your father was born. [*Laughs.*] Why, I was already head butler at the time of the emancipation, but I wouldn't take my freedom, I stayed on with the master and mistress. . . . [*Pause.*] I remember everyone was happy at the time, but what they were happy about, they didn't know themselves.

LOPAHIN That was the good life all right! All the peasants were flogged!

FEERS [*Not having heard him.*] That's right! The peasants belonged to their masters, and the masters belonged to the peasants; but now everything's all confused, and people don't know what to make of it.

GAEV Be quiet, Feers. Tomorrow I've got to go to town. I've been promised an introduction to some general or other who might lend us some money for the mortgage.

LOPAHIN Nothing will come of it. And how would you pay the interest, anyway?

LYUBOV He's talking nonsense again. There aren't any generals. [*Enter* TROFIMOV, ANYA *and* VARYA.]

GAEV Here come the children.

ANYA There's Mamma.

LYUBOV Come here, my dears. Oh, my darling children. . . . [*Embraces* ANYA *and* VARYA.] If you only knew how much I love you! Here now, sit down beside me. [*All sit down.*]

LOPAHIN Our perennial student is always with the girls.

TROFIMOV It's none of your business.

LOPAHIN He'll soon be fifty, and he's still a student.

TROFIMOV Oh, stop your stupid jokes.

LOPAHIN What's bothering you? My, you *are* a strange fellow!

TROFIMOV Why do you keep pestering me?

LOPAHIN [*Laughs.*] Just let me ask you one question: what's your opinion of me?

TROFIMOV My opinion of you, Yermolay Alexeyevich, is this: you're a rich man, and soon you'll be a millionaire. For the same reason that wild beasts are necessary to maintain nature's economic laws, you are necessary, too—each of you devours everything that gets in his way. [*Everybody laughs.*]

VARYA You'd better talk about the planets, Petya.

LYUBOV No, let's go on with the conversation we had yesterday.

TROFIMOV. What was that?

GAEV About pride.

TROFIMOV We talked for a long time yesterday, but we didn't agree on anything. The proud man, the way you use the word, has some mysterious quality about him. Perhaps you're right in a way, but if we look at it simply, without trying to be too subtle, you have to ask yourself why should we be proud at all? Why be proud when you realize that Man, as a species, is poorly constructed physiologically, and is usually coarse, stupid, and profoundly unhappy, too? We ought to put an end to such vanity and just go to work. That's right, we ought to work.

GAEV You'll die just the same, no matter what you do.

TROFIMOV Who knows? And anyway, what does it mean—to die? It could be that man has a hundred senses, and when he dies only the five that are known perish, while the other ninety-five go on living.

LYUBOV How clever you are, Petya!

LOPAHIN [*Ironically.*] Oh, very clever!

TROFIMOV Humanity is continually advancing, is continually seeking to perfect its powers. Someday all the things which we can't understand now, will be made clear. But if this is to happen, we've got to work, work with all our might to help those who are searching for truth. Up until now, here in Russia only a few have begun to work. Nearly all of the intelligentsia that I know have no commitment, they don't do anything, and are as yet incapable of work. They call themselves "the intelligentsia," but they still run roughshod over their servants, and they treat the peasants like animals, they study without achieving anything, they read only childish drivel, and they don't do a thing. As for their knowledge of science, it's only jargon, and they have no appreciation of art either. They are all so serious, and they go about with solemn looks on their faces; they philosophize and talk about important matters; and yet before our very eyes our workers are poorly fed, they live in the worst kind of squalor, sleeping not on beds, but on the floor thirty to forty in a room—with roaches, odors, dampness, and depravity everywhere. It's perfectly clear that all our moralizing is intended to deceive not only ourselves, but others as well. Tell me, where are the nursery schools we're always talking about, where are the libraries? We only write about them in novels, but in actuality there aren't any. There's nothing but dirt, vulgarity, and decadent Orientalism. . . . I'm afraid of those serious faces, I don't like them; I'm afraid of serious talk. It would be better if we'd just keep quiet.

LOPAHIN Well, let me tell you that *I'm* up before five every morning, and I work from morning till night. I always have money, my own and other people's, and I have lots of opportunities to see what the people around me are like. You only have to start doing something to realize how few honest, decent people there are. Sometimes, when I can't sleep, I start thinking about it. God's given us immense forests, and wide-open fields, and unlimited horizons —living in such a world we ought to be giants!

LYUBOV But why do you want giants? They're all right in fairy tales, anywhere else they're terrifying.

[EPIHODOV *crosses the stage in the background, playing his guitar.*]

LYUBOV [*Pensively.*] There goes Epihodov. . . .

ANYA [*Pensively.*] There goes Epihodov. . . .

GAEV The sun's gone down, my friends.

TROFIMOV Yes.

GAEV [*In a subdued voice, as if reciting a poem.*] Oh, glorious Nature, shining with eternal light, so beautiful, yet so indifferent to our fate . . . you, whom we call Mother, the wellspring of Life and Death, you live and you destroy. . . .

VARYA [*Imploringly.*] Uncle, please!

ANYA You're doing it again, Uncle!

TROFIMOV You'd better bank the red into middle pocket.

GAEV All right, I'll keep quiet.

[*They all sit deep in thought; the only thing that can be heard is the muttering of* FEERS. *Suddenly there is a sound in the distance, as if out of the sky, like the sound of a harp string breaking, gradually and sadly dying away.*]

LYUBOV What was that?

LOPAHIN I don't know. Sounded like a cable broke in one of the mines. But it must've been a long way off.

GAEV Perhaps it was a bird . . . a heron, maybe.

TROFIMOV Or an owl. . . .

LYUBOV [*Shudders.*] Whatever it was, it sounded unpleasant . . . [*A pause.*]

FEERS It was the same way before the disaster: the owl hooted and the samovar was humming.

GAEV What disaster?

FEERS Before they freed us. [*A pause.*]

LYUBOV We'd better get started, my friends. It's getting dark and we should get home. [*To* ANYA.] You're crying, my darling! What's wrong? [*She embraces her.*]

ANYA Nothing, Mamma. It's nothing.

TROFIMOV Someone's coming.

[*Enter* A TRAMP *in a battered white hunting cap and an overcoat; he's slightly drunk.*]

TRAMP Excuse me, but can I get to the station through here?

GAEV Yes, just follow the road.

TRAMP. Much obliged to you, sir. [*Coughs.*] It's a beautiful day today. [*Declaiming.*] "Oh, my brother, my suffering brother! . . . Come to the Volga, whose groans . . ." [*To* VARYA.] Mademoiselle, could a poor starving Russian trouble you for just enough to . . . [VARYA *cries out, frightened.*]

LOPAHIN [*Angrily.*] Really, this is too much!

LYUBOV [*At a loss what to do.*] Here, take this . . . here you are. [*Looks in her purse.*] I haven't any silver . . . but that's all right, here's a gold one. . . .

TRAMP Thank you very much! [*Goes off. Laughter.*]

VARYA [*Frightened.*] I'm going. . . . I'm going . . . Oh, Mamma, you know there's not even enough to eat in the house, and you gave him all that!

LYUBOV Well, what can you do with a silly woman like me? I'll give you everything I've got as soon as we get home. Yermolay Alexeyevich, you'll lend me some more, won't you?

LOPAHIN Why of course I will.

LYUBOV Come, it's time to go now. By the way, Varya, we've just about arranged your marriage. Congratulations!

VARYA [*Through her tears.*] Don't joke about things like that, Mother!

LOPAHIN Go to a nunnery, Okhmelia! . . .

GAEV Look at how my hands are trembling: I haven't had a game for so long.

LOPAHIN Okhmelia, nymph, remember me in your prayers!

LYUBOV Come along, everybody. It's almost supper time.

VARYA That man frightened me so. My heart's still pounding.

LOPAHIN My friends, just one thing, please just a word: the cherry orchard's to be sold on the 22nd of August. Remember that! Think of what. . . .

[*All go out except* TROFIMOV *and* ANYA.]

ANYA [*Laughs.*] We can thank the tramp for a chance to be alone! He frightened Varya so.

TROFIMOV Varya's afraid—she's afraid we might fall in love—so she follows us about all day long. She's so narrow-minded, she can't understand that we're above falling in love. To free ourselves of all that's petty and ephemeral, all that prevents us from being free and happy, that's the whole aim and meaning of our life. Forward! We march forward irresistibly towards that bright star shining there in the distance! Forward! Don't fall behind, friends!

ANYA [*Raising her hands.*] How beautifully you talk! [*A pause.*] It's wonderful here today.

TROFIMOV Yes, the weather's marvelous.

ANYA What have you done to me, Petya? Why don't I love the cherry orchard like I used to? I used to love it so very much I used to think that there wasn't a better place in all the world than our orchard.

TROFIMOV The whole of Russia is our orchard. The earth is great and beautiful and there are many wonderful places in it. [*A pause.*] Just think, Anya: Your grandfather, and your great grandfather, and all your ancestors were serf owners—they owned living souls. Don't you see human beings staring at you from every tree in the orchard, from every leaf and every trunk? Don't you hear their voices? . . . They owned living souls—and it has made you all different persons, those who came before you, and you who are living now, so that your mother, your uncle and you yourself don't even notice that you're living on credit, at the expense of other people, people you don't admit any further than your kitchen. We're at least two hundred years behind the times; we have no real values, no sense of our past, we just philosophize and complain of how depressed we feel, and drink vodka. Yet it's obvious that if we're ever to live in the present, we must first atone for our past

orchard ugly because of serfs that were killed

and make a clean break with it, and we can only atone for it by suffering, by extraordinary, unceasing work. You've got to understand that, Anya.

ANYA The house we live in hasn't really been ours for a long time. I'll leave it, I promise you.

TROFIMOV Yes, leave it, and throw away the keys. Be free as the wind.

ANYA [*In rapture.*] How beautifully you say things.

TROFIMOV You must believe me, Anya, you must. I'm not thirty yet, I'm young, and I'm still a student, but I've suffered so much already. As soon as winter comes, I'll be hungry and sick and nervous, poor as a beggar. Fate has driven me everywhere! And yet, my soul is always—every moment of every day and every night—it's always full of such marvelous hopes and visions. I have a premonition of happiness, Anya, I can sense it's coming. . . .

ANYA [*Pensively.*] The moon's coming up.

[EPIHODOV *is heard playing the same melancholy tune on his guitar. The moon comes up. Somewhere near the poplars* VARYA *is looking for* ANYA *and calling.*]

VARYA [*Off-stage.*] Anya! Where are you?

TROFIMOV Yes, the moon is rising. [*A pause.*] There it is—happiness—it's coming nearer and nearer. Already, I can hear its footsteps. And if we never see it, if we never know it, what does it matter? Others will see it!

[VARYA'*s voice.*] Anya! Where are you?

TROFIMOV It's Varya again! [*Angrily.*] It's disgusting!

ANYA Well? Let's go to the river. It's lovely there.

TROFIMOV Yes, let's. [TROFIMOV *and* ANYA *go out.*]

[VARYA'*s voice.*] Anya! Anya!

[*Curtain.*]

ACT III

The drawing room separated by an arch from the ballroom. The same Jewish orchestra that was mentioned in Act II, is playing off-stage. The chandelier is lighted. It is evening. In the ballroom they are dancing the Grand-rond. SEMYONOV-PISHCHIK *is heard calling: "Promenade à une paire!" Then they all enter the drawing room.* PISHCHIK *and* CHARLOTTA IVANOVNA *are the first couple, followed by* TROFIMOV *and* LYUBOV, ANYA *and a* POST-OFFICE CLERK, VARYA *and* THE STATION MASTER, *etc.* VARYA *is crying softly and wipes away her tears as she dances.* DUNYASHA *is in the last couple.* PISHCHIK *shouts: "Grand rond balancez!" and "Les cavaliers à genoux et remerciez vos dames!"* FEERS, *wearing a dress coat, crosses the room with soda water on a tray.* PISHCHIK *and* TROFIMOV *come back into the drawing room.*

PISHCHIK I've got this high blood-pressure—I've had two strokes already, you know—and it makes dancing hard work for me; but, as they say, if you're one of a pack, you wag your tail, whether you bark or not. Actually I'm as strong as a horse. My dear father —may he rest in peace—had a little joke. He used to say that the ancient line of Semyonov-Pishchik was decended from the very same horse that Caligula made a member of the Senate. [*Sitting down.*] But my trouble is, I haven't any money. A starving dog can think of nothing but food . . . [*Starts to snore, but wakes up almost at once.*] That's just like me—I can't think of anything but money . . .

TROFIMOV You know, you're right, there *is* something horsy about you.

PISHCHIK Well, a horse is a fine animal, you can sell a horse. . . .

[*The sound of someone playing billiards is heard in the next room.* VARYA *appears under the arch to the ballroom.*]

TROFIMOV [*Teasing her.*] Madame Lopahin! Madame Lopahin!

VARYA [*Angrily.*] The "moth-eaten man!"

TROFIMOV Yes, I am a moth-eaten man, and I'm proud of it.

VARYA [*Thinking bitterly.*] Now we've hired an orchestra—but how are we going to pay for it? [*Goes out.*]

TROFIMOV [*To* PISHCHIK.] If all the energy you've spent during your life looking for money to pay the interest on your debts had been used for something useful, you'd have probably turned the world upside down by now.

PISHCHIK The philosopher Nietzsche, the greatest, the most famous—a man of the greatest intelligence, in fact—says its quite allright to counterfeit.

TROFIMOV Oh, you've read Nietzsche?

PISHCHIK Of course not, Dashenka told me. But right now I'm in such an impossible position that I could forge a few notes. The day after tomorrow I've got to pay 310 roubles. I've borrowed 130 already. . . . [*Feels in his pockets, in alarm.*] The money's gone! I've lost the money. [*Tearfully.*] Where's the money? [*Joyfully.*] Oh, here it is, inside the lining! I'm so upset, I'm sweating all over! . . . [*Enter* LYUBOV *and* CHARLOTTA.]

LYUBOV [*Humming the "Lezginka."*] What's taking Leonid so long? What's he doing in town? [*To* DUNYASHA.] Dunyasha, offer the musicians some tea.

TROFIMOV The auction was probably postponed.

LYUBOV The orchestra came at the wrong time, and the party started at the wrong time . . . Oh, well . . . never mind . . . [*She sits down and hums quietly.*]

CHARLOTTA [*Hands a deck of cards to* PISHCHIK.] Here's a deck of cards—think of any card.

PISHCHIK I've thought of one.

CHARLOTTA Now shuffle the deck. That's right. Now give it to me, my dear Monsieur Pishchik. *"Ein, zwei, drei!"* Why look! There it is, in your coat pocket.

PISHCHIK [*Takes the card out of his coat pocket.*] The eight of spades, that's right! [*In astonishment.*] Isn't that amazing!

CHARLOTTA [*Holding the deck of cards on the palm of her hand, to* TROFIMOV.] Quickly, which card's on the top?

TROFIMOV Well . . . ahh . . . the queen of spades.

CHARLOTTA You're right, here it is! Now, which card?

PISHCHIK The ace of hearts.

CHARLOTTA Right again! [*She claps her hand over the pack of cards, which disappears.*] What beautiful weather we're having today! [*A woman's voice, as if coming from underneath the floor, answers her.*]

VOICE Oh yes, indeed, the weather's perfectly marvelous!

CHARLOTTA [*Addressing the voice.*] How charming you are! I'm fond of you!

VOICE And I like you very much, too.

STATION MASTER [*Applauding.*] Bravo, Madame ventriloquist! Bravo!

PISHCHIK [*Astonished.*] Isn't that amazing! Charlotta Ivanovna, you're absolutely wonderful! I'm completely in love with you!

CHARLOTTA [*Shrugging her shoulders.*] In love? What do you know about love? *"Guter Mensch, aber schlechter Musikant."*

TROFIMOV [*Slaps* PISHCHIK *on the shoulder.*] He's just an old horse, he is!

CHARLOTTA Your attention please! Here's one more trick. [*She takes a shawl from a chair.*] Now there's this very nice shawl . . . [*Shakes it out.*] Who'd like to buy it?

PISHCHIK [*Amazed.*] Imagine that!

CHARLOTTA *"Ein, zwei, drei!"*

[*She lifts up the shawl and* ANYA *is standing behind it;* ANYA *curtsies, runs to her mother, gives her a hug, and runs back to the ballroom. Everybody's delighted.*]

LYUBOV [*Clapping.*] Bravo, bravo!

CHARLOTTA Once more. *"Ein, zwei, drei!"*

[*Lifts the shawl again; behind it is* VARYA, *who bows.*]

PISHCHIK [*Amazed.*] Isn't that amazing!

CHARLOTTA It's all over! [*She throws the shawl over* PISHCHIK, *curtsies, and runs into the ballroom.*]

PISHCHIK [*Going after her.*] You little rascal! . . . Have you ever seen anything like her? What a girl . . . [*Goes out.*]

LYUBOV Leonid's still not here. I can't understand what's keeping him all this time in town. Anyway, by now everything's been settled; either the estate's been sold or the auction didn't take place. Why does he wait so long to let us know?

VARYA [*Trying to comfort her.*] Uncle's bought it, I'm sure he did.

TROFIMOV [*Sarcastically.*] Why of course he did!

VARYA Our great-aunt sent him power of attorney to buy it in her name, and transfer the mortgage to her. She's done it for Anya's sake . . . God will look after us, I'm sure of it—Uncle will buy the estate.

LYUBOV Your great-aunt sent us fifteen thousand to buy the estate in her name—she doesn't trust us—but that's not enough to even pay the interest. [*She covers her face with her hands.*] My fate is being decided today, my fate. . . .

TROFIMOV [*To* VARYA, *teasingly.*] Madame Lopahin!

VARYA [*Crossly.*] The perpetual student! Why, you've been thrown out of the University twice already!

LYUBOV But why get so cross, Varya? He's only teasing you about Lopahin, there's no harm in that, is there? If you want to, why don't you marry him; he's a fine man, and he's interesting, too. Of course, if you don't want to, don't. No one's trying to force you, darling.

VARYA I'm very serious about this, Mother . . . and I want to be frank with you . . . he's a good man and I like him.

LYUBOV Then marry him. What are you waiting for? I don't understand you at all.

VARYA But, Mother, I can't propose to him myself, can I? It's been two years now since everybody began talking to me about him, and everybody's talking, but he doesn't say a word, or when he does, he just jokes with me. I understand, of course. He's getting rich and his mind's busy with other things, and he hasn't any time for me. If only I had some money, even a little, just a hundred roubles, I'd leave everything and go away, the farther the better. I'd go into a convent.

TROFIMOV How beautiful!

VARYA [*To* TROFIMOV.] Of course, a student like you has to be so intelligent! [*Quietly and tearfully.*] How ugly you've become, Petya, how much older you look! [*To* LYUBOV, *her tearfulness gone.*] The only thing I can't stand, Mother, is not having any work to do. I've got to stay busy.

[*Enter* YASHA.]

YASHA [*With difficulty restraining his laughter.*] Epihodov's broken a cue! . . . [*Goes out.*]

VARYA But what's Epihodov doing here? Who let him play billiards? I don't understand these people. . . . [*Goes out.*]

LYUBOV Please don't tease her, Petya. Don't you see she's upset already?

TROFIMOV Oh, she's such a busy-body—always sticking her nose into other people's business. She hasn't left Anya and me alone all summer. She's afraid we might fall in love. What difference should it make to her? Besides, I didn't give her any reason to think so. I don't believe in such trivialities. We're above love!

LYUBOV And I suppose I'm below love. [*Uneasily.*] Why isn't Leonid back? If only I knew whether the estate's been sold or not. It's such an incredible calamity that for some reason I don't know what to think, I feel so helpless. I think I'm going to scream this very minute . . . I'll do something silly. Help me, Petya. Talk to me, say something!

TROFIMOV What difference does it make whether the estate's sold today or not? It was gone a long time ago. You can't turn back, the path's lost. You mustn't worry, and above all you mustn't deceive yourself. For once in your life you must look the truth straight in the face.

LYUBOV What truth? You know what truth is and what it isn't, but I've lost such visionary powers. I don't see anything. You're able to solve all your problems so decisively—but, tell me, my dear boy, isn't that because you're young, because life is still hidden from your young eyes, because you can't believe anything horrible will ever happen to you and you don't expect it to? Oh, yes, you're more courageous and honest and serious than we are, but put yourself in our position, try to be generous—if only a little bit—and have pity on me. I was born here, you know, and my father and mother lived here, and my grandfather, too, and I love this house—I can't conceive of life without the cherry orchard, and if it really has to be sold, then sell me with it . . . [*Embraces* TROFIMOV, *kisses him on the forehead.*] You know, my little boy was drowned here. . . . [*Weeps.*] Have pity on me, my dear, kind friend.

TROFIMOV You know that I sympathize with you from the bottom of my heart.

LYUBOV But you should say it differently . . . differently. [*Takes out her handkerchief and a telegram falls on to the floor.*] There's so much on my mind today, you can't imagine. It's so noisy around here that my soul trembles with every sound, and I'm shaking all over—yet I can't go to my room because the silence of being alone frightens me. . . . Don't blame me, Petya. . . . I love you as if you were my own son. I'd gladly let Anya marry you, honestly I would, but, my dear boy, you must study, you've got to graduate. You don't do anything, Fate tosses you from one place to another —it's so strange—Well, it is, isn't it? Isn't it? And you should do something about your beard, make it grow somehow. . . . [*Laughs.*] You look so funny!

TROFIMOV [*Picks up the telegram.*] I don't care how I look. That's so superficial.

LYUBOV This telegram's from Paris. I get one every day . . . Yesterday, today. That beast is sick again, and everything's going wrong for him. . . . He wants me to forgive him, he begs me to return, and, really, I suppose I should go to Paris and stay with him for awhile. You're looking very stern, Petya, but what am I to do, my dear boy, what am I to do? He's sick, and lonely, and unhappy, and who'll take care of him, who'll stop him from making a fool of himself, and give him his medicine at the right time? And anyway, why should I hide it, or keep quiet about it? I love him; yes, I love him. I do, I do. . . . He's a stone around my neck, and I'm sinking to the bottom with him—but I love him and I can't live without him. [*She presses* TROFIMOV*'s hand.*] Don't think I'm evil, Petya, don't say anything, please don't. . . .

TROFIMOV [*With strong emotion.*] Please—forgive my frankness, but that man's swindling you!

LYUBOV No, no, no, you mustn't talk like that. . . . [*Puts her hands over her ears.*]

TROFIMOV But he's a scoundrel, and you're the only one who doesn't know it! He's a despicable, worthless scoundrel. . . .

LYUBOV [*Angry, but in control of herself.*] You're twenty-six or twenty-seven years old, but you're talking like a schoolboy!

TROFIMOV Say whatever you want!

LYUBOV You should be a man at your age, you ought to understand what it means to be in love. And you should be in love. . . . Tell me, why haven't you fallen in love! [*Angrily.*] Yes, yes! Oh, you're not so "pure," your purity is a perversion, you're nothing but a ridiculous prude, a freak. . . .

TROFIMOV [*Horrified.*] What is she saying?

LYUBOV "I'm above love!" You're not above love, you're useless, as Feers would say. Imagine not having a mistress at your age! . . .

TROFIMOV [*Horrified.*] This is terrible! What's she saying? [*Goes quickly towards the ballroom, clutching his head between his hands.*] This is dreadful. . . . I can't stand it, I'm going. . . . [*Goes out, but returns at once.*] Everything's over between us! [*Goes out through the door into the hall.*]

LYUBOV [*Calls after him.*] Petya, wait! You funny boy, I was only joking! Petya!

[*Someone can be heard running quickly downstairs and suddenly falling down with a crash.* ANYA *and* VARYA *scream, and then begin laughing.*]

What's happened?

[ANYA *runs in.*]

ANYA [*Laughing.*] Petya fell down the stairs. [*Runs out.*]

LYUBOV What a strange boy he is!

[*The* STATION MASTER *stands in the middle of the ballroom and begins to recite "The Sinner" by Alexey Tolstoy. The others listen to him, but he's hardly had time to recite more than a little bit when a waltz is played, and he stops. Everyone dances.* TROFIMOV, ANYA, VARYA *come in from the hall.*]

Poor Petya . . . there, my dear boy . . . Please forgive me . . . Come, let's dance . . . [*She dances with* PETYA. ANYA *and* VARYA *dance. Enter* FEERS, *then* YASHA. FEERS *leans on his cane by the side door.* YASHA *looks at the dancers from the drawing room.*]

YASHA How are you, old boy?

FEERS Not too well . . . We used to have generals, barons,

and admirals at our parties . . . long ago, but now we send for the post-office clerk and the station master, and even they don't want to come it seems. I seem to be getting weaker somehow . . . My old master, the mistress' grandfather, used to make everyone take sealing wax no matter what was wrong with them. I've been taking it every day for the last twenty years, maybe even longer. Perhaps that's why I'm still alive.

YASHA How you bore me, old man! [*Yawns.*] Why don't you just go away and die . . . It's about time.

FEERS Eh, you! . . . You're useless . . . [*Mutters.*]

[TROFIMOV *and* LYUBOV *dancing, come into the drawing room.*]

LYUBOV Thank you. I think I'll sit down for a bit. [*Sits down.*] I'm tired.

[*Enter* ANYA.]

ANYA [*Agitated.*] There's a man in the kitchen who's been saying that the cherry orchard was sold today.

LYUBOV Sold? To whom?

ANYA He didn't say. He's gone.

[*She and* TROFIMOV *dance into the ballroom.*]

YASHA There was some old man gossiping there. A stranger.

FEERS Leonid Andreyevich isn't back yet, he hasn't come yet. And he's only got his light overcoat on; he'll probably catch a cold. Oh, these youngsters!

LYUBOV I've got to know, or I think I'll die. Yasha, go and find out who bought it.

YASHA But the old guy went away a long time ago. [*Laughs.*]

LYUBOV [*With a touch of annoyance.*] What are you laughing at? What's so humorous?

YASHA Epihodov's so funny—he's so stupid. Two-and-twenty misfortunes!

LYUBOV Feers, if the estate's sold, where will you go?

FEERS I'll go wherever you tell me to go.

LYUBOV Why are you looking like that? Aren't you well? You ought to be in bed.

FEERS Yes . . . [*With a faint smile.*] But if I went to bed, who'd take care of the guests and keep things going? There's no one in the house but me.

YASHA [*To* LYUBOV.] Lyubov Andreyevna! I want to ask you something! If you go back to Paris, will you please take me with you? I couldn't stand staying here. [*Looking round and speaking in a low voice.*] I don't have to say it, you can see for yourself how uncivilized everything is here. The people are immoral, it's frightfully dull, and the food is terrible. And then there's that Feers walking about the place and muttering all sorts of stupid things. Take me with you, please!

[*Enter* PISHCHIK.]

PISHCHIK May I have this dance, beautiful lady . . . [LYUBOV *gets up to dance.*] I'll have that 180 roubles from you yet, you enchantress . . . Yes, I will . . . [*Dances.*] Just 180 roubles, that's all . . . [*They go into the ballroom.*]

YASHA [*Sings quietly.*] "Don't you understand the passion in my soul? . . .

[*In the ballroom a woman in a grey top hat and check trousers starts jumping and throwing her arms about; shouts of*: "Bravo, Charlotta Ivanovna!"]

DUNYASHA [*Stops to powder her face.*] Anya told me to dance: there are so many men and not enough ladies; but I get so dizzy from dancing and it makes my heart beat so fast. Feers Nikolayevich, the post-office clerk said something to me just now that completely took my breath away. [*The music stops.*]

FEERS What did he say?

DUNYASHA You're like a flower, he said.

YASHA [*Yawns.*] What ignorance! . . . [*Goes out.*]

DUNYASHA Like a flower . . . I'm so sensitive, I love it when people say beautiful things to me.

FEERS You'll be having your head turned if you're not careful.

[*Enter* EPIHODOV.]

EPIHODOV Avdotya Fyodorovna, you act as if you don't want to see me . . . as if I were some kind of insect. [*Sighs.*] Such is life!

DUNYASHA What do you want?

EPIHODOV But then, you may be right. [*Sighs.*] Of course, if one looks at it from a certain point of view—if I may so express myself, and please excuse my frankness, you've driven me into such a state . . . Oh, I know what my fate is; every day some misfortune's sure to happen to me, but I've long since been accustomed to that, so I look at life with a smile. You gave me your word, and though I . . .

DUNYASHA Please, let's talk later, just let me alone now. I'm lost in a dream. [*Plays with her fan.*]

EPIHODOV Some misfortune happens to me every day, but I—how should I put it—I just smile, I even laugh.

[VARYA *enters from the ballroom.*]

VARYA Are you still here, Semyon? Your manners are abominable, really! [*To* DUNYASHA.] You'd better go now, Dunyasha. [*To* EPIHODOV.] First you play billiards and break a cue, and now you're going about the drawing room, like one of the guests.

EPIHODOV Permit me to inform you, but you have no right to attack me like this.

VARYA I'm not attacking, I'm telling you. You just wander from one place to another, instead of doing your work. We've hired a clerk, but why no one knows.

EPIHODOV [*Offended.*] Whether I work, wander, eat, or play billiards, the only people who are entitled to judge my actions are those who are older than me and have some idea of what they're talking about.

VARYA How dare you say that to me? [*Beside herself in anger.*] You dare to say that? Are you suggesting that I don't know what I'm talking about? Get out of here! Right now!

EPIHODOV [*Cowed.*] I wish you'd express yourself more delicately.

VARYA [*Beside herself.*] Get out this minute! Get out! [*He goes to the door, she follows him.*] Two-and-twenty misfortunes! Get out of here! I don't want ever to see you again!

EPIHODOV [*Goes out; his voice is heard from outside the door.*] I'm going to complain.

VARYA Oh, you're coming back, are you? [*She seizes the stick which* FEERS *left by the door.*] Well, come along, come in . . . I'll show you! So, you're coming back . . . are you? There, take that . . . [*Swings the stick, and at that moment* LOPAHIN *comes in.*]

LOPAHIN [*Whom the stick did not, in fact, touch.*] Thank you very much!

VARYA [*Angry and ironically.*] I'm sorry!

LOPAHIN Don't mention it. I'm much obliged to you for the kind reception.

VARYA That's quite all right. [*Walks away and then looks around and asks gently.*] I haven't hurt you, have I?

LOPAHIN No, not at all. . . . But there's going to be a huge bump, though.

VOICES [*In the ballroom.*] Lopahin's here! Yermolay Alexeyevich!

PISHCHIK There he is! You can see him, do you hear him? . . . [*Embraces* LOPAHIN.] You smell of cognac, my good fellow! . . . Well we're having a party here, too.

[*Enter* LYUBOV.]

LYUBOV It's you, Yermolay Alexeyevich? What's taken you so long? Where's Leonid?

LOPAHIN Leonid Andreyevich's here, he'll be along in a minute.

LYUBOV [*Agitated.*] Well, what happened? Was there an auction? Tell me!

LOPAHIN [*Embarrassed, afraid of betraying his joy.*] The auction was over by four o'clock . . . We missed our train and had to wait until nine-thirty. [*Sighs heavily.*] Ugh! I feel a little dizzy . . .

[*Enter* GAEV; *he carries packages in his right hand and wipes away his tears with his left.*]

LYUBOV Leonia, what happened? Leonia? [*Impatiently, with tears.*] Tell me quickly, for God's sake! . . .

GAEV [*Doesn't answer, but waves his hand. To* FEERS, *crying.*] Here, take these . . . it's some anchovies and Kerch herrings . . . I haven't eaten all day . . . What I've been through!

[*Through the open door leading to the ballroom a game of billiards can be heard and* YASHA'*s voice is heard.*]

YASHA Seven and eighteen.

GAEV [*His expression changes and he stops crying.*] I'm very tired. Come, Feers, I want to change my things. [*Goes out through the ballroom, followed by* FEERS.]

PISHCHIK Well, what happened at the auction? Come on, tell us!

LYUBOV Has the cherry orchard been sold?

LOPAHIN It has.

LYUBOV Who bought it?

LOPAHIN I did.

[*A pause.* LYUBOV *is overcome; only the fact that she is standing beside a table and a chair keeps her from falling.* VARYA *takes the keys from her belt, throws them on the floor in the middle of the room and goes out.*]

I bought it. Wait a moment, ladies and gentlemen, please. I'm so mixed up, I don't quite know what to say . . . [*Laughs.*] When we got to the auction, Deriganov was already there. Leonid had only fifteen thousand roubles, and immediately Deriganov bid thirty thousand over and above the mortgage. I saw how things were, so I stepped in and raised it to forty. He bid forty-five, I went to fifty-five; he kept on raising five thousand and I raised it ten thousand. Well, finally it ended—I bid ninety thousand over and above the mortgage, and it went to me. The cherry orchard's mine now! All right, tell me I'm drunk, tell me I'm crazy and that I'm just imagining all this. . . . [*Stamps his feet.*] Don't laugh at me! If only my father and grandfather could rise from their graves and see all that's happened . . . how their Yermolay, their ignorant, beaten Yermolay, the little boy that ran around in his bare feet in the winter . . . if only they could see that he's bought this estate, the most beautiful place in the world! Yes, he's bought the very estate where his father and grandfather were slaves and where they weren't even admitted to the kitchen! I must be asleep, I'm dreaming, it only seems to be true . . . it's all just my imagination, my imagination must be confused . . . [*Picks up the keys, smiling gently.*] She threw these down because she wanted to show that she's not the mistress here anymore. [*Jingles the keys.*] Well, never mind. [*The orchestra is heard tuning up.*] Hey there! you musicians, play something for us! I want some music! My friends, come along and soon you'll see Yermolay Lopahin take an axe to the cherry orchard, you'll see the trees come crashing to the ground! We're going to build hundreds of summer cottages, and our children and our grandchildren will see a whole new world growing up here . . . So play, let's have some music!

[*The band plays.* LYUBOV *has sunk into a chair and is crying bitterly. Reproachfully.*]

Why, why didn't you listen to me? My poor, dear lady, you'll never get it back now. [*With tears.*] Oh, if only all this could be over soon, if only we could change this unhappy and disjointed life of ours somehow!

PISHCHIK [*Taking his arm, in a low voice.*] She's crying. Come into the ballroom, let her be by herself . . . Come on . . . [*Takes his arm and leads him away to the ballroom.*]

LOPAHIN What's the matter! Where's the music? Come on, play! Play! Everything will be as *I* want it now. [*Ironically.*] Here comes the new owner, here comes the owner of the cherry orchard! [*He tips over a little table accidentally and nearly upsets the candelabra.*] Don't worry about it, I can pay for everything! [*Goes out with* PISHCHIK. *There is no one left in the ballroom or drawing room, but* LYUBOV, *who sits huddled up in a chair, crying bitterly. The orchestra continues to play quietly.* ANYA *and* TROFIMOV *enter quickly;* ANYA *goes up to her mother and kneels beside her,* TROFIMOV *remains at the entrance to the ballroom.*]

ANYA Mamma! . . . Mamma, you're crying. Dear, kind, good Mamma, my precious one, I love you! God bless you, Mamma! The cherry orchard's sold, that's true, it's gone, but don't cry, Mamma, you still have your life ahead of you, you still have your good, innocent heart. You must come with me, Mamma, away from here! We'll plant a new orchard, even more wonderful than this one—and when you see it, you'll understand everything, and your heart will be filled with joy, like the sun in the evening; and then you'll smile again, Mamma! Come, dearest one, come with me! . . .

[*Curtain.*]

ACT IV

The same setting as for Act I. There are no pictures on the walls, or curtains at the windows; most of the furniture is gone and the few remaining pieces are stacked in a corner, as if for sale. There is a sense of desolation. Beside the door, suitcases and other luggage have been piled together. The voices of VARYA *and* ANYA *can be heard through the door on the left, which is open.* LOPAHIN *stands waiting;* YASHA *is holding a tray with glasses of champagne. In the hall* EPIHODOV *is tying up a large box. Off-stage there is a low hum of voices; the peasants have called to say good-bye.* GAEV*'s voice from off-stage.*

GAEV Thank you, friends, thank you.

YASHA The peasants have come to say good-bye. In my opinion, Yermolay Alexeyevich, they're good people, but they don't know much.

[*The hum subsides.* LYUBOV *and* GAEV *enter from the hall;* LYUBOV *is not crying but her face is pale and it quivers. She is unable to speak.*]

GAEV You gave them everything you had, Lyuba. You shouldn't have done that. You really shouldn't.

LYUBOV I couldn't help it! I couldn't help it! [*Both go out.*]

LOPAHIN [*Calls after them through the door.*] Please, have some champagne, please do! Just a little glass before you go. I didn't think to bring some from town, and at the station I could find only this one bottle. Please have some. [*A pause.*] You don't want any, my friends? [*Walks away from the door.*] If I'd known that, I wouldn't have brought it. . . . Well, then I won't have any either. [YASHA *carefully puts the tray on a chair.*] Have a drink, Yasha, nobody else wants any.

YASHA To the travelers! And to those staying behind. [*Drinks.*] This champagne isn't the real thing, believe me.

LOPAHIN What do you mean, eight roubles a bottle. [*A pause.*] God, it's cold in here.

YASHA The stoves weren't lit today. What difference does it make since we're leaving? [*Laughs.*]

LOPAHIN Why are you laughing?

YASHA Because I feel good.

LOPAHIN It's October already, but it's still sunny and clear, just like summer. Good building weather. [*Looks at his watch, then at the door.*] Ladies and gentlemen, the train leaves in forty-seven minutes. We've got to start in twenty minutes. So hurry up.

[TROFIMOV, *wearing an overcoat, comes in from outdoors.*]

TROFIMOV It's time we get started. The horses are ready. God knows where my goloshes are, they've disappeared. [*Calls through the door.*] Anya, my goloshes aren't here; I can't find them.

LOPAHIN I've got to go to Kharkov. I'm taking the same train. I'll be spending the winter in Kharkov: I've stayed around here too long, and it drives me crazy having nothing to do. I can't be without work: I just don't know what to do with my hands; they hang there, as if they didn't belong to me.

TROFIMOV We'll be gone soon, then you can start making money again.

LOPAHIN Have a drink.

TROFIMOV No, thanks.

LOPAHIN So, you're going to Moscow?

TROFIMOV Yes, I'll go with them to town, and then, tomorrow I'll leave for Moscow.

LOPAHIN I suppose the professors are waiting for you to come before they begin classes.

TROFIMOV That's none of your business.

LOPAHIN How many years have you been studying at the university?

TROFIMOV Can't you say something new for a change, that's getting pretty old. [*Looks for his goloshes.*] By the way, since we probably won't see each other again, let me give you a bit of advice, as we say good-bye: stop waving your arms! Try to get rid of that habit of making wide, sweeping gestures. And another thing, all this talk about building estates, these calculations about summer tourists that are going to buy property, all these predictions —they're all sweeping gestures, too. . . . You know, in spite of everything, I like you. You've got beautiful delicate fingers, like an artist's, you've a fine, sensitive soul. . . .

LOPAHIN [*Embraces him.*] Good-bye, my friend. Thanks for everything. I can give you some money for your trip, if you need it.

TROFIMOV What for? I don't need it.

LOPAHIN But you haven't got any!

TROFIMOV Yes, I have, thank you. I got some money for a translation. Here it is, in my pocket. [*Anxiously.*] But I can't find my goloshes.

VARYA [*From the other room.*] Here, take the nasty things! [*She throws a pair of rubber goloshes into the room.*]

TROFIMOV What are you so angry about, Varya? Hm . . . but these aren't my goloshes!

LOPAHIN I sowed three thousand acres of poppies last spring, and I've made forty thousand on it. And when they were in bloom, what a picture it was! What I mean to say is that I've made the forty thousand, so now I can lend you some money. Why be so stuck up? So I'm a peasant . . . I speak right out.

TROFIMOV Your father was a peasant, mine was a druggist. What's that got to do with it? [LOPAHIN *takes out his wallet.*] Forget it, put it away . . . Even if you offered me two hundred thousand, I wouldn't take it. I'm a free man. And all that you rich men—and poor men too—all that you value so highly doesn't have the slightest power over me—it's all just so much fluff floating about in the air. I'm strong and I'm proud! I can get along without you, I can pass you by. Humanity is advancing towards the highest truth, the greatest happiness that it's possible to achieve on earth, and I'm one of the avant-garde!

LOPAHIN Will you get there?

TROFIMOV Yes. [*A pause.*] I'll get there myself, or show others the way to get there.

[*The sound of an axe hitting a tree is heard in the distance.*]

LOPAHIN Well, my friend, it's time to go. Good-bye. We show off in front of one another, and all the time life is slipping by. When I work all day long, without resting, I'm happier and sometimes I even think I know why I exist. But how many people there are in Russia, my friend, who exist for no reason at all. But, never mind, it doesn't matter. They say Leonid Andreyevich has a job at the bank, at six thousand a year. That won't last long; he's too lazy. . . .

ANYA [*In the doorway.*] Mamma begs you not to let them cut down the orchard until we've left.

TROFIMOV Really, haven't you got any tact? [*Goes out through the hall.*]

LOPAHIN All right, I'll take care of it. . . . These people! [*Follows* TROFIMOV.]

ANYA Has Feers been taken to the hospital?

YASHA I told them to take him this morning. He's gone, I think.

ANYA [*To* EPIHODOV, *who passes through the ballroom.*] Semyon Pantaleyevich, will you please find out whether Feers has been taken to the hospital?

YASHA [*Offended.*] I told Yegor this morning. Why ask a dozen times?

EPIHODOV That old Feers—frankly speaking, I mean—he's beyond repair, it's time he joined his ancestors. As for me, I can only envy him. [*He places a suitcase on top of a cardboard hatbox and squashes it.*] There you are, you see! . . . I might have known it! [*Goes out.*]

YASHA [*Sardonically.*] Two-and-twenty misfortunes!

VARYA [*From behind the door.*] Has Feers been taken to the hospital?

ANYA Yes.

VARYA Why wasn't the letter to the doctor taken then?

ANYA I'll send someone after them with it . . . [*Goes out.*]

VARYA [*From the adjoining room.*] Where's Yasha? Tell him his mother is here and wants to say good-bye to him.

YASHA [*Waves his hand.*] This is too much! I'll lose my patience.

[*While the foregoing action has been taking place,* DUNYASHA *has been busy with the luggage; now that* YASHA *is alone, she comes up to him.*]

DUNYASHA If only you'd look at me just once, Yasha! You're

going . . . you're leaving me! . . . [*She cries and throws her arms round his neck.*]

YASHA What are you crying for? [*Drinks champagne.*] In a week I'll be in Paris again. Tomorrow we'll get on the train—and off we'll go—gone! I can't believe it. "*Vive la France!*" I can't stand it here and could never live here—nothing ever happens. I've seen enough of all this ignorance. I've had enough of it. [*Drinks.*] What are you crying for? Behave yourself properly, then you won't cry.

DUNYASHA [*Looking into a handmirror and powdering her nose.*] Please, write to me from Paris. You know how much I've loved you, Yasha. Oh, I've loved you so much! I'm very sensitive, Yasha!

YASHA Sshh, someone's coming. [*Pretends to be busy with a suitcase, humming quietly.*]

[*Enter* LYUBOV ANDREYEVNA, GAEV, ANYA *and* CHARLOTTA IVANOVNA.]

GAEV We've got to leave soon. There isn't much time left. [*Looks at* YASHA.] What a smell! Who's been eating herring?

LYUBOV We'll have to leave in the carriage in ten minutes. [*Looks about the room.*] Good-bye, dear house, the home of our fathers. Winter will pass and spring will come again, and then you won't be here any more, you'll be torn down. How much these walls have seen! [*Kisses her daughter passionately.*] My little treasure, how radiant you look, your eyes are shining like diamonds. Are you glad? Very glad?

ANYA Oh, yes, very glad, Mamma! Our new life is just beginning!

GAEV [*Gaily.*] Really, everything's all right now. Before the cherry orchard was sold we were all worried and upset, but as soon as things were settled once and for all, we all calmed down and even felt quite cheerful. I'm working in a bank now, a real financier. . . . The red into the side pocket . . . And say what you like, Lyuba, you're looking much better. No doubt about it.

LYUBOV Yes, that's true, my nerves are better. [*Someone helps her on with her hat and coat.*] I'm sleeping better, too. Take out my things, Yasha, it's time. [*To* ANYA.] My little darling, we'll be seeing each other again soon. I'm going to Paris—I'll live on the money which your Grandmother sent us to buy the estate—God bless Grandmamma!—but that money won't last very long either.

ANYA You'll come back soon, Mamma . . . won't you? I'll study and pass my exams and then I'll work and help you. We'll read together, Mamma . . . all sorts of things . . . won't we? [*She kisses her mother's hands.*] We'll read during the long autumn evenings. We'll read lots of books, and a new wonderful world will open up before us . . . [*Dreamily.*] Mamma, come back soon . . .

LYUBOV I'll come back, my precious. [*Embraces her.*]

[*Enter* LOPAHIN. CHARLOTTA *quietly sings to herself.*]

GAEV Happy Charlotta! She's singing.

CHARLOTTA [*Picks up a bundle that looks like a baby in a blanket.*] Bye-bye, little baby. [*A sound like a baby crying is heard.*] Hush, be quiet, my darling, be a good little boy. [*The "crying" continues.*] Oh, my baby, you poor thing! [*Throws the bundle down.*] Are you going to find me another job? If you don't mind, I've got to have one.

LOPAHIN We'll find you one, Charlotta Ivanovna, don't worry.

GAEV Everybody's leaving us, Varya's going away . . . all of a sudden nobody wants us.

CHARLOTTA There's no place for me to live in town. I'll have to go. [*Hums.*] Oh, well, what do I care. [*Enter* PISHCHIK.]

LOPAHIN Look what's here!

PISHCHIK [*Gasping for breath.*] Oohhh, let me get my breath . . . I'm worn out . . . My good friends. . . . Give me some water . . .

GAEV I suppose you want to borrow some money? I'm going . . . Excuse me . . . [*Goes out.*]

PISHCHIK I haven't seen you for a long time . . . my beautiful lady . . . [*To* LOPAHIN.] You're here, too . . . glad to see you . . . you're a man of great intelligence . . . here . . . take this . . . [*Gives money to* LOPAHIN.] Four hundred roubles . . . I still owe you eight hundred and forty. . . .

LOPAHIN [*Shrugging his shoulders in amazement.*] It's like a dream. . . . Where did you get it?

PISHCHIK Wait a minute . . . I'm so hot . . . A most extraordinary thing happened. Some Englishman came along and discovered some kind of white clay on my land. . . . [*To* LYUBOV.] Here's four hundred for you also, my dear . . . enchantress . . . [*Gives her the money.*] You'll get the rest later. [*Takes a drink of water.*] A young man on the train was just telling me that some great philosopher advises people to jump off roofs. You just jump off, he says, and that settles the whole problem. [*Amazed at what he has just said.*] Imagine that! More water, please.

LOPAHIN What Englishmen?

PISHCHIK I leased the land to them for twenty-four years. . . . And now you must excuse me, I'm in a hurry and have to get on. I'm going to Znoikov's, then to Kardamonov's . . . I owe them all money. [*Drinks.*] Your health. I'll come again on Thursday . . .

LYUBOV We're just leaving for town, and tomorrow I'm going abroad.

PISHCHIK What's that? [*In agitation.*] Why to town? Oh, I see . . . this furniture and the suitcases. . . . Well, never mind . . . [*Tearfully.*] What difference does it make. . . . These Englishmen, you know, they're very intelligent . . . Never mind. . . . I wish you all the best, God bless you. Never mind, everything comes to an end eventually. [*Kisses* LYUBOV'*s hand.*] And when you hear that my end has come, just think of a horse, and say: "There used to be a man like that once . . . his name was Semyonov-Pishchik—God bless him!" Wonderful weather we're having. Yes . . . [*Goes out embarrassed, but returns at once and stands in the doorway.*] Dashenka sends her greetings. [*Goes out.*]

LYUBOV Well, we can get started now. I'm leaving with two worries on my mind. One is Feers—he's sick. [*Glances at her watch.*] We've still got five minutes. . . .

ANYA Mamma, Feers has been taken to the hospital. Yasha sent him this morning.

LYUBOV The other is Varya. She's used to getting up early and working, and now, with nothing to do, she's like a fish out of water. She's gotten so thin and pale, and she cries a lot, the poor dear. [*A pause.*] You know very well, Yermolay Alexeyevich, that I've been hoping you two would get married . . . and everything pointed to it. [*Whispers to* ANYA *and motions to* CHARLOTTA, *and they both go out.*] She loves you, and you're fond of her, too . . . I just don't know, I don't know why you seem to avoid each other. I don't understand it.

LOPAHIN Neither do I, I admit it. The whole thing's so strange. . . . If there's still time, I'm ready to. . . . Let's settle it at once— and get it over with! Without you here, I don't feel I'll ever propose to her.

LYUBOV That's an excellent idea! You won't need more than a minute. I'll call her at once.

LOPAHIN And there's champagne here, too, we'll celebrate. [*Looks at the glasses.*] They're empty, someone's drunk it all. [YASHA *coughs.*] They must have poured it down.

LYUBOV [*With animation.*] Oh, I'm so glad. I'll call her, and we'll leave you alone. Yasha, "*allez!*" [*Through the door.*] Varya, come here for a minute, leave what you're doing and come here! Varya! [*Goes out with* YASHA.]

LOPAHIN [*Looking at his watch.*] Yes. . . .

[*A pause. Whispering and suppressed laughter are heard behind the door, then* VARYA *comes in and starts fussing with the luggage. At last she says:*]

VARYA That's strange, I can't find it. . . .

LOPAHIN What are you looking for?

VARYA I packed it myself, and I can't remember . . . [*A pause.*]

LOPAHIN Where are you going to now, Varvara Mihailovna?

VARYA I? To the Rogulins. I've taken a job as their housekeeper.

LOPAHIN That's in Yashnevo, isn't it? Almost seventy miles from here. [*A pause.*] So this is the end of life in this house. . . .

VARYA [*Still fussing with the luggage.*] Where could it be? Perhaps I put it in the trunk? Yes, life in this house has come to an end . . . there won't be any more. . . .

LOPAHIN And I'm going to Kharkov. . . . On the next train. I've got a lot of work to do there. I'm leaving Epihodov here. . . . I've hired him.

VARYA Really! . . .

LOPAHIN Remember, last year at this time it was snowing already, but now it's still so bright and sunny. Though it's cold . . . Three degrees of frost.

VARYA I haven't looked. [*A pause.*] Besides, our thermometer's broken. . . .

[*A pause. A voice is heard from outside the door.*]

VOICE Yermolay Alexeyevich!

LOPAHIN [*As if he had been waiting for it.*] I'm coming! Right away! [*Goes out quickly.*]

[VARYA *sits on the floor, with her head on a bundle of clothes, crying quietly. The door opens,* LYUBOV *enters hesitantly.*]

LYUBOV Well? [*A pause.*] We must be going.

VARYA [*Stops crying and wipes her eyes.*] Yes, Mamma, it's time we got started. I'll just have time to get to the Rogulins today, if we don't miss the train.

LYUBOV [*Calls through the door.*] Anya, put your things on.

[*Enter* ANYA, *followed by* GAEV *and* CHARLOTTA. GAEV *wears a heavy overcoat with a hood. Servants and coachmen come into the room.* EPIHODOV *is picking up the luggage.*] Now we can begin our journey!

ANYA [*Joyfully.*] Our journey!

GAEV My friends, my dear, beloved friends! As I leave this house forever, how can I be silent, how can I refrain from expressing to you, as I say good-bye for the last time, the feelings which now overwhelm me. . . .

ANYA [*Begging.*] Uncle!

VARYA Uncle, please don't!

GAEV [*Downcast.*] I put the red into the corner and then . . . I'll keep quiet.

[*Enter* TROFIMOV *and* LOPAHIN.]

TROFIMOV Well, ladies and gentlemen, it's time we get started.

LOPAHIN Epihodov, my coat!

LYUBOV I'll just stay for one more minute. It seems as if I'd never seen the walls and ceilings of this house before, and now I look at them with such longing, such love. . . .

GAEV I remember when I was six—it was Trinity Sunday . . . I was sitting here at this window watching father on his way to church. . . .

LYUBOV Have they taken everything out?

LOPAHIN It looks like it. [*To* EPIHODOV, *as he puts on his coat.*] Be sure to take care of everything, Epihodov.

EPIHODOV [*In a husky voice.*] Don't worry, Yermolay Alexeyevich!

LOPAHIN What is wrong with your voice?

EPIHODOV I just had some water, and it went down the wrong throat.

YASHA [*With contempt.*] What a fool!

LYUBOV After we leave, there won't be a soul here. . . .

LOPAHIN Not until spring.

[VARYA *pulls an umbrella from a bundle of clothes;* LOPAHIN *pretends to be afraid.*] What are you doing that for? . . . I didn't mean to. . . .

TROFIMOV Ladies and gentlemen, hurry up, it's time. The train will be here soon.

VARYA Pyeta, here are your goloshes beside the suitcase. [*Tearfully.*] How dirty and old they are! . . .

TROFIMOV [*Puts them on.*] Hurry up, ladies and gentlemen!

GAEV [*Greatly embarrassed, afraid of breaking into tears.*] The train, the station . . . The red off the white into the middle pocket. . . .

LYUBOV Let us go!

LOPAHIN Are we all here? No one left? [*Locks the door on the left.*] There are some things stored in there, best to keep it locked up. Come along!

ANYA Good-bye, old house! Good-bye, old life!

TROFIMOV Welcome to the new life! . . . [*Goes out with* ANYA.]

[VARYA *looks around the room and goes out slowly.* YASHA *and* CHARLOTTA, *with her little dog, follow.*]

LOPAHIN And so, until the spring. Come, my friends. . . . *Au revoir!* [*Goes out.*]

[LYUBOV *and* GAEV *alone. They seem to have been waiting for this moment, and now they embrace each other and cry quietly, with restraint, so as not to be heard.*]

GAEV [*In despair.*] Sister, my sister. . . .

LYUBOV Oh, my orchard, my beloved, my beautiful orchard! My life, my youth, my happiness . . . good-bye! . . . Good-bye!

ANYA [*Off-stage, calling gaily.*] Mamma! . . .

TROFIMOV [*Off-stage, gaily and excitedly.*] Yoo-hoo! . . .

LYUBOV Just one last time—to look at these walls, these windows. . . . Mother loved to walk in this room. . . .

GAEV Sister, my sister . . .

ANYA [*Off-stage.*] Mamma!

TROFIMOV [*Off-stage.*] Yoo-hoo!

LYUBOV We're coming . . . [*They go out.*]

The stage is empty. The sound of doors being locked and then of carriages driving off. Silence. In the stillness the dull sounds of an axe striking on a tree can be heard. They sound mournful and sad. Footsteps are heard and from the door on the right FEERS *enters. He is dressed, as usual, in a coat and white waistcoat, and is wearing slippers. He is ill.*

FEERS [*Walks up to the middle door and tries the handle.*] Locked. They've gone . . . [*Sits down on a sofa.*] They've forgotten me. Never mind. . . . I'll sit here for a bit. I don't suppose Leonid Andreyevich put on his fur coat, he probably wore his light one. [*Sighs, preoccupied.*] I didn't take care of it . . . These young people! . . . [*Mutters something unintelligible.*] My life's slipped by as if I'd never lived. . . . [*Lies down.*] I'll lie down a bit. You haven't got any strength left, nothing's left, nothing. . . . Oh, you . . . you old good-for-nothing! . . . [*Lies motionless.*]

A distant sound that seems to come out of the sky, like a breaking harp, slowly and sadly dying away. Then all is silent, except for the sound of an axe striking a tree in the orchard far away.

[*Curtain.*]

Rinehart Editions

Addison and Steele, SEL. FROM THE TATLER & THE SPECTATOR 87
AMERICAN THOUGHT: CIVIL WAR TO WORLD WAR I 70
ANTHOLOGY OF ENGLISH DRAMA BEFORE SHAKESPEARE 45
ANTHOLOGY OF GREEK DRAMA: FIRST SERIES 29
ANTHOLOGY OF GREEK DRAMA: SECOND SERIES 68
ANTHOLOGY OF ROMAN DRAMA 101
Arnold, SELECTED POETRY AND PROSE 62
Austen, NORTHANGER ABBEY; Walpole, THE CASTLE OF OTRANTO; Radcliffe, THE MYSTERIES OF UDOLPHO (Abridged) 121
Austen, PRIDE AND PREJUDICE 22
Balzac, PÈRE GORIOT 18
Benét, S. V., SELECTED POETRY & PROSE 100
THE BIBLE: SEL. FROM OLD & NEW TESTAMENTS 56
Brontë, Charlotte, JANE EYRE 24
Brontë, Emily, WUTHERING HEIGHTS 23
Brown, C. B., ARTHUR MERVYN 112
Browning, Robert, SELECTED POETRY 71
Bunyan, THE PILGRIM'S PROGRESS 27
Burke, REFLECTIONS ON THE REVOLUTION IN FRANCE 84
Butler, THE WAY OF ALL FLESH 7
Byron, SELECTED POETRY AND LETTERS 54
Chaucer, THE CANTERBURY TALES 65
Chekhov, SIX PLAYS OF CHEKHOV 117
Coleridge, SELECTED POETRY AND PROSE 55
COLONIAL AMERICAN WRITING 43
Conrad, LORD JIM 85
Conrad, NOSTROMO 111
Cooper, THE PIONEERS 99
Cooper, THE PRAIRIE 26
Crane, RED BADGE OF COURAGE, SEL'D PROSE & POETRY 47
Dante, THE DIVINE COMEDY 72
Defoe, MOLL FLANDERS 25
De Forest, MISS RAVENEL'S CONVERSION 74
Dickens, GREAT EXPECTATIONS 20
Dickens, HARD TIMES 95
Dickens, OLIVER TWIST 115
Dostoevsky, THE FRIEND OF THE FAMILY and THE ETERNAL HUSBAND 119
Dreiser, SISTER CARRIE 86
Dryden, SELECTED WORKS 60
Eliot, ADAM BEDE 32
Eliot, SILAS MARNER 114
ELIZABETHAN FICTION 64
Emerson, SELECTED PROSE AND POETRY 30
ENGLISH PROSE AND POETRY 1660–1800: A SELECTION 110
Fielding, JOSEPH ANDREWS 15
FIFTEEN MODERN AMERICAN POETS 79
Flaubert, MADAME BOVARY 2
FOUR MODERN PLAYS: FIRST SERIES, Rev. Ibsen, Shaw, O'Neill, Chekhov 90
FOUR MODERN PLAYS: SECOND SERIES, Ibsen, Wilde, Rostand, Gorky 109
Franklin, AUTOBIOGRAPHY AND SELECTED WRITINGS 12
Frederic, THE DAMNATION OF THERON WARE 108
Frost, SELECTED POEMS OF ROBERT FROST 120
Garland, MAIN-TRAVELLED ROADS 66
Godwin, CALEB WILLIAMS 103
Goethe, FAUST: PART I 75
Goethe, SORROWS OF YOUNG WERTHER, NEW MELUSINA, NOVELLE 13
Gogol, DEAD SOULS 5
GREAT ENGLISH AND AMERICAN ESSAYS 34
Hardy, FAR FROM THE MADDING CROWD 98
Hardy, THE MAYOR OF CASTERBRIDGE 9
Hardy, THE RETURN OF THE NATIVE 39
Hauptmann, THREE PLAYS: The Weavers, Hannele, The Beaver Coat 52
Hawthorne, THE HOUSE OF THE SEVEN GABLES 89
Hawthorne, THE SCARLET LETTER 1
Hawthorne, SELECTED TALES AND SKETCHES 33